un-kill creativity

ALSO BY YORAM SOLOMON:

Bowling with a Crystal Ball (2nd Ed.)

From Startup to Maturity

Worst Diet Ever

Dedicated to Moshe and Margalit,
who always believed that I can, even when I thought I couldn't.

un-kill creativity

How Corporate America can Out-Innovate Startups

Copyright © 2016 Yoram Solomon
All rights reserved.
ISBN: 1535525282
ISBN-13: 978-1535525282
Library of Congress Control Number: 2016915887
CreateSpace Independent Publishing Platform, North Charleston, SC
An Amazon Company

ALL RIGHTS RESERVED. No Part of this book publication may be reproduced, stored in a retrieval system, or transmitted in any form or by any means—electronic, mechanical, photo-copy, recording, or any other—except brief quotation in reviews with attribution to the author, without the prior permission of the author.

un-kill creativity

how Corporate America can out-innovate startups

Yoram Solomon, PhD

2016

what? where?

CONTENTS

Introduction 1

PART 1: IS INNOVATION IMPORTANT? 13
   1. What is Innovation? 15
   2. Is innovation important to the CEO? 23
   3. Why are we killing creativity? 31
   4. Why innovation-through-acquisition fails 49
   5. Organic Innovation is possible 59

PART 2: UN-KILL CREATIVITY 65
   6. 3,000 ideas, one success story 67
   7. knowledge is not the issue… 71
   8. Who is Responsible for Innovation? 85
   9. Corporate Climate Starts with You 91
   10. Dynamics of a Creative Team 131
   11. The Role of the Team Leader 173
   12. Why do we get the best ideas in the shower 189

PART 3: FROM CREATIVITY TO RESULTS 221
   13. Management's degrees of freedom 223
   14. Introspection: who, me? 231
   15. Intervention: you first 261
   16. Ideation: The next big thing 293
   17. Implementation: rubber meets the road 317
   18. Do it again 327
   Epilogue: myth busting 331
   Post-Epilogue: three takeaways 335
   Acknowledgements 339
   Index 343
   Other Books by Yoram Solomon 345

hello.

INTRODUCTION

Two significant things happened to me in the summer of 2008. One, I was about to take my PhD comprehensive exam, and needed to start thinking about a topic for my research. The other was that a recruiter for Interphase Corporation approached me, while I was still employed by Texas Instruments, and asked me if I would be interested in interviewing for the position of Vice President of Corporate Strategy in that company. For a while I realized that Texas Instruments would not be implementing some of my ideas, and also that the impact of a new 500 million dollar business on a 14 billion dollar company was going to be marginal. Maybe this was the reason I needed to look for a smaller company. One that could be *dramatically* impacted by a 500 million dollar idea. Even a 100 million one. All of a sudden it hit me. Books and articles were written about how startups innovate, while mature companies don't. But nobody, to the best of my knowledge, ever asked *why*. Why are startups more innovative than mature companies?

So I decided to make this the topic of my dissertation. I set out to study whether people experienced more creativity in startup companies than they did in mature ones, and if so—why? After two years of research, I found the answer to both questions[1]. Chapter 3 of this book covers my study and its findings in greater detail, but for now I won't leave you in suspense—people *do* experience higher creativity in startups, and the climate in startups is more conducive to creativity than the climate in mature companies. For every single participant who experienced more creativity in a large, established

---

[1] The dissertation was published in: *From Startup to Maturity: A Case Study of Employee Creativity Antecedents in High Tech Companies.*

company, six experienced more creativity in startups. I defended my dissertation in front of my committee, and after 87 minutes I heard the three words that every PhD student works hard to hear: "congratulations, *Doctor* Solomon…" The smile on my face was parallel only to the one I had when I married Anat, when Maya and Shira were born, and right after takeoff on my first solo flight.

However, and despite the fact that the "Ph" in PhD comes from the word "philosophy", I consider myself a very practical and pragmatic person, and the feeling of accomplishment quickly made room for a nagging acronym: SWWC. *So What? Who Cares?* There had to be a purpose for my research, and there had to be a way to put its findings to good use. There had to be value in it for someone, beyond proving a point, as hard as it took to prove it.

Before I continue the discussion about mature companies, let me stop for a second and define the term. In my research, to be able to identify the differences, I went to extremes. The startups I chose were less than 5 years old, pre-revenue (or at least pre-profit). The mature companies were large, more than 20 years old, all Fortune 200 (with revenue greater than $1 billion in 2008), and all public. However, the term *mature companies* in this book fits a broader definition. It describes "Corporate America". I couldn't find an official definition for Corporate America, other than the name of the rock band Boston's fifth album, so I'll use mine. To me, "Corporate America" is what American companies become after reaching a certain level of maturity and stability, when corporate life takes center field over what happens outside the walls of the company. Corporate America was described greatly, although cynically, by the NBC prime time TV comedy series *The Office*, and in Scott Adams comic strips and books *Dilbert*. So, to me, the line between startups and mature companies is defined by the point in time in which "corporate life" takes over.

The first epiphany from my study was that not *all* participants experienced better creativity in startups. Almost all of them described an environment much more conducive to creativity in startups than in matures companies, but not *all* of them. So all was not lost! This was probably where my inclination towards qualitative research allowed me to dig deeper and understand the subtleties of the environmental differences.

I worked for small, startup, and early stage companies. I even started one myself (Solram Electronics) in the third bedroom of my apartment in Kfar-Saba, east of Tel-Aviv. Most of my career, though, was spent in mature companies. Companies that were already public (such as Texas Instruments and Interphase), and companies who just became public (such as PCTEL in Silicon Valley). I felt firsthand the differences between those companies, but I wanted to ground my knowledge and experience in research.

A few years passed since I completed my research, and the SWWC question kept bothering me, until I realized what I had to do. For years I've been helping entrepreneurs and very early stage startup companies get investments (as a private investor and one of the founding members of the *North Texas Angel Network* I invested my own money in some) or government grants. As exciting as it was, it wasn't my mission. A Harvard Business Review article by Professor Teresa Amabile, titled *How to kill creativity*, inspired me. It described what Corporate America was doing, unintentionally, to kill creativity. I realized that my research and personal experiences hold the key to help mature companies who gave up on innovation. My new mission became: *helping Corporate America un-kill creativity and out-innovate startups*. This is what this book is about, and this is what my keynote speaking and corporate training practice[2] focus on. Amabile's article also inspired the name for this book.

---

[2] www.LargeScaleCreativity.com

PENVEU

In the fall of 2008, I finally left Texas Instruments and joined Interphase. Interphase was, at that time, 34 years old, publicly traded in NASDAQ since 1984. It was a small company, but it was definitely *mature*. It had detailed processes and policies for everything, and those processes were followed to the letter. At the time, the company had served the largest telecom equipment manufacturers such as Nokia Siemens Networks, Nortel, and Alcatel-Lucent. It maintained very high standards of quality, which imposed some of the strictest processes the company employees followed.

I have to admit that when the recruiter approached me in the summer of 2008, I looked at the company's website, but didn't find it interesting. It was a company that built electronic boards. There were different types of boards, but they were all just electronic boards. Nothing flashy. Those were no cool-looking Apple products. Here I was, on the phone with the recruiter, about to tell him that I was not interested, when I hit the company's *Contact Us* page. I stopped. The company's headquarters was in my home zip code in Plano! This must sound very superficial right now, but you need to understand that when I joined Texas Instruments in 2002, I worked out of the company's office in Santa Rosa, California. While in beautiful wine country of Sonoma County, it was 100 miles (actually, 99.9 miles according to my car odometer) away from my home in Sunnyvale, at the heart of Silicon Valley, and I was not planning to move north. My wife's support network of ex-Israeli friends was in and around Sunnyvale, so we were going to stay there. The commute took one hour and forty minutes in the morning, and two hours driving back in the evening. Don't get me wrong—it was a beautiful commute. The scenic Highway 280, the colorful 19th avenue in San Francisco, the Golden Gate Bridge and the scenic Interstate 101 and highway 12 in the North Bay. I didn't have to drive to the office every day, since my job involved a lot of travel from the much-closer *San Jose Mineta International Airport*, and I worked from home at least one day a week.

Right now, on the call with the recruiter for Interphase, I realized that the company was in my home zip code, so I decided to accept a meeting with the CEO. We had a pleasant lunch at an Italian restaurant in North Plano, and I told him that I wasn't very excited about the company's telecom business. As it turned out—neither was he. Then I asked him: "so, what do you need me for?" He replied: "to come up with the next big thing for this company." Those were words to my ears. If there is one thing that defines me, my passion, and my professional interest, it would have to be those four words: "the next big thing". To make a long story short—after a few rounds of interviews with the rest of the executive team members and the board of directors, Interphase extended an offer, which I accepted, and worked there for the next seven years, inventing the next big thing: *penveu*®. My departure from Texas Instruments coincided with a reduction in force there, which only made me a stronger believer that things happen for a reason. penveu was publicly launched on April 17, 2012. It was one of my better ideas. Unlike all the previous products conceived at Interphase, this one was as cool as an Apple product.

What does penveu have to do with this book? When put into chronological context, I had just defended my PhD dissertation in February 2010, and hired the first members of the penveu team in May, three months later. This was just about the same time I realized that my research is more applicable to mature companies than to startups. I benefitted from all that I learned while implementing it at Interphase, with the penveu team. I felt I had a front row seat to how applicable everything was to this 36 year old company. In many cases, the penveu team dynamics proved what I already knew. However, in some cases I noticed the subtleties of implementing the framework described in this book in a mature company, and adjusted it accordingly. More than anything, I was able to practice what I had just learned with a team that eventually delivered an amazingly innovative product that required many creative ideas to be conceived, and many nearly-impossible problems solved throughout the development process. I was not the perfect leader, as my team members could testify, but I learned not only from what I did right, but also from what I did *wrong*.

THE MOST INNOVATIVE COMPANY IN THE WORLD

In 2008, the Boston Consulting Group (BCG) published the results of its fifth annual global survey of innovative companies[3]. They surveyed 2,957 executives who, using subjective ranking, financial measures, and general criteria, selected Apple as the most innovative company in the world. In fact, Apple has consistently occupied the top spot on the list between 2005 and 2015. Bloomberg, too, identified Apple as the most innovative company in 2009 and 2010[4].

But wait, weren't mature companies supposed to be *less* innovative than startups? Not always. A small percentage of my research participants experienced a higher degree of creativity in a mature company compared to a startup they worked in. There are exceptions to the rule, and Apple, a 40 year old company, is definitely such an exception. And so are 3M, Toyota, and others. There is still hope.

Why not simply learn what Apple has done to be as innovative as it is, and emulate it? Because Apple is also one of the most secretive companies in the world, and finding information about its inner-

---

[3]Andrew, J. P., Haanaes, K., Michael, D. C., Sirkin, H. L., & Taylor, A. (2008). *Innovation 2008: Is the tide turning? A BCG senior management survey*. Boston, MA: The Boston Consulting Group, Inc.
[4]http://www.businessweek.com/interactive_reports/innovative_companies_2010.html

workings is extremely hard. Few case studies were written about the company, but they were almost exclusively based on publicly available information, such as financial reports and press releases, combined with external opinions of people not directly involved in the company. Steve Jobs' biography[5] opened a small window into the operation of this company and the innovation and creativity of its people and founder. Fascinated by this company and its former leader, I read that biography within two weeks after it was published. It was only fair that I read the electronic version of it on an iPad. This biography and a few of the articles helped confirm some of the elements of the framework I offered in this book, and I used them accordingly.

However, I used another company in the book as well. Actually, a group within a company. The Skunk Works® group in Lockheed (now Lockheed Martin) that delivered some of the most amazing airplanes and technologies the world has ever seen, such as the P-80 Shooting Star, the U2 and SR71 "spy planes", and the F-117A Stealth Fighter. That group was founded by the visionary Clarence ("Kelly") Johnson. Some of the practices used in that group were discussed in greater detail in this book.

MYTHS

To set the stage, I decided to open with some of the common myths associated with innovation and creativity in the corporate context. Throughout the book I will bust them, one by one.

1. *Innovation = creativity.* Those two words are used interchangeably.
2. *Innovation = entrepreneurship and startups.* Innovation can be achieved only by entrepreneurs in startups and not in mature, large companies.

---

[5] Walter Isaacson (2011) *Steve Jobs*. Simon & Schuster, New York.

3. ***You were either born creative, or not***. Creativity cannot be learned or exercised. If you don't have it—you never will. If you have it—you could never lose it.

4. ***There is nothing you can do to increase innovation organically in your company***. If your company "lost its innovative edge," it is irreversible and the only way to increase innovation would be through acquiring innovative startups.

5. ***You must drive innovation***. Innovation will not happen by itself. If employees are given a choice, they would choose not to innovate. You, the executive, must be the driving force behind innovation.

6. ***You must Establish innovation space and allocate time for innovation***. Innovation cannot happen while an employee is performing his "day job" in his office. You must build an innovation lab and move employees there to be innovative. It has to be a special place that inspires innovation. Furthermore, one of the most innovative companies, Google, is famous for giving its employees one day a week in which they are required to work on new things. If this worked for them—you must implement it in your company.

7. ***Financial incentives increase creativity***. People work here for the money. So, why not promise bonuses for great ideas? Often companies offer patent-filing bonuses. It seems to be working because they have generated many patents that way.

8. ***Innovation requires significant resources and funding***. Innovation is measured by the percentage of revenue that goes into R&D. The more R&D dollars you spend, the more innovative your company is. You should give your creative people every resource they need. Don't hold back, or they would not be able to innovate.

9. ***Innovation initiatives must be implemented throughout the entire organization***. The first problem with innovation is that it must be implemented throughout the entire organization. You cannot implement it "locally." It's either all or nothing. The second problem is that the last thing you want is a creative accounting department, or a manufacturing department that doesn't follow processes.

WHO IS THIS BOOK FOR?

This book is for *you*. You are now working in a large, mature, established company. You feel that the company is not as innovative as it used to be, but you are not ready to throw in the towel. You may be any employee in the company, a middle manager, an executive, or even the CEO. I wrote this for you in both your capacities: as someone who *can*, and should be more creative, and as someone who can help the organization be more innovative. I will, interchangeably, talk about what you could do to increase your *personal* creativity, even outside of the office, and about how you could help others in your company, and the company as a whole.

TOOLS THAT EVOLVED FROM THIS BOOK

While writing this book, I didn't plan to develop any new tool, but nevertheless two new tools have emerged from it. One of them is a new method for measuring product innovation. I felt that using "the percentage of revenue that comes from products that didn't exist five years ago" was not enough. Not by a stretch. There needed to be something better, and through the process of searching for a better metric, I reviewed many scholarly articles describing existing metrics and proposing new ones. I didn't like any of them, so I decided to develop my own, which I named the *Growth Innovation Index*. Over a period of several months I introduced it to different companies and gathered input from them, while continuing the metric development. I believe I have something worth using now, and it is covered in chapter 14. I decided not to provide the exact method for a simple reason: the tool has not stopped evolving and I don't know if I reached the final version. It will be available, at its latest version, on my website[6].

---

[6] https://www.largescalecreativity.com/growth-innovation-index-gii

Team diversity is discussed in chapter 10. I found that the diversity is critical for team creativity, and when the time came to write chapter 15 and propose how you should optimize team diversity, a second tool was developed: the *Creative Diversity Optimizer*. This tool, for the most part, is described there. Any revisions to it, as minor as they might be, would be available too, on my website[7].

STRUCTURE OF THIS BOOK

This book has three parts. The first part (*is innovation important?*) creates a common language and terminology that you and I could share. It discusses the importance of innovation in reality and in perception, and the tight relationship (although not interchangeability) between innovation and creativity. It then explains *why* Corporate America, the focus of this book, kills creativity, and *how* it does that. It also analyzes the problematic innovation-through-acquisition path that many large companies take, after giving up on organic innovation. The first part ends on a positive note: organic innovation *is* possible!

The second part (*un-kill creativity*) provides a comprehensive review of the factors that affect creativity (and thus innovation) in the company. It focuses on the individual employee as the source of creative ideas, and shows how that individual could be *motivated* to be creative. Money is not enough. In fact, money can have a detrimental effect on creativity. The factors are divided into three groups: corporate climate, team dynamics, and individual actions. The second part provides the theoretical background and empirical investigation of those factors, and how they affect creativity. It answers the

---

[7] https://largescalecreativity.squarespace.com/creative-team-optimizer

question: why do some factors positively affect creativity, some affect it negatively, and other don't affect it at all?

The third and final part (*from creativity to results*) is the practical one. It holds the answer to my nagging SWWC (so what, who cares?) question. It is the *who, how, when,* and *where* of increasing both creativity and innovation in the company. It starts with a discussion of management's degrees of freedom, how they could impact creativity, and where they cannot. It is the blueprint for your innovation improvement plan, through a focus on increasing individual and team creativity. In general, it goes through four stages: *introspection, intervention, ideation,* and *implementation.*

I promise you four things that I intend to fulfill throughout this book. The first is that the book explains the factors that affect the generation of creative ideas in the organization, and the transformation of those ideas into company-level innovation. My second promise is that everything in this book is grounded in research and in practice. I included research done by others before me (and parallel to me), as well as my own doctoral research conducted in 2008-2010, and my research since then. It also included my own, firsthand experiences, and the experiences of others, as shared with me. Third, I promise to provide you with practical, pragmatic, and actionable information. You would be able to act on what you learned from this book. I promise not to be purely academic. Finally, I promise that a lot of what you read would make sense. Whenever I described the premises of this book in keynote speeches, workshops, and corporate training, I heard that what I said made sense. Sometimes it may be counter-intuitive, but it still makes sense. It's just that now everything is provided to you in one package—this book.

With that, let's start.

PART 1: IS INNOVATION IMPORTANT?

1.
WHAT IS INNOVATION?

Life is full of seemingly accidental encounters with new and interesting people. A friend of mine and a world-class leadership consultant, Lee Colan, introduced me to an editor at *Inc. Magazine*. It wasn't long before the Los Angeles Bureau Chief, Lindsay Blakely, was ready to take me on as a columnist at the *Innovate* channel. However, there was a catch. On her first email to me she wrote: "our readers... don't care much for the word innovation. In their eyes, it's jargon. So we really try to avoid headlines about innovation." Sounds odd, considering that the channel name is *innovate* and my articles were mostly going to be about innovation and creativity in companies. But I complied, and as of the writing of this chapter only two of the sixty-plus articles I wrote for *Inc.* had some derivative of the word innovation in their titles.

Well, how do you write about innovation without using the word? Lindsay was right. It dawned on me that the word *innovation* was used (and abused) too often. What does it really mean?

The dictionary definition of the verb *to innovate* is: "to introduce something new; make changes in anything established." Pretty simple. However, it misses the true meaning and importance of innovation. When I worked at Texas Instruments and pushed the company to innovate and differentiate, I was very specific. Texas Instruments is a company that, for the most part, builds semiconductor components, integrated circuits, that constitute the majority of the capabilities, intelligence, and performance of most electronic products. They look like small black square chips. Innovation could mean that TI would be the only company in the world that built *purple* chips (instead of black ones). This would fit the dictionary definition of innovation. Purple chips are new, and represent a change from the established black chips. But would anyone care? Would the fact that the chips are purple bring *value* to anyone?

Articles and books were written about the definition of the word. West and Farr book *Innovation and creativity at work*[8] provided the following definition for workplace innovation:

> "The intentional introduction and application within a role, group or organization of ideas, processes, products or procedures, new to the relevant unit of adoption, designed to significantly benefit the individual, the group, organization or wider society."

Different authors defined innovation differently. Some definitions focused on the *generation* of ideas inside the organization that impacted the world outside it. Others focused on *adoption* of external innovation inside the organization. Finally, some focused on the innovation *process* itself.

Yet another definition of innovation emerged from the general requirements of patentability: the invention has to be *new*, *useful*, and *feasible* to make.

Innovation is not a binary term. Some new products are merely a slight improvement over previous products. When the *iPhone 6S* first came out, I had a hard time justifying the need to spend the extra $100 to buy the iPhone 6S over the iPhone 6, which was still available for purchase. The camera was somewhat better. The processor was faster. It added the "3D Touch" feature which, although I hardly ever used it, was the only completely new feature that didn't exist in the iPhone 6.

---

[8] West, M. A., & Farr, J. L. (1990). *Innovation and creativity at work: Psychological and organizational strategies*. New York: Wiley.

To me, as a consumer, the difference was mostly *incremental*, even though Apple stated that "the only thing that's changed is everything."[9] This shows you that different people can see the same innovation differently. To some (typically the inventors) an idea may seem radical, disruptive, and game-changing. To others (typically the users of that invention), the same idea may seem incremental, because the added *value* was marginal. Both perspectives are valid, and this point is brought to life through the discussion of the innovation index in chapter 14.

RADICAL INNOVATION

And then there is the other extreme, called *Radical Innovation*. Harvard Business School Professor Clayton Christensen explained that mature companies lost their market share to startups that have no "baggage" and no respect to the "rules of the game" by which mature companies, established in their markets, play.

Often, during a speech or a workshop, when I have to make a point about the importance of radical innovation, I open with the words:

"Those who live by the sword…"

Can you finish the sentence for me before you turn the page?

---

[9] http://www.trustedreviews.com/opinions/iphone-6s-vs-iphone-6

"... get *shot* by those who don't..."

I can only guess that you finished it the way the original, from the Gospel of Matthew, ended with "... die by the sword". But I like the way Stanford University strategy Professor and consultant Gary Hamel completed it in an executive briefing in 1998, the year I moved from Israel to Silicon Valley: "Those who live by the sword get *shot* by those who don't." This was one of the most influential quotes of my professional life. It epitomizes the essence of radical innovation. The original intention of "those who live by the sword die by the sword" was to suggest that the way you lived your life would be the way you end it. If you lived life violently, you would die a violent death. However, Hamel's modification suggested something else. It also brings a picture to mind.

In a scene from the 1981 Steven Spielberg movie *Raiders of the lost ark*, Indiana Jones (Harrison Ford) found himself in the middle of a 1936 Cairo Square, facing an Arab assassin sent by the Nazis to kill him. The swordsman assassin skillfully waved his sword in front of Ford, challenging him to a swords duel. According to the story, the original script called for Ford to reach out to a nearby sword, and with the sword and his whip win the fight. However, with Ford himself (and most of the crew at the scene) already suffering from dysentery, feeling impatient, he realized that in this scene he still had his revolver in his side holster. Believing this would likely end up on the cutting room floor or the gag reel—he pulled out the revolver and shot the assassin. Everybody cracked up, but the director decided to keep this humoristic scene in the movie as is.

What did Hamel mean when he said "those who live by the sword get shot by those who don't"? Hamel celebrated radical innovators. Those who do not play by the rules. Those who do not innovate incrementally by creating "a better mouse trap", but rather inventing something completely different, and changing the behavior of the market, completely disregarding "the rules of the game".

Radical innovation is nothing new. The Austrian-American economist Joseph Schumpeter called it *Creative Destruction* in his 1934 book. He stated that radical innovation "...strikes not at the margins of the profits and the outputs of the existing firms but at their foundations and their very lives."

As an investor, I often saw entrepreneurs present their "radical" ideas as game-changing, but for the most part I considered those merely incremental. It's not that users don't have anything else that can perform similar functions today. Granted, the ideas presented were innovative, different, more effective, but they didn't create new markets or new wealth. If a product is not radically innovative (like the first cellular phone, the first PC, the Internet), users would not pay more than they pay today for products or services that fulfill similar needs. They would, however, be willing to shift a budget they already have towards the new product. As a result, investors typically ask entrepreneurs to identify the budget currently spent on *existing* products (or services, processes, or business models) and show how the new product or service could attract that existing budget (or parts of it).

True radical innovation is the type of innovation that creates new markets and new budgets. It's the kind that creates new dimensions of value to applications that didn't have those before. The first cellular phone added the value dimension of *mobility* that didn't exist before. I remember walking to the neighborhood pay phone. I remember using a rotary phone in the living room. Recently I gave up my landline because I didn't need more than my mobile phone. Mobile phones created a market that didn't exist before. So did personal computers and the Internet. However, innovations like those are few and far between. They are hard to develop. They require significant user education. And they have a much higher probability of failure.

Sometimes they involve major capital write-offs. When the DSL (Digital Subscriber Line) broadband Internet was introduced, several companies burned through billions of dollars and went bankrupt before the market developed.

Unlike other books on innovation, *un-kill creativity* doesn't show you how to let go of orthodoxies, change the rules of the game, or develop true radical innovation. This book focuses on the premise that *knowledge* is not the issue. *Motivation* is. I assumed that you already know what innovation means, and your problem is that your employees simply don't deliver it. The book concentrates on how to allow established companies to innovate at all, through the perspective of the human factor.

INNOVATION AND CREATIVITY

My two-year doctoral research focused on creativity and innovation in two types of organizations: startups and mature companies. When developing the proposal for the dissertation I had to define innovation. The definition I eventually used in my dissertation, based on review of many definitions created before I started, including the ones I quoted above, was:

> "Innovation is the *organizational process* that begins with a *creative idea* that is *implemented* to deliver a *new product, service, process*, or *business model* to the market place."

It is a process-based definition, and it serves this book well.

This definition introduced two additional terms beyond innovation: *creativity* and *implementation*, and categorized them on two dimensions: *where* they occur, and the *relationship* between them. I often found that the words innovation and creativity were used interchangeably. They are not interchangeable. They are closely related, though, and the following image illustrates how I see the differences and the relationships between them.

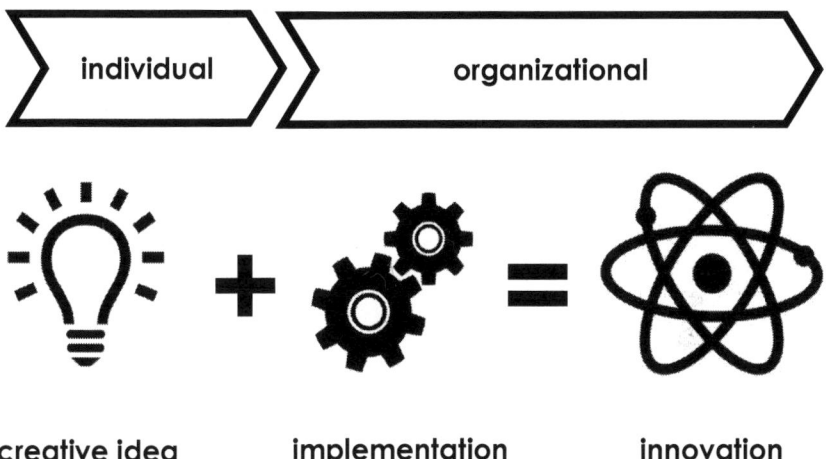

Based on that definition and illustration, innovation is an *organizational* function, while creativity is a personal, *individual* function. Implementation, too, is an organizational function, and serves to transform individually-generated creative ideas into the organizational output called innovation.

Harvard University Professor Teresa Amabile defined *creativity* as "the production of novel and useful ideas by an individual or small group of individuals working together." This definition is important, since it expands the individual aspect of creativity to a small group, a team, while reminding you that the team is made of individuals. That was the definition I used consistently throughout my dissertation, and was the basis for the definition I used in this book. Here are the definitions of the three terms in the way they are used.

> **Innovation** is the organizational process that begins with a creative idea that is implemented to deliver a new product, service, process, or business model to the market place.
>
> **Creativity** is the individual (or team of individuals) function that incorporates the cognitive ability to transcend traditional ideas, rules, patterns, and create meaningful and original ideas.
>
> **Implementation** is the organizational function that includes the selection of a viable idea, and application of resources to turn that idea into an innovative company output.

If you read any of the best innovation books (such as Clayton Christensen's classic, *The Innovator's Dilemma*), you were taught what established companies were doing wrong, and why startups were "eating their lunch." Most books focused on how *companies* innovate, as if innovation begins at the organizational level. However, if you accept the premise of *un-kill creativity* that innovation is the implementation of creative ideas, which were generated in a person's brain, you would realize that the focus has to be on the individual, and whatever makes that individual creative. What *motivates* that individual to be creative.

As a practical matter, the definition of the word "innovation" includes the word *useful*. It is an important part of innovation, and the true purpose of innovation, and why we care about it. It is also a perfect segue to the next chapter.

2.

IS INNOVATION IMPORTANT TO THE CEO?

THE PERCEPTION

It's not enough for *me* to know that something is important. Specifically, to know that innovation is important to mature companies. I want to know that it is important to *you*, and that you *perceive* it as such. When I was a part of the PCTEL executive team in late 2000, we used to hold monthly executive team retreats. This was before the 2001 dot-com bust and 9/11, after which very few companies continued holding strategic planning retreats, which seemed wasteful, possibly redundant, and that could impact "only" the future. We became very short-sighted. But in 2000, thinking about the future and improving executive team dynamics seemed important, and therefore we held those off-site retreats monthly. A part of that retreat, facilitated by our Vice President of Human Resources, Tom Capizzi, was the "hot seat" session. In it, we took turns sitting in the "hot seat" and getting feedback from our peers. It wasn't a comfortable feeling, since negative feedback was very hard to take. To make it easy to swallow, Tom reminded us that of everything we heard from our peers, maybe 10% was true in *reality*, but that 100% was true in *perception*. So even if what people said about me was not entirely true, it was what people thought about me. Perception is very important. And this is why it's not enough for *me* to know that innovation is important to your company—it is important that *you* believe it to be so.

The Boston Consulting Group (BCG) has been researching innovation for many years [10]. When I began developing my dissertation proposal in 2008, I relied on a BCG survey of executives done that year. BCG has been conducting this survey since 2005. In it, they asked corporate executives how important they considered innovation was to their companies, and whether it was one of their top three priorities, or even the single top priority. Those numbers went up consistently over the years. In 2005, 66% of the surveyed executives said that innovation was one of their top three priorities. That number grew approximately 2% annually over a decade to 79% in 2015. 19% of the surveyed executives in 2005 responded that innovation was the single top priority for their company. That number grew as well, to 22% in 2015.

In 2015, KPMG, another large consulting firm, conducted its own survey of 1,200 CEOs of companies with annual revenue greater than $500 million, to gain insight into the outlook of those CEOs, their priorities, and their concerns[11]. The executives in that survey were not asked to specifically prioritize innovation for their company, but nevertheless 86% of them (the highest finding from that report) were concerned about customer loyalty, mainly (66%) due to relevance (or lack thereof) of their products and services, and (72%) due to their company struggling to keep up with new technologies. 74% of them (the second highest key finding) were concerned about new entrants disrupting their business model and their competitors' ability to take business away. All findings indicated strong concerns about the lack of innovation in their companies.

---

[10] https://www.bcgperspectives.com/content/articles/growth-lean-manufacturing-innovation-in-2015/

[11] https://www.kpmg.com/Global/en/IssuesAndInsights/ArticlesPublications/ceo-outlook/Documents/global-ceo-outlook-2015-v2.pdf

A third top-tier consulting firm, McKinsey & Company, conducted its own innovation and commercialization survey in 2010[12]. Surveying 2,240 executives around the world, representing the full range of industries, functional specialties, and seniority, 84% responded that innovation was extremely or very important to their companies' growth strategy. The majority of the surveyed executives said they sought *organic* growth in their companies through new products or services (68%), or new customers within their existing markets (63%), rather than pursuing growth through new markets or mergers and acquisitions (M&A).

One final study, conducted by Adobe in 2012[13], revealed a growing gap between the *need* for creativity and the *ability* to deliver it. The study included 5,000 respondents from 5 countries (US, UK, Germany, France, and Japan; 1,000 participants each). The study showed that while 8 in 10 people felt that creativity was critical to economic growth and two-thirds felt it was valuable to society overall, only 1 in 4 participants believed that they were living up to their own creative potential. Three out of every four participants felt pressured to be *productive* more than *creative* at work.

The conclusion is simple: top executives in established companies *believe* that innovation is very important to their companies, and they wish to pursue it organically. However, were they saying that only because it was the politically-correct thing to say? After all, wouldn't it sound bad if they said that innovation was not important or, even worse—that they didn't believe their companies were capable of delivering it? Did they understand the real impact of innovation on their companies? At the risk of alienating potential future clients, but

---

[12] http://www.mckinsey.com/business-functions/strategy-and-corporate-finance/our-insights/innovation-and-commercialization-2010-mckinsey-global-survey-results

[13] State of Create global benchmark study. http://www.adobe.com/aboutadobe/pressroom/pdfs/Adobe_State_of_Create_Global_Benchmark_Study.pdf

based on my experience, I chose to believe the former. Innovation is one of those buzz words you must use and say is important to you and that you are pursuing it. That is one of the reasons the word is used publically so much, and top executives engage in *driving* innovation initiatives so much. But do they truly believe it is important? And is *driving* innovation effective? I'll get back to that later. I promise. For now, let's see if innovation is really important. Beyond perception.

THE REALITY

For my own study, I reviewed many research articles and books outlining the importance and implications of innovation to companies. They provided four reasons why innovation was important to companies. First, innovation can help companies *survive*. Without innovation, companies were at risk of being cannibalized by their competitors. "Innovate or die." The second reason was the competitive advantage and *financial performance* that resulted from innovation. The majority of research articles cited this as the main reason for innovation. The third reason was that innovation was considered the appropriate response to environmental and technological *change*. Finally, the fourth reason was an altruistic one: innovation provides economical and quality of life improvements to society as a whole. Only few articles described the latter as the main reason to innovate, but nevertheless—it was still a viable reason. It was hard for me to think of many cases in which for-profit companies innovated and introduced new products, services, processes, or business models purely to advance society and not for any financial (or otherwise company-related) gain. In fact, I've seen cases in which companies put shareholder and profit goals above their customers' welfare, as the infamous case of Turing Pharmaceutical[14] suggested.

Of all the cited reasons for why innovation is important, it seemed that, in the for-profit world, the link between innovation and financial results was the most important to executives and shareholders. If I could prove to you that the link exists in a significant way, I could talk you into putting an earnest effort into innovation. Or, at least, into finishing this book.

Not much research was done in recent years to measure the impact of innovation on profitability, with the exception of the following two studies done in the UK and the US.

The first study was done by Paul Geroski at the London Business School, and Steve Machin and John Van Reenen at the University College in London, and published in the RAND Journal of Economics[15]. The researchers took a sample of 721 large, public UK companies, and correlated their financial performance against innovation data from the Economic and Social Science Research Council (ESRC). They set out to find not only if there was a relationship between innovation and profitability, but also whether this relationship was temporary or permanent. Essentially, the distinction would determine whether it is the *product* of the innovative process that affected profitability (in which case the impact would be *temporary*), or the innovation *process* itself (which would therefore repeat itself and have a *permanent*, or at least a long-term impact). The data for the 721 manufacturing companies was collected for the period 1972 - 1983. During that period, 117 companies produced at least one new innovative product.

---

[14] The company that raised its AIDS and cancer drugs 5,000% from $13.50 to $750, because it could.
[15] *The Profitability of Innovating Firms*, Paul Geroski, Steve Machin and John Van Reenen. The RAND Journal of Economics Vol. 24, No. 2 (Summer, 1993), pp. 198-211

The researchers found that every single innovative product released by a company increased, on average, the profit margin by 6.1%. However, the effect of previously introduced innovative products (consistent innovation) showed a profit margin increase of 16.5%. Perhaps the most important findings were that—

- The market share of *consistently* innovative companies was six times higher than those of non-innovators;
- The difference in profitability was minimal at the beginning of the period, but grew as innovations "spilled over" to future years over a period of 12 years. As the innovation process created a *permanent* advantage, profitability of the innovative companies were 50% better than the non-innovative ones; and—
- Innovative companies had profits that were much more resilient (50% better) to economic downturns than non-innovative companies.

The second study was conducted by Peter Roberts at the Carnegie Mellon University in 1999[16]. Roberts' study focused on the US Pharmaceutical industry. Product data covering the period 1977 - 1993 was retrieved from the *Intercontinental Medical Statistics America* (IMS) data base. The data included, for each product, the introduction year, annual sales from it, and overall market data. At any given year, each company covered in the study sold more than 100 different drugs, so to make the study more manageable, only drugs that generated at least $1 million in sales at any given year were included. 4,914 drugs were included in the study as a result, accounting for more than 95% of the total US pharmaceutical sales for the period. According to the consulting firm Booz, Allen and Hamilton, only 10% of the products introduced to the market could really be considered completely "new to the world" and were therefore designated "significantly innovative," as opposed to incrementally and

---

[16] Product Innovation, Product-Market Competition and Persistent Profitability in the U.S. Pharmaceutical Industry, Peter W. Roberts, *Strategic Management Journal*, Vol. 20, No. 7 (Jul., 1999), pp. 655-670

minimally innovative. The findings, once again, should not surprise you. The significantly innovative products generated annual sales of $71.7 million, six times more than the average sales of the less innovative products. Another non-surprising fact was that 98% of the significantly innovative drugs were non-generic.

The main conclusion from Roberts' study was that only companies who *consistently* innovate could enjoy consistent high profitability. In some cases, the introduction of a radically innovative drug led to a temporary market monopoly position, with all its benefits. Specifically, the model developed as a result of the study (illustrated in the graph below) showed that if the profitability of the consistently innovative company and the average company were normalized for year 1, then by year 5 the innovative company would generate 300% higher profits than the non-innovative company, and 400% more in year 20. To put it in simple terms:

A persistently-innovative company generates 5 times more profit than a non-innovative company.

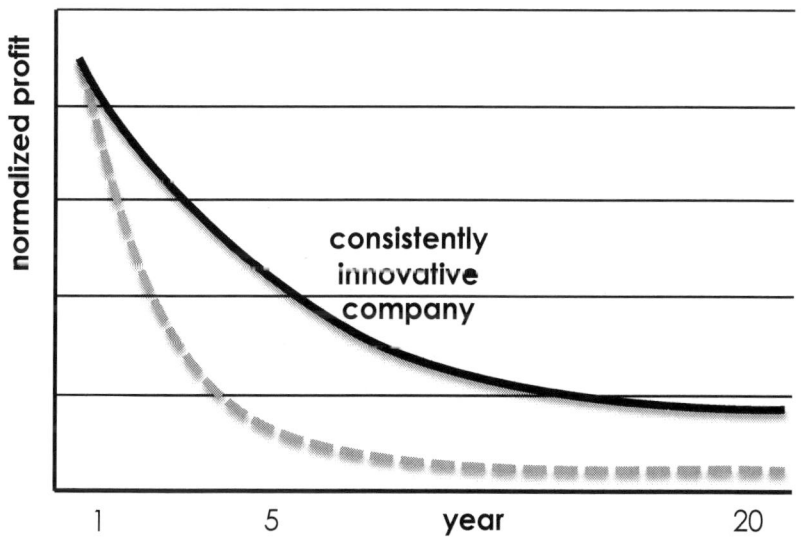

While profits from new products erode over time, as copycats emerge and competition increases, they erode much slower for consistently innovative companies (that continue to introduce new innovative products) than for companies that are either not innovative, or not *consistently* innovative.

In the 1980s and 1990s, Sony was considered one of the world's most innovative companies[17]. That's where you could find the newest electronic gadgets such as the transistor radio, Walkman, flat-screen TV, and more. However, in the consumer electronics industry it is very hard to maintain sustainable competitive advantage with any new product, because technology evolves very rapidly, and so does market adoption of new products[18]. Sony consistently maintained superior market share and profitability through persistent innovative culture and refusal to lie on the laurels of one product's success. Once Sony introduced a product, it enjoyed a rapid increase in sales and profits from it as the product entered the growth stage in its life cycle. Quickly thereafter, competitors began to reverse-engineer Sony's products and introduce imitations. Commoditization begun and profits eroded. The competitive advantage and profitability were short-lived. However, by that time, Sony had introduced the next innovative product. At any point in time, Sony had at least one product at the highly profitable growth stage of its life cycle. As a result, Sony was consistently profitable as a company, and its continuous innovation became sustainable.

Hopefully, by now, you are convinced that innovation is essential to your company's most important value: its financial performance. But how do you measure "innovative?" That's in chapter 14.

---

[17] Barney, J. (1995). *Looking inside for competitive advantage*, Academy of Management Executive, 9, pp. 49–61.
[18] Suarez, F., & Lanzolla, G. (2005). *The Half-Truth of First-Mover Advantage*. Harvard Business Review, 83(4), 121-127.

3.

WHY ARE WE KILLING CREATIVITY?

HOW ARE WE KILLING CREATIVITY?

If you followed the previous chapters carefully, which I'm sure you have, you know that innovation in your company is merely the implementation of creative ideas that employees conceived. I'm also sure that if anyone asked you if innovation was important to your company, you would say yes. Right? Say yes. However, somehow almost every time I asked an executive in a large company whether he believed that his company was innovative, the answer was no. Rarely the answer was yes, and even when it was, it was driven by pride more than by reality. Harsh words, I know.

ORGANIZATIONAL CLIMATE AND CREATIVITY

If employee creativity is so important, and executives believe it to be so, why is it being killed in Corporate America? To answer that, another question must be asked first: *how* can the company's culture affect creativity in the first place? While my two-year doctoral research covered that, a lot was studied before I ever started. Most companies focus on the importance of *strategy* for business success, but only few realize the importance of corporate climate to it. This was best described by the following words, attributed to Peter Drucker (although he was arguably not the first person to make this statement): *Culture eats strategy for breakfast*[19].

Regardless of whether companies are mature or startups, the following are the factors proven to affect creativity. They represent a wide range, from born creativity to individual context (such as mood, support or pressure from home, etc.) and, of course, team dynamics and corporate climate. I started my research with a long laundry list of factors that were studied before, which had the potential of making my interviews insanely long. However, in this book I used the 80:20 rule and focused on the factors that appeared to have made the most significant impact on employee creativity in companies, and contributed to the highest difference in creativity between startups and mature companies. Some of the personal factors, such as mood and pressure (or support) from home, seemed to have had very little impact on employee creativity, so I eliminated them from the following discussion. Other factors, such as supervisor encouragement and recognition, seemed to have had some impact on employee creativity, but the impact was similar at startup and mature companies, so I didn't discuss those either.

Following is the list of factors that were found to be the most impactful on employee creativity, and that were implemented differently in mature versus startup companies. That's what I wanted to learn in my study, and those factors explained why startups are innovative and mature companies are less so. A more detailed discussion of those factors was included in chapters 9 thru 11, and recommendations of how to affect them was in chapter 15.

---

[19] http://www.thecultureworks.com/wp-content/uploads/2014/01/Culture_Eats_Strategy_for_Breakfast_Whitepaper.pdf

- ***Organizational factors***
  - Autonomy and freedom
  - Bureaucracy, formalization, structure, and processes
  - External challenges
  - Resources
- ***Team dynamics***
  - Conflict vs. Debate
  - Internal Competition
  - Open communications

These factors did not include individual activities that any person could (and should) perform to increase his or her level of creativity. More on that later.

FROM STARTUP TO MATURITY

Clayton Christensen's *The Innovator's Dilemma* remains one of my favorite books ever. It explained exactly what mature companies did wrong that caused them to miss opportunities, and exactly what startups did to seize those same opportunities, force market disruptions, and cause mature companies to eventually fail. He explained *how*, but not *why*. Why would mature companies allow this to happen? Given the simple relationship between employee creativity and company innovation described earlier, I hypothesized that the source of the problem lies with limited employee creativity in mature companies, and that's what I decided to study in my doctoral research.

"A good dissertation is a *done* dissertation," I was told at the university. Many PhD students end up with the title ABD (All But Dissertation) next to their name, indicating they have completed all the requirements of their PhD program, except for the dissertation. You see, doctoral coursework is not much different than it was in high school. You have a very specific schedule, assignments, and an instructor who keeps you on track. Miss an assignment and you would be called on it. The comprehensive exam is nothing more than any other exam. Multiple questions, that took four weeks to complete, but very structured. The dissertation is a different story. You are almost completely on your own. Even your mentor doesn't keep you on schedule. Sometimes you feel that you are fighting the university and the dissertation committee just to complete the dissertation. This is one of the reasons why so many PhD students choose the quantitative methodology of using existing (for the most part) survey instruments to prove (or reject) a hypothesis (or few). The average quantitative dissertation is 120 pages long, and takes 6 to 9 months to complete. If yours was a quantitative dissertation that took much longer to complete, or has many more than 120 pages, you don't have to call me to set the record straight. For the most part, you are the exception.

My mentor, Dr. Corty (Cortlandt) Cammann, referred to the two methodologies by the names *explanatory* (quantitative) and *exploratory* (qualitative). The explanatory dissertation lets you prove or reject your hypotheses, while the exploratory dissertation, as its name suggests, allows you to explore areas that were not explored before, and thus learn something new. I'm glad I took this latter route. Because of it, I learned that some of the known factors behaved somewhat differently in the two types of companies. My dissertation was 348 pages long, and took almost two years to complete. A word I had to add about Corty: he was a great mentor to me. We spent hours over the phone talking about my research. He never gave me answers—he always asked me more questions, but those questions helped me focus my research better. Finally, I finished writing the last chapter of the dissertation. I spoke with him over the phone on Sunday and told him that I needed one more week to review it one last time, before I was ready to send it to him the following weekend. He never lived to read it. Corty passed away peacefully in his sleep Monday night.

My dissertation was designed to answer three research questions:

> 1. How do employees who worked in both startup and mature companies experience the differences in their own creativity between the two types of organizations?
> 2. How do employees who worked in both startup and mature companies experience the differences in the organizational climate for creativity between the two types of organizations?
> 3. How do employees who worked in both startup and mature companies experience the differences in their personal context between the two types of organizations?

This book does not discuss the third question, because there was no observable difference in the personal context for employees when they worked in startup companies or in mature companies.

There was a fourth question that wasn't included in my research, which I discussed later in this book, though:

> 4. Are creative people more likely to work for startups?

As I stated above, my study was qualitative-exploratory. Instead of offering my participants questionnaires, I interviewed them in person. The interviews took anything from 45 minutes to more than two hours. When I found something interesting that I didn't ask previous participants, I often contacted them again to ask this one additional question.

I realized that asking two different people, one who worked only in a startup and another who worked only in a mature company, to compare their environments, could mislead me. After all, different people could see the same things differently. One might describe the level of autonomy he experienced at the mature company as high since he expected less, while the other might describe the autonomy level in the startup as low, because she expected more, even though the autonomy level she experienced in the startup was, objectively, higher than what the first participant experienced in the mature company. To eliminate this potential bias, I selected participants who have worked in *both* types of environments, and were therefore in a position to truly compare the two. My sample was made of 21 participants. Each had to have worked in relatively similar positions in both companies (business or technical), filled individual contributor roles, and both companies had to have been in the electronic product hardware or software industry. This last point was a sticky one, which my dissertation committee rejected initially. "The study has to be *generalizable* to a large enough population to have value," they said. After a quick Google search I found that the electronic product industry generated $1.4 trillion in 2008. Whatever I found in that study would be applicable to a $1.4 trillion industry. Once I brought this data point to the committee, they allowed me to proceed.

The following figure illustrates the comparative nature of my study. It shows that the companies (both startup and mature) have three degrees of freedom to control innovation: hiring (and selecting) creative people, establishing an environment supportive of creativity, and establishing processes to transform creative ideas into innovative products, services, processes, or business models. The focus of my study, as the diagram shows, was on the climate that could allow (or prevent) an employee to generate creative ideas.

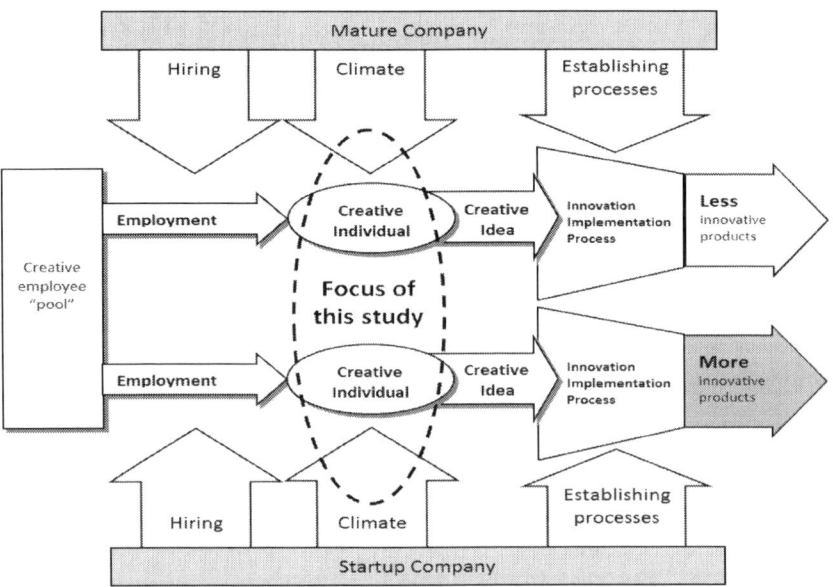

Overall, the participants in my study worked in 19 different startups and 8 different mature companies. All startups were private, ranging from 10 to 150 employees. All mature companies were public, with annual revenue ranging from $1 billion to $75 billion, and from 5,000 to 125,000 employees.

One consideration was that employees, like everyone else, evolve over time. They mature, gain more experience, their personal circumstances change, and their personality changes. However, to control the effect of this evolution as much as possible, the participant selection was done such that: (1) the sample included employees who moved from startups to mature companies, as well as employees who moved in the opposite direction; and (2) the participants must have moved *directly* between the two companies, with no significant gap between them. With the exception of four participants—all made the transition between the years 2000 and 2007, and spent at least two years in each company, so their experiences were considered recent and relevant. Only four participants made the transition from one company to the other outside of those 8 years, but none of them was earlier than 1997 or later than 2008. Only two participants spent less than two years in one of the companies: one spent 20 months in one of them, and the other spent 15 months. Only two participants had an employment gap between the two companies: one had a 6-month unemployment gap, and the other had a 10-month gap in which he worked in a medium size company.

I prepared 12 main interview questions and 46 secondary questions that allowed me to probe into every area of creativity factors and not miss anything. Once I asked a question, I kept on "peeling the onion" until I got to the bottom of every issue.

In February 2010, I finally "defended" my study, at the end of which I heard the words that were three and a half years in the making: "congratulations, *Doctor* Solomon…"

CONCLUSIONS

Summarizing prior research in organizational climate for creativity, I narrowed the list down to 12 *input* factors, and one outcome (level of creativity). The following table describes the findings at a high level.

Factor (outcome)	Domain	Effect	Higher in-
Creativity (outcome)	Outcome	N/A	Startup
Autonomy	Organizational	**Strong Positive**	Startup
Supervisor encouragement	Organizational	Positive	Unnoticeable
Recognition	Organizational	Positive	Unnoticeable
External challenges	Organizational	**Strong Positive**	Startup
Organizational impediments	Organizational	**Strong Negative**	Mature
Resource Quantity	Organizational	Negative	Mature
Positive team dynamics (and trust)	Organizational	**Strong positive**	Startup
Dynamism and involvement	Organizational	**Strong positive**	Startup
Job satisfaction (outcome)	Personal context	**Strong Positive**	Startup
Mood and affect	Personal context	Unclear	Unnoticeable
Support from home	Personal context	Positive	Unnoticeable
Pressure from home	Personal context	Negative	Unnoticeable

57% of the respondents experienced higher creativity in startup companies. 33% felt equally creative in both types of companies. 10% felt more creative in mature companies. Simply put: for every single participant who felt more creative in the mature company there were six who felt more creative in the startup company.

The strongest *positive* factors affecting creativity were: autonomy, external challenges (market, technology, etc.), team dynamics, and involvement (seeing the "big picture" and feeling the impact of their work on company performance). The single strongest *negative* factor affecting creativity was organizational impediments (bureaucracy, formalization, and rigid processes). Job satisfaction was found to be positively correlated to creativity, but through the interviews it became apparent that all other factors affected both creativity and job satisfaction equally, so I concluded that job satisfaction was an *output* rather than an input. Other factors were found to have much lower impact on creativity than reported in previous studies. One factor (availability of resources) was found to have an opposite effect on creativity than previously described. This finding was discussed further in chapter 9.

The findings from the study are illustrated in the conceptual model in the next page. Some of the factors are bold and underlined, indicating that their effect on creativity was strong. Other factors were printed in standard font, indicating that they had lower impact on participants' creativity. For each factor, there is an arrow from it to the "spine" (the link between individuals and the creative ideas they generate), showing a positive (+) or negative (-) impact on creativity, as experienced and described by the participants.

At the top right of the model are the external challenges, with a positive impact on creativity. These challenges are intellectual, technical, survival-related, and market-related. Organizational impediments to creativity are shown (on the left) to have a negative effect on creativity, and are made of *internal* challenges, formalization, bureaucracy, and complex and unsupportive processes. Different team dynamics had different impact on creativity: open communications and free idea debating have a positive effect on creativity, while internal competition and personal conflict have a negative effect. This study revealed that *trust* was a key element of team dynamics that affected all four, and thus it was illustrated as a core element in team dynamics, affecting the other factors. Although not shown in this diagram, trust was shown to be affected by geographical and cultural differences, time together, friendships, churn, and perceived competency of team members. The relationship between trust and creativity is discussed in greater detail in chapter 10.

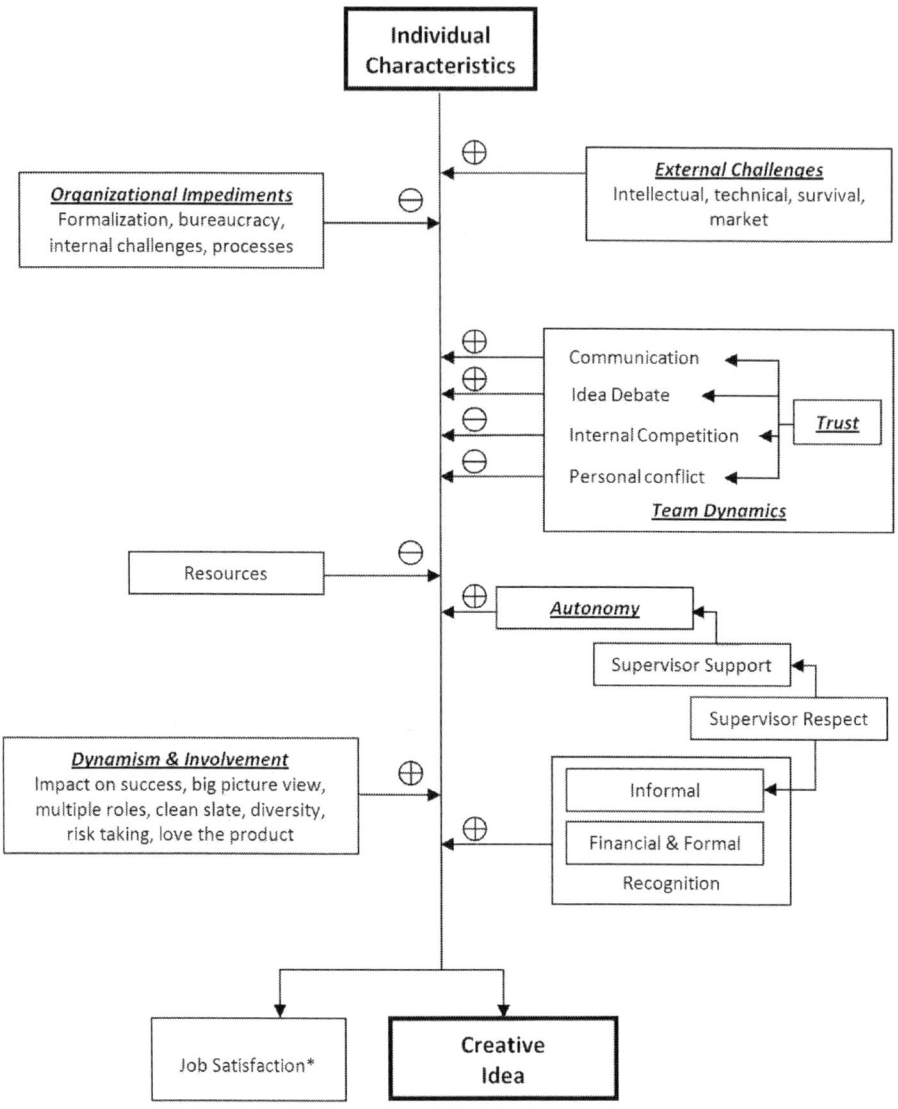

Resources were initially reported as having a *negative* impact on creativity (the less resources available to the participants, the more they felt creative), although not a very strong one. Later I found, as detailed in chapter 9, that the relationship between the two appears to look like an upside-down U-shaped curve. Autonomy has a strong, positive effect on creativity, but it is affected by supervisory *support*

which, in turn, is affected by the *respect* that employees had towards their supervisors. The respect towards the supervisor also affected one of the three types of recognition described by participants—*informal* recognition. In mature companies, participants who described lack of respect towards their supervisors did not appreciate informal recognition by them. It should be noted, though, that participants cared less about informal recognition in startups, even when they respected their supervisors. All three types of recognition have positive effect on creativity.

Dynamism was a new factor to the framework of my study, and emerged out of the interview narratives. As described by the participants—dynamism had seven important elements: (1) the impact participants felt they had on the success of the company or project; (2) their ability to see the big picture; (3) filling multiple roles; (4) starting with a clean slate; (5) the diversity of backgrounds, experience and knowledge; (6) risk taking; and (7) loving the product and the positive impact it has on *society*.

Several final conclusions came out of my study (and from the work I conducted in the following years):

1. While the majority of participants felt more creative in startups, one-in-six felt more creative in established companies, indicating that all is not lost for mature companies;
2. In order to "un-kill" creativity in established companies, work must be done at three levels: the company climate, the team dynamics, and the individual;
3. Increasing levels of creativity and innovation does not necessarily require a high investment in research and development ; and—
4. Some of the factors (e.g., autonomy) may be conflicting with "normal" company business imperatives (such as coordination, efficiency, and compliance), but are not required to apply to the *entire* company, only to the creative core.

The rest of the book details how these factors affect creativity, and what must an established, mature company do so that those factors have a positive effect. If you are interested in greater details of my study, you can read the entire dissertation and the stories of the 21 participants in *From Startup to Maturity*.[20]

WHY DOES CORPORATE AMERICA KILL CREATIVITY?

Now you know that organizations kill creativity. You know exactly how, which leaves a simple, yet very important question—*why*? To answer this, I'll start with four short stories with a common theme.

I served on several industry boards of directors, such as the Wi-Fi Alliance, WiMedia Alliance, the North Texas Regional Center for Innovation and Commercialization, and more. Doing that, you get to know employees from other companies, be it your competitors, customers, suppliers, or companies who are neither of those. At that time, I worked for Texas Instruments. One evening I had dinner with an employee of one of the major cellular phone manufacturers. He was notorious for treating TI people badly. During that dinner, out of the blue, he said to me: "you are the only person in TI that I enjoy having a technical conversation with." I enjoyed the compliment, but asked "why?" He explained: "because everybody I met at TI wanted to know what I wanted, and promises to build it, no questions asked. It's as if nobody had an original thought there. You were the only person who didn't seem to mind calling BS on what I asked for, and offer things that might be the opposite."

PCTEL was a Silicon Valley startup founded in 1995. It took a leap of faith and developed dial-up modems (do you remember those?) which, instead of relying on the expensive Digital Signal Processor

---

[20] Yoram Solomon (2010), *From startup to Maturity: a case study of employee creativity antecedents in high tech companies*

(DSP), were relying on the available processing power that the main PC processor had. As a result, the PCTEL modem was significantly cheaper than existing modems. By 2000, this startup reached almost $100 million in sales, and was named the second fastest growing company in Silicon Valley, following Yahoo! It went through an IPO in 1999, and soon reached a market value of $2.2 billion, with barely 200 employees. Every employee in the company was "worth" 10 million dollars within a month following the IPO! Before I sold Voyager Technologies to PCTEL in 2000, the company embarked on a challenging project: replicate their success, but this time with DSL modems. I attended an all-employee meeting in which the vice president of marketing said "we did it once with dial-up modems, and we will do it again with DSL!" The employees got excited. You could feel the energy in the air. At that time the Voyager acquisition was complete, and a few months later I became the DSL product line director. We were building an *internal* DSL modem. Do you, by any chance, own a computer with an *internal* broadband modem? Do you know anyone who does? I didn't think so. And there is a reason for that. Several, actually. As I started meeting potential customers, broadband Internet service providers, and other value-chain partners, I realized that the value proposition of an internal DSL modem was flawed. We were building a product that was destined to fail. As I dug into the reasons the company embarked on developing this product to start with, I found that it was because two of the leading PC manufacturers issued an RFQ for internal DSL modems. Nobody really challenged them. Nobody considered the statistic that users who are likely to purchase and pay for DSL services are also likely to have more than one computer at home, and would like to give all of them access to DSL services, and therefore the modem had to be *external*, like they are to this date. The customer asked for it, the customer is always right, and like a good company—that's what PCTEL built.

The story of USB 3.0 was much more successful, as it did lead to the launch of a connection that is 10 times (now 20 times[21]) faster than USB 2.0 was before it. However, when in 2005 I forecasted the need for a much faster interface, one of the first questions I was confronted with at Texas Instruments was: "did any of our customers ask for it?" After all, if none of our customers had asked for it—why should we develop it? Needless to say that I fought an uphill battle to get USB 3.0 developed. Eventually, it was developed, and today every computer and peripheral uses it, with billions of ports shipping every year. But at that time, like every good company, we were not going to develop it unless a customer asked for it. Specifically.

Finally, when I first joined Interphase in 2008 as the Vice President of Corporate Strategy, I conducted a company assessment. I met with many of our engineers to see how well did the company deliver on projects. One of the questions I asked employees was: "at what level in the customer's organization do you spend most of your time communicating? Was it at the strategic level, including the Chief Technology Officer or Chief Strategy Officer? Was it at the engineering level? Marketing level?" I found, much to my surprise, that Interphase employees spent more than 60% of their customer-facing time with *purchasing* managers. The purchasing manager is the person who delivers specifications, RFQ, and business terms to suppliers, but is not involved in strategic planning. As a result, the company was always *reactive* and late to market, as there was very little exposure to the forefront of technology demand at the customer's site. It also explained why many projects failed to deliver positive return on investment. The customers' purchasing managers provided product specifications, and while Interphase focused on delivering to those (rather than understanding what *drove* those

---

[21] With USB 3.1.

specifications), the customers often changed specifications half-way through a project, or cancelled orders, leaving Interphase with the development bill.

Do you now see the common theme of these four stories? Each one is an example of a company that, instead of developing products that their customers would *need*, whether they knew it or not, opted to develop the products to the exact specifications provided by the customers without questioning them. In other words—they developed what the customer *wanted*, like good suppliers do. The customer is always right. And that was their mistake.

The stories above tell you that there is a very simple reason why Corporate America kills both innovation and creativity, which both Harvard Professors Clayton Christensen and Teresa Amabile pointed out. Christensen defined the *innovator's dilemma* as the fact that—

> "The logical, competent decisions of [established companies'] management that are critical to the success of their companies are also the reasons why they lose their positions of leadership,"

Amabile wrote that—

> "... creativity gets killed [in established companies] much more often than it gets supported... ...creativity is undermined unintentionally every day in work environments that were established—for entirely good reasons—to maximize business imperatives such as coordination, productivity, and control."

What other reasons do companies have to kill creativity?

Employees need a certain climate to be creative. Teresa Amabile is one of the key researchers of organizational climate for creativity. She found that one of the main factors in that climate is the *autonomy* given to employees, which includes the ability to deviate from plans, lose some of the control structures in the organization, take exemptions from bureaucracy and rigid processes, and get visibility to the "big picture" rather than to small pieces of it. Why is it so hard for large companies to give employees the autonomy they so desperately need? Here are three reasons.

AUTONOMY MAY CAUSE CHAOS

When each employee pursues his own path and tries different things in a small startup, the CEO could still keep track of all projects throughout the entire company. There are only a handful of employees, and typically only one main product or project, so it's easy to know the details. However, in a public company with 30,000 employees and hundreds, if not thousands of product lines, having each employee take the freedom they need from company processes and structure could quickly get out of hand, and managers could easily lose control, leading to chaos. That is a risk that managers are simply not willing to accept. They have to know what goes on, and the only way to do that is if the employees followed their directions. After all, their jobs are on the line, and they don't trust the employees enough to leave it in their hands.

INCREASED REGULATION

Even before Sarbanes Oxley, regulations kept creeping up on companies. Especially large, public companies with deep pockets. There is no doubt that companies brought this on themselves through operating unethically and in the "grey areas" of the law. As a result, quality, reporting, and operating regulations have increased, to the point that employees sometimes spend more time reporting what they are about to do and what they have done, than actually doing it. Reporting does not generate new value, and is not a creativity-inspiring activity. It may improve *productivity* and *efficiency*, but those are not synonymous with *creativity*.

THE QUALITY MOVEMENT

Part of quality philosophies and standards such as TQM and ISO9000 is the translation of what the customer *wants* into what the company builds. As a result, employees in companies focus more on what the customer specifically asked for, than on what the customer really needed to be successful. Front line employees spend more time documenting what customers *want* than trying to understand their business and offer solutions they may not have asked for, or showed interest in, even if those solutions were better for the customers' success. After all, you never get fired for launching and developing a failing project, sinking millions of dollars, if you actually have a customer who asked for it. Especially if that request was well documented. On the other hand, you may (or may not) be a hero for developing something the customer needed but didn't ask for, but if you were wrong—you may lose your job. So why even try?

You see, there are perfectly good reasons for preventing employee autonomy, and for maintaining the bureaucracy and processes large companies have. The loss of autonomy and thus creativity that results from it—well, this is just an unfortunate side effect...

4.
WHY INNOVATION-THROUGH-ACQUISITION FAILS

When my daughter Maya was 4 years old she dislocated her left elbow. It must have not been painful all the time, only when she tried to move her left arm, so she didn't cry. Instead, as we took her to the emergency room, she simply started using her right arm. Kids quickly learn to adapt. So do companies. Many companies realized that something was wrong with their ability to innovate. However, they learned to accept that they might never be as innovative as startups. Some of them even realized that the reason they couldn't innovate was that they didn't provide the environment required by their employees to be creative. And for the most part, for the reasons described in the previous chapter, they believe they never will. Employees in large companies often envy their counterparts in startups, especially when those reach their "exit strategy" and, for the most part, get acquired. They are jealous of people who became rich overnight.

In December 2010, Groupon (www.groupon.com), the very successful online coupon and deal-sharing startup, rejected an acquisition offer made by Google, a deal valued at 6 billion dollars. When asked about the offer by NBC's *The Today Show* anchor, Matt Lauer, 30 year old CEO Andrew Mason cleverly avoided answering by telling childhood stories. Groupon's success was meteoric: from 30 million dollar in 2009 to 713 million in 2010, and 645 million in the first quarter of 2011[22]. In June 2011 Groupon filed for an initial public

---

[22] Making it the fastest growing company in history at the time, according to Forbes (http://www.forbes.com/forbes/2010/0830/entrepreneurs-groupon-facebook-twitter-next-web-phenom.html)

offering (IPO) at the NASDAQ stock exchange, a clear indication that the company intended to stay in business independently rather than be acquired by another company. With the company valued at 10 billion dollars at the IPO, and with Mason's share estimated at 50%, he would have likely been richer faster by accepting the acquisition offer from Google than "going it alone" in a public offering, but he chose the latter, and harder path.

However, in the last decade or two, the Groupon story was the exception, and not the rule. When I founded Solram Electronics in 1995, I was inspired by the success of Vocaltec, CheckPoint, and other Israeli startups through their IPOs in the US stock markets. Israel had (and still has) the second largest number of companies traded publicly in US stock markets, following only the US itself. That was the essence of the Israeli high-tech dream: have a successful IPO in the US. The dream was to build a *sustainable* company. I dreamed of an IPO on NASDAQ when I launched Solram Electronics.

But that all changed, and not only in Israel. Four Israeli friends founded Mirabilis. You probably don't recognize the name. The brand name of their product would sound more familiar: ICQ. They created the first PC-based instant messaging system, which had a profound impact on how we communicate today. I don't know if we would have enjoyed mobile text messaging today if it wasn't for the PC instant messaging that preceded it. What was their business model? How were they going to generate revenue? Profit? Shareholder value? The truth was that they didn't generate any revenue prior to their acquisition by AOL in 1998. They didn't even have plans to generate revenue. They only wanted to develop a product that people would use. But with 12 million subscribers they were acquired for the unimaginable (at the time) sum of 407 million dollars. What role did Mirabilis (and others) play in changing the IPO paradigm? They showed that valuation could be very different than a simple multiple of revenue or profit. It could be based on the promise of the future. It could be some other value to the acquiring company, which the acquired company could not realize by itself. The ICQ team wanted to create something *cool*, which they did. But AOL did not acquire something cool. They acquired direct access to 12 million subscribers for $34 per subscriber. They also showed that entrepreneurial success could be measured by metrics other than the sustainability of the company or its business model. They also made aspiring entrepreneurs think. When a company raises funds through an IPO, those funds go to the *company*. Not to the founders. Sure, the valuation of the company, multiplied by the ownership percentage of the founders determines the "value" of those founders. However—this value is "on paper." The founders cannot simply "dump" their stock holdings in the stock market, as the stock value of their company (and thus the value of their fractional ownership in it) would plummet due to the oversupply of shares. The shareholders in a public company pay attention to trades made by founders, executives, and other major owners of the company (otherwise called "insiders"). When the insiders sell—they indicate to the market that they do not expect the company value (and thus its shares) to increase anymore. This is why SEC regulations require all insiders to publish any trade they make with the company stock (through filing Form 4). So, after all the hardship that the founders went through in creating the company, growing it, and taking it public—the value of their ownership in the company is "on paper" only.

On the other hand, when a company is acquired—the founders are paid immediately and directly. The 407 million dollars paid by AOL for Mirabilis went directly to the founders' pockets (well, except for the taxes they had to pay, which I had to estimate as part of my final tax law exam at law school in 1998). Any further ICQ success or failure would not affect their personal gain. If AOL would completely destroy the value created through ICQ—the four founders would not lose a dime. Building your company to be acquired offers more tangible wealth and liquidity to the founders than taking the hard way of the IPO and building a sustainable company.

Of course, there are always the exceptions. Bill Gates, Steve Jobs, Michael Dell, Bill Joy, Bill Boeing, and others built great companies. They could probably have sold them for much less than they are worth today, but they decided to grow their companies to the successful giants they became. They are obviously much wealthier than they would have been if they sold early. But those are the exceptions, and not the rule. Only a small number of startups ever reached this level of success.

And thus a new term was born: *exit strategy*. It is a strategy that allows the founders and investors in the company to sell their ownership position during an acquisition. It would be unfair to attribute the desire to build the company for an acquisition solely to the founders' desire to get rich quickly. Sometimes the startup simply can't go it alone. Sometimes the acquiring company has unique resources, market access, or any other value that would scale the startup's offering. The startup might have a great technological advantage, but no market access. An acquiring company in the same industry may have the market access and brand recognition, but not the product. Once they acquire the new product—they could capitalize on it much better than if the startup was to go it alone.

In 2015, $3.8 trillion were spent on mergers and acquisitions, the highest number since 2007. Of those, $1.3 trillion were spent in the fourth quarter of the year alone[23]. Large companies with strong balance sheets use their cash to buy innovation, and they spend a lot of money for it. But does it work? Acquisitions puts significant amount

---

[23] http://www.bloomberg.com/news/articles/2016-01-05/2015-was-best-ever-year-for-m-a-this-year-looks-pretty-good-too

of cash into the startup founders' and investors' pockets, but do acquiring companies get their money's worth?

There are two sides to every acquisition, especially when a large, established company acquires a technology startup. For the startup, given the increased difficulty of an IPO and the immediate gratification required by investors, acquisition became the "standard" exit strategy. In fact, one of the most typical questions asked by early stage investors during a pitch is: who will potentially acquire you, and what were the details of comparable acquisitions?

However, different studies put the acquisition failure rates between 50% and 90%. The majority of those are between 70% and 90%. In 2009, Cisco, considered by many a leader in innovation-through-acquisition, acquired *Pure Digital*, the creator of the *Flip* camera for $590 million. In the 2009 press release, Cisco stated that—

> "The acquisition of Pure Digital is key to Cisco's strategy to expand our momentum in the media-enabled home and to capture the consumer market transition to visual networking."

A short two years later, Cisco shut down that business unit and wrote off the purchase price.

A 2011 *Harvard Business Review* article[24] and a 2012 article in *Business Insider*[25] stated the following as the main reasons why acquisitions fail:

- The acquisition was done for the wrong reasons;
- The price was wrong and did not present a positive ROI;
- The business model didn't work out; and—
- The integration failed (due to business model and process mismatch).

---

[24] Clayton Christensen, Richard Alton, Curtis Rising, and Andrew Waldeck. *The Big Idea: The New M&A Playbook*. Harvard Business Review. https://hbr.org/2011/03/the-big-idea-the-new-ma-playbook
[25] http://www.businessinsider.com/why-acquisitions-fail-2012-10

My experience with mergers and acquisitions (both as a seller and as a buyer), and stories told by participant in my two-year study, suggested that the real reasons were somewhat different, and related to the *people* involved in both companies. Those reasons are focused mainly on the personalities involved in the post-acquisition effort. Specifically, the dynamics of the relationships between the startup team and the large company's team that needed to work together right after the acquisition. Here are four people-related reasons why acquisitions fail.

FORCED INTEGRATION

In 2000, a large American semiconductor company spent $300 million to acquire a small fabless semiconductor startup with a complementary product. During the due-diligence process the projected release date of that product was presented by the startup founders. After the integration, the acquiring company insisted that the new component be released using the large company's processes, instead of the 3rd party process that was used by the startup originally. As a result, the release date of the new component was delayed by 18 months, losing both companies significant competitive position and allowing competitors to gain market share. Forcing a tighter integration than was needed could break the assumptions made prior to the acquisition.

NONEXISTENT TRUST

Acquisition negotiations (especially when one or both companies are public) are very sensitive and confidential, and involve only the highest levels of management. If word of the acquisition got out before it was done, it could be disruptive to both companies. There is always the possibility that the acquisition negotiations would fall apart, too. The employees who would have to work together on both sides after the acquisition are often unaware of the upcoming merger.

Immediately after the acquisition is complete, those employees are informed of the acquisition, often for the first time. Both teams would now be forced to begin collaborating, and a lot of pressure would be put on them due to the typically high acquisition price and expectations from it. But *trust* cannot be built overnight. The lack of pre-existing trust between the teams would prevent true productive cooperation. Trust is built over time, and is seeded by mutual respect. Chapter 10 discusses this dynamic in greater detail. Making a "sudden" introduction between the teams after the acquisition would not promote such respect. In fact, both teams (especially those in the acquiring company, who were kept in the dark more often than the smaller startup team) would begin to lose trust in their own management that kept them in the dark. Trust in management would be important for them to be creative, even without the acquisition. Damage was already done.

THIS IS HOW WE DO THINGS AROUND HERE

The team at the acquiring company now feels unappreciated by their own management due to the acquisition. The implied message from management was clear: you were not innovative enough, forcing us to acquire an external team.

Moreover, their management had just told them, although not in so many words, that they could not be *trusted* with knowledge of the acquisition before it happened. Management continued to tell them how great the acquired team is, which hurts the local team's self-esteem. Their way of gaining some self-esteem back is through using internal processes to whip "the new guys," and show everyone how valuable they (the internal team) were, and why they should have been consulted with *before* the acquisition. The local team would use every move in their play book to prove their own value. The words "this is how things are done here" would be heard more often than ever before. They would undermine every effort made by the newly acquired startup team to succeed. This would not help the acquired team gain respect for them or trust them. On the contrary, I know a founder of a startup company who left the acquiring company before fully earning his acquisition payout. He received enough money, and couldn't stand the constant "harassment" by the local team which, in his opinion, was driven by anything other than good productive intentions.

ARROGANCE OF STARTUP PEOPLE

At the same time, the acquired startup team had just received the ultimate validation of their "greatness." The large company had just paid an obscene amount of money for the value they brought. They entered the relationship from a position of superiority, and they show it through *arrogance*. They downplay everything the local team had done to date. "Obviously, if you knew what you were doing, your management wouldn't need to acquire us." Furthermore, key players in the startup company received so much money that they don't really need to work anymore. They could retire now, and they brag about it, adding insult to injury. The phrase "I don't have to take this crap anymore" would be heard quite often by the newly acquired startup team. They don't have to take the abuse anymore. It furthers their arrogance, or at least as perceived by the acquiring company's local team, who prefers to see it that way. Needless to say, this doesn't help grow respect or trust in either direction.

THIS CAN NEVER HAPPEN HERE

Don't assume it could never happen to you. You are not immune to these statistics. You are not doing anything so different and special that the other 70-90% weren't doing. Instead, think ahead about how to make the two teams work well together. Neglecting the dynamics of the two teams of strangers, their different cultures and motivation, would prove to be your biggest Achilles heel, and probably the most important reason why acquisitions fail. I have ideas on what you need to do to avoid this acquisition pitfall, but that's a topic for another book.

WHAT IF YOU ARE SUCCESSFUL?

What if somehow you are, against all odds, in the 10-30% of successful acquirers, and the integration went without a glitch? You got your money's worth, and the return on investment exceeded your predictions. Did innovation-through-acquisition work for you?

I have never seen a startup create multiple product lines, or one that was founded to create a "machine" that continuously innovates. The process of funding startup companies prevents that. Investors never ask the founders "how consistently will your company innovate?" Instead, investors focus on one product, service, process, or business model. The few times I've seen, as an investor, a company that offered several possible product lines, as close to one another as they may have been, I heard the other investors ask the company to focus on *one*. There is a perfectly good reason for that. Succeeding as a startup in the "grownup" world takes everything you've got, and then some. The startup is too small, too fragile, and has too few people and very limited resources to spread them across multiple product lines. As a result, when a startup company gets acquired by a mature company it brings a *single* product, service, process, or business model. It may be highly innovative, and possibly dramatically disruptive, but it is still only a *single* innovation.

The research covered in chapter 2 showed that in order to achieve superior financial results the company had to be *consistently* innovative. A single product may provide superior results only for a short period of time, but once the market for the product matures, competition increases, profit margins collapse, and the company stops enjoying the benefits of the single acquisition it made.

So even if you happened to be in the 10-30% of successful acquisitions—acquiring a single company would not provide the consistent innovation you need to gain superior financial results. Even if the *Flip* camera company acquisition by Cisco in 2009 was successful, it would have provided Cisco with one more product line. It would not have had any impact on the company's consistent level of innovation.

5.

ORGANIC INNOVATION IS POSSIBLE

If I were you, working in an established, mature, large company, I would feel pretty discouraged after reading the book to this point. While I made a pretty strong case for why innovation is important to your company (both in perception and in reality), I also explained *why* your company was killing it. I even showed you exactly *how!* What you are feeling is what I heard from executives and managers in many companies when I met them for the first time to discuss innovation.

And just when you accepted that the only way for your company to innovate is through acquiring innovative startups, I stole that glimmer of hope too, and shared with you the poor innovation-through-acquisition success statistics, and the little value of acquiring a single-product company.

However, understanding all of that was important. You had to know why innovation is important, have a common language of what innovation and creativity are, understand why and how they are killed, and come to the realization that acquisition was not the solution. Only now, we can move past that.

In April 2002, while living in Silicon Valley, right after I decided to leave PCTEL, I received an offer letter from Texas Instruments to be the Director of Strategy for the Wireless Networking Business Unit. Although the position offered was in North California, my wife asked me if we would have to move to Dallas. After all, TI's headquarters are in Dallas. "Dallas?" I asked, "Why would we need to move to Dallas? Nobody knows me there." She insisted: "what if they wanted you to become general manager of a business unit located in Dallas, but insist that you move there?" Again, I couldn't see that happening. However, there is something to be said about a woman's intuition, and I'm saying that with all due respect. Just over a year into my position at TI, I received a call from "the ranch" in Dallas. A new business unit was being formed, and I was asked to run it. Of course—I would have to move to Dallas… I flew to Dallas several times and went through the interview process.

The last interview was with C.S. Lee, a Senior Vice President in TI, and two levels above me. I walked into his office for an interview that lasted less than 10 minutes. He looked at my resume, and asked me one simple question: "You seem to have been working for quite a few startup companies. How would you deal with the slow pace in which a large company moves?" I had to think for a second, before I replied: "I believe there are three ways to handle this. One—accept that things are not going to move as fast as in a startup. Learn to take things slow. Two—get frustrated and leave. I believe I will choose the third one." "And what's that?" Lee asked. "I would do something about it. Things don't *have* to go slow simply because that's how they are in a large company." He seemed to have liked that answer, because I got the job, and against my better judgement—we moved to Dallas…

Lee's acceptance of that "fait accompli"[26] was not unique to him. It is pervasive in mature companies (not only large ones). What struck me as odd was how many large and mature companies seemed to accept the fact that they have heavy bureaucracies, heavy processes, and that they move slowly. Even their employees accepted those facts with their detrimental consequences. They don't try to do anything about it, for the most part. As my research found (and described in chapter 3, and further explained in chapter 9)—bureaucracy, formalization, and inflexible processes correlate directly to lower

---

[26] From French in 1845: something that is already done and is beyond alteration.

levels of creativity experienced by employees in mature companies which, in turn, explains why mature companies are generally significantly less innovative than startups.

IS THERE STILL HOPE?

My study showed that for every single person who experienced high creativity levels in a large, mature, established company, there were six who experienced higher creativity in startups. But you could look at the glass one-seventh full (it's not really half full…): I met participants who convinced me after two-hour interviews that they were more creative when they worked in a *mature* company than when they worked in a startup. I also met participants who did not experience any difference in their creativity between the two types of companies.

Hope is not lost!

Here are some good news. The Boston Consulting Group's list of the most innovative companies for 2015[27] includes:

BCG 2015 Ranking	Company	Year founded	2015 Revenue
1	Apple	1976	$228b
2	Google	1998	$78b
3	Tesla	2003	$4.3b
4	Microsoft	1975	$87b
5	Samsung	1938	N/A
6	Toyota	1933	N/A
7	BMW	1929	N/A
8	Gilead	1987	$33b
9	Amazon	1994	$113b
10	Daimler	1896	N/A

---

[27] https://www.bcgperspectives.com/content/interactive/innovation_growth_most_innovative_companies_interactive_guide/

Apple has been consistently #1 on BCG's list for the past 10 years. Google has been #2 for 9 out of the last 10 years. Microsoft was consistently hovering around #4, while Samsung, Toyota, BMW, Amazon, and Daimler have all maintained their top 10 (or top 20) positions over that period. Among the top 10 list, only 2 companies (Tesla and Gilead) were not on this list at all 3 years ago.

The average age of the 10 most innovative companies was 53 years. The youngest of them was 13 years old (Tesla), and the oldest was 120 years old (Daimler). Revenue of all 10 was in the billions, tens of billions, and even hundreds of billions of dollars. I could dig up more statistics, but you get the picture—you could be large, mature, established, and still be innovative! Apple, although occupying the top spot, does show some worrying signs of innovation decline now. While the company experienced 68.3% annual revenue growth and 373% annual profit growth in 2005, it reported only 7% revenue growth and 7.2% profit growth in 2015.

In full disclosure, the fact that only large companies were listed was driven by the methodology used in the BCG survey: the researchers asked executives to list the most innovative companies *they knew*, and the probability that enough of them knew the same innovative *startups* was low.

Regardless, the companies occupying the top of the list still meet the criteria for being consistently innovative. They command a large market share in their respective industries (sometimes even monopoly positions), and continue to deliver new products and services on a regular basis. And if *they* can do it—nothing prevents your company from being as innovative as they are.

This is the end of Part 1. The most important takeaways from this part are:

- Startup companies are generally more innovative than established, mature, large companies;
- Innovation is the organizational function of implementing employees' creative ideas;
- Company executives clearly understand that innovation is important to their companies;
- Empirically, innovative companies command 6 times the market share and 3 times the profitability of non-innovative companies, and are more resilient to recessions;
- Only *consistent* innovation delivers those desired financial results;
- Large companies "kill" employee creativity, the core building block of company innovation, by doing the *right* things—listening to their customers and following rules and regulations;
- 70-90% of acquisitions fail, and even when successful—they only add one more product line, and not the consistent innovation required for superior financial performance; and finally—
- Organic innovation *is* possible. Some of the most innovative companies are mature, established, and large ones.

Throughout Part 1, I did my best to show you *why* and *how* your mature company is killing creativity and innovation. However, I left you with a ray of hope: large companies *can* innovate. In Part 2, I will show you *how*.

PART 2: UN-KILL CREATIVITY

part 2:
un-kill creativity

6.

3,000 IDEAS, ONE SUCCESS STORY

How many ideas do you need to generate so you can have one successful product launch? What is your *success rate?*

Little did Michigan's Greg Stevens and James Burley imagine that their study[28] of that very question would be cited so many times. They wanted to help set the expectations of how many ideas were required to have one commercially successful product. Their measure of success was that the concept generated profit for the company in which it was conceived or, in other words, it would have a positive return on investment (ROI). They noticed that some companies reported success rates of 1-in-3,000, while others counted 60%. Both were true, depending on how you defined an *idea*. As a result, Stevens and Burley used four data sources to create their universal *success curve:* patent activity, project activity, venture capitalist (VC) activity, and independent inventor activity. They reviewed databases (patent applications, company financial data, etc.), and interviewed people in companies who could share insights. They pieced together all the different bits of information they collected to create that one single *success curve* that would be consistent and representative of the idea-to-success funnel.

Stevens and Burley found that there were at least 10 raw ideas for every single one that was submitted to the company's internal patent committee to decide whether it should be filed with the patent office.

---

[28] Stevens, G., & Burley, J. (1997, May). *3,000 raw ideas = 1 commercial success!* Research Technology Management, 40(3), 16.

The company's innovation funnel (review committee) screened those ideas for some of the obvious characteristics: the novelty of the idea, peer review, literature review, experimentation, and review by the marketing department that showed a glimmer of commercial viability. In general, before the company committed the $10,000 to $100,000 to file the patent, it had to be screened internally. When I worked for Texas Instruments I witnessed both sides of this process. As an inventor, I submitted several patent disclosures to the committee. The committee decided to proceed with three of them, which since then were issued. As a technology strategist, I audited patent committee meetings in which patent disclosures were presented by inventors and screened by reviewers. What I witnessed supported the statistic that 1-in-10 ideas were presented to the patent committee. Stevens and Burley interviewed employees from several companies and found that 50% of the ideas submitted to the internal patent committees were later submitted to the US Patent and Trademark office (USPTO), of which 37.5% were issued as patents. Of those, a total of 3% were determined (inside the company) to have *some* commercial viability. Finally, the rate of ideas that represented the company's "crown jewels," offering significant financial returns, the kind that makes you go to work for that company, was 0.03%. After piecing all the data together, Stevens and Burley generated the following "success curve":

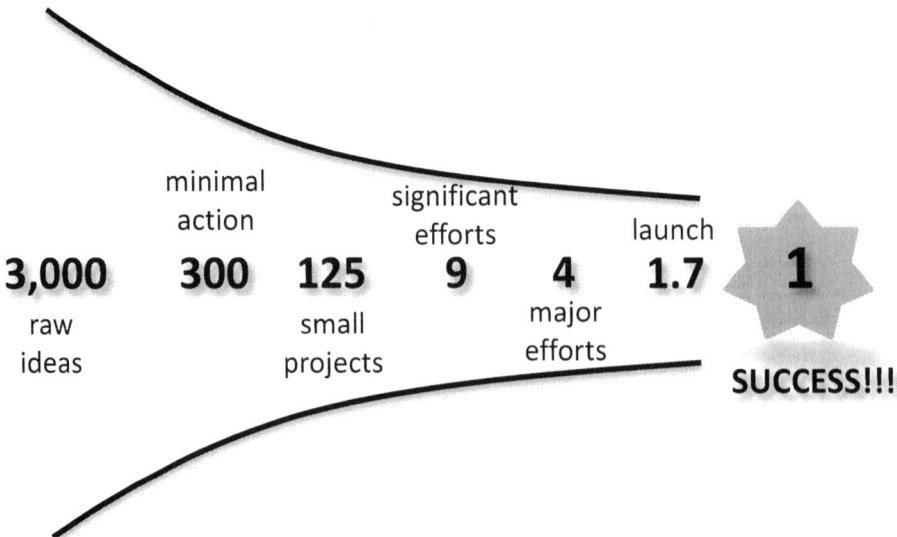

The curve starts with 3,000 raw ideas in stage one. Those ideas may come out of ideation workshops (discussed in chapter 16). They are technology- or market-driven, unscreened, un-researched, and before market-segmentation was ever done. Of those, 300 (10%) are submitted as disclosures to patent committees, seeking minimal funding, and involving tiny, "under the radar" level of research and development at stage 2, requiring less than one man-year. Ideas are then screened, and secondary market research is often used (third-party market reports), before they are filed as patents. On average, 125 (4.2% of the original 3,000) are issued patents, and/or allocated 1-3 man-years to continue development work in stage 3. In this stage, an analysis of fit-to-the-organization, market size, competitive advantage, and probability of success is conducted. As a result of that analysis, only 9 (0.3%) would typically survive and move on to stage 4, which represents a more significant expenditure of resources, allocating an R&D team of 10 or more engineers, and detailed specifications and requirements documentation are developed. Of those, 4 projects (0.1%) would undertake major development efforts, involving larger teams, major funding, pilot production, and test marketing with test customers in stage 5. From those, 1.7 projects (0.06%) would move to stage 6—a major, full scale commercial launch. Finally, only one project (0.03%) is expected to be commercially successful. Only one idea… The statistics are very demotivating: the probability of an idea leading to commercial success is a mere 0.03%. I know—it makes you want to quit, doesn't it? And if you think that 1-in-3,000 is bad, you should know that Stevens and Burley found that pharmaceutical companies have success rate of 1 in 6,000 to 8,000 ideas…

But here is how I look at it: when you bring an idea and find that it's a bad one, you now only have to produce 2,999 more ideas before you reach commercial success. This, of course, is as true as saying that your odds of getting "heads" in a coin toss increase if you just tossed "tails." Neither is true.

There is another problem resulting from this success curve. If only one market success comes out of 3,000 raw ideas, or even out of the 300 that were submitted internally—what do you think is the probability of the internal "screening" committee making a mistake and allowing a bad idea to move forward through the funnel (false positive), getting resources that should have been allocated to better projects, or that a good idea is thrown away (false negative)? They are very high. You can see the results of false positives in the high number of projects that never yield good return on investment. Unfortunately, you don't know how many false negative you had, because those ideas never got funded. Without my continuous drive to realize USB 3.0, it would have been a false negative and never see the light of day. Instead, billions of USB 3.0 ports are shipping in electronic products every year.

The insight you should take from Stevens and Burley's success curve is that for every successful commercial product launch you need to generate 3,000 ideas, so it is really important that you develop a system to generate high *quality* and *quantity* of ideas. And that's what the next few chapters are about.

7.

KNOWLEDGE IS NOT THE ISSUE...

Almost every summer my wife, Anat, and our two daughters, Maya and Shira, fly to Israel for a three-to-four week vacation to visit the family. Since my parents are long gone, and as much as I get along with my in-laws, I don't typically join them. It's hard for me to get away from my work and community involvement for such a long time, not to mention that I have the opportunity to build (or fix) my radio-controlled airplanes in every room of the house for at least three weeks. However, we typically combine their trip to Israel with a destination in the US or Europe. Here is how we do it: they fly to Israel, and on their way back we extend their connection by five or so days. I then fly to meet them at their connecting airport, rent a car, and we make a trip out of it. In 2012 they stayed in New York for five days. I joined them, and we planned a packed five-day trip to Washington DC and New York City.

On the last day, given that our flight back to Dallas was not until the evening, we left our luggage at the hotel and took the subway to the Rockefeller Plaza. I should add that we wake up to NBC's *The TODAY Show* every morning. So, that last morning we headed to the Plaza. We stood by the fence and waved when the anchors came out. After a while, we went up to NBC's "experience store" on the second floor of the GE building. This was during the 2012 London Olympics, and the store was loaded with memorabilia and accessories associated with *Team USA*. As I browsed through different shirts, three people approached me. One was wearing makeup for "on air" performance (I did not recognize her at the time, but she was NBC's nutrition editor, Madelyn Fernstrom), and the other two carried clipboards.

"Would you like to be on *The TODAY Show* this morning?" one of them asked.

"What do you want me on the show for?" I replied with a question.

"It's about weight loss," they carefully answered. I looked down to see what was it that made them seek me out for a show about weight loss. But hey—any reason is a good reason to be on TV, right? And this was not just any TV show, it was *The TODAY show*!

"What do you need me to do?"

"Every morning we turn to the audience to see if there are any questions. We need you to ask a question about weight loss. If you have a question we like, we would like you to ask it on air".

I thought for a second and realized I actually had a good question—a *very* good question.

"OK, how's this," I started: "I know what I have to do to lose weight. I know how I need to eat, and I know how I need to exercise. I know what I should and shouldn't do. *Knowledge* is not the issue! Where do you get the *motivation?*"

"Oh, this is a great question! Let's put him on air," said Madelyn Fernstrom with excitement. The others immediately took notes on their clipboards, and invited me to another room, where I would get some makeup myself. After all, we don't want me to shine on TV too much (pun intended).

Maya and I went to the preparation room and then to a room where many others, who were invited to ask questions on the show too, were standing. We weren't the only ones. However, they did put us in the front row, and we got to ask the first question. The answer was pretty generic: "You need to take small steps. Those will motivate you. And you also need to get the support of others." And that was it. After we got the answer we left that room, finished our shopping at the NBC experience store, collected our luggage from the hotel, and flew back to Dallas. During that flight I realized that something *big* had happened. I realized that I was right. Knowledge was *not* the issue. *Motivation* was. It didn't matter that I knew what I had to do. What mattered was how I could motivate myself to do the right things.

You can find the rest of the story[29] and how I lost 32 pounds over the following 6 months, exactly as planned, in my book *Worst Diet Ever*. But that's not why I told you this story.

The same concept applies to creativity and innovation in organizations. Most innovation books would tell you exactly what the *company* has to do, as far as innovation goes. They tell you that you must develop radical ideas. That you have to be less encumbered by orthodoxies and be willing to take risks. However, just like my diet, knowledge is *not* the issue. *Motivation* is. All this knowledge is worthless if you cannot motivate your employees to be creative, and this is what this book is about.

If you are a sports fan, maybe the following analogy would be better. Curling is not a sport often watched at the Olympics. I remember watching it for the first time trying to understand what was happening there. It didn't seem like a real sport. Curling was first introduced at the 1924 Olympic Games, but was on-and-off for many years, until it became an official part of the 1998 Winter Olympics. Curling may look like bowling, but is nothing like it. In bowling you give the ball whatever push, throw, and roll you can and let go. There is nothing you can do once the ball is out of your hand. Other than watch… You gave the ball the initial thrust, and now it is up to the ball. Curling is more subtle than that. Once the "stone" is thrusted,

---

[29] http://www.today.com/id/48210533

two players (sweepers) with brooms (yes, brooms) would alter the state of the ice in front of the stone to affect its path. By the way—I don't think you lose many calories in curling.

I have to confess now. I never played golf. I know, I know, who doesn't play golf? Well, I don't. However, I know enough to tell that there are different types of golf clubs. The ones that propel the golf ball the farthest (up to 350 yards) are the wood clubs. They are called that because they were originally made out of wood, although they are not anymore. The club that hits the ball the farthest is the #1 club, also called the driver[30].

---

[30] http://blog.golfsmith.com/golf-equipment/types-of-golf-clubs-their-uses/#.V2PyLNUrLnA

Creativity is more like curling and less like golf. You don't *drive* the ball, you make room for it to slightly change direction, and you have very little control over it. Even if it drives you crazy. Creative bosses don't try to *force* their employees to be creative. It doesn't work. They don't try to give their employees 20% of their time to be creative, or build an innovation lab for them, because those don't work either. Instead, creative bosses *allow* their employees to create naturally and individually.

In her 1998 article *How to Kill Creativity*, Teresa Amabile described individual creativity with the following Venn diagram, showing creativity as the overlap of expertise, creative thinking skills, and motivation.

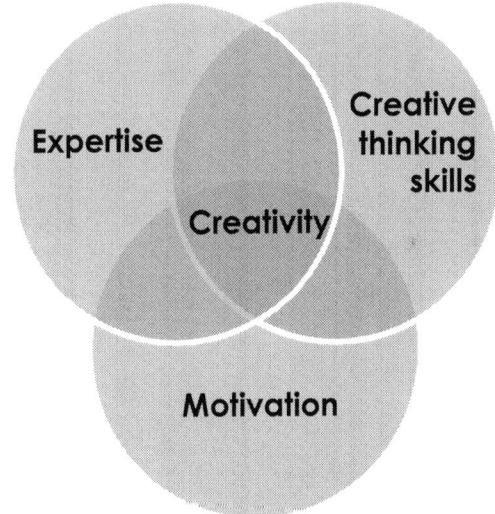

(Source: Teresa Amabile, How to Kill Creativity, Harvard Business Review, 1998)

Expertise includes the technical skills related to the problem at hand. If you need to solve an electronic problem, an electronics engineering degree, knowledge, and/or experience are the expertise you need. You don't have to be a Nobel Prize laureate in the field, but you have to know enough.

Creative thinking skills include the cognitive abilities required to solve problems. Different people solve problems differently. Introverts like to (and can) solve problems alone, while extroverts (like me) need sounding boards to bounce ideas. Amabile referred to expertise and creative thinking skills as the "raw materials" that you have.

However, it is the third factor that turns those raw materials into creativity: *motivation*. Much like I had the knowledge I needed to lose weight but it wasn't enough—I needed the motivation to turn that knowledge into real weight loss. The *right* motivation. And this is where motivation for creativity is different from motivation for weight loss. While the motivation needed for my weight loss was *extrinsic*, the one required for creativity is *intrinsic*. I feel that I need to define those two new terms, don't I?

Extrinsic motivation is external to your person. It's the "carrot and stick" motivation. It includes financial incentives, threats of termination, promise of promotions, and others things that are completely external to you, controlled by someone else (your boss), and have nothing to do with the task at hand. Intrinsic motivation, on the other hand, comes from within you. It is the passion you have, your curiosity to see the end result, the satisfaction and sense of accomplishment when conquering a difficult challenge, and other similar things that nobody else can control or provide you with. If you think about it, intrinsic motivation ranks at the highest level of Maslow's hierarchy of needs (self-actualization), while extrinsic motivation ranks somewhat lower than that.

The importance of making that distinction comes from Amabile's own four-decade-long research, in which she found that intrinsic motivation had a much stronger effect on creativity than extrinsic motivation. Not only that, but she found that while intrinsic motivation had a *positive* effect on creativity, extrinsic motivation had a *negative* effect. The candle problem illustrates this best.

THE CANDLE PROBLEM

The candle problem was a cognitive performance test, developed by psychologist Karl Duncker and published in 1945[31]. In this test, participants were given a candle, matches, and a box of thumbtacks. The objective was to fix a lit candle on the wall, such that wax would not drip from it onto the floor. Before you keep reading, think about it for a second; how would *you* do it?

The answer is: take the thumbtacks out of their box, use them to fix the box itself to the wall, and then put the lit candle in that box. Simple, isn't it? If you reached that conclusion before reading the answer, you *are* creative (or at least would have been considered creative in 1945) and less affected by "functional fixedness" (limiting your imagination to the normal use of things, such as the box being used only to hold the thumbtacks).

The test could be made simpler by removing the thumbtacks from their box. When they are outside the box, it is clear to see that the box could be used for other purposes (such as holding the candle) and, therefore, more test participants would reach this obvious solution faster. Not much creativity or complex thought was required in this case.

In 1962, psychologist Sam Glucksberg[32] added another factor to the test: he offered a $5 reward ($40 in today's values) to the fastest 25% of those who solved the candle problem, and $20 to those who

---

[31] http://en.wikipedia.org/wiki/Candle_problem
[32] Glucksberg, S. (1962). *The influence of strength of drive on functional fixedness and perceptual recognition.* Journal of Experimental Psychology, 63 (1), 36-41: http://whywereason.com/2011/09/01/how-misguided-incentives-negatively-affect-productivity-and-well-being/

were the fastest of all. He now had a total of four groups: one pair of groups *with* the monetary incentives and one pair of groups without them. In each pair there was one group for which the thumbtacks were inside the box (requiring higher creativity level to solve) and one group for which the thumbtacks were outside the box (more obvious, requiring less creativity). Glucksberg expected the incentives to improve performance regardless of the task/test complexity, but to his surprise he found the opposite: offering the incentives *decreased* performance sometimes. I'll repeat this: the incentives *decreased* performance.

In 2005, the Federal Reserve Bank of Boston commissioned a study to find the impact of contingent pay incentives on productivity and performance[33]. The research was conducted by Dan Ariely (MIT), Uri Gneezy (University of Chicago), George Lowenstein (Carnegie Mellon University), and Nina Mazar (MIT). The experiments were conducted in several locations: at MIT, at the University of Chicago, and in rural India. The participants were given six games to play, with varying levels of complexity and varying need for creative thinking. Based on the results of the games, the test groups were offered incentives (in contrast with the control groups that were not offered any incentives). The highest possible performance rewarded participants a sum equal to a median monthly wage. The results were consistent with Glucksberg's findings in 1962: while performance has improved with incentives at the simple tasks, it deteriorated at the more complex tasks that required creativity. To use the researchers' own words:

---

[33] Ariely, D., U. Gneezy, G. Lowenstein and N. Mazar (2009): *Large Stakes and Big Mistakes*, Review of Economic Studies 76, 451-469: http://www.bostonfed.org/economic/wp/wp2005/wp0511.pdf

"It now appears that beyond some threshold level, raising incentives may increase motivation to supra-optimal levels and result in perverse effects on performance."

The results are summarized in the following chart:

	WITH incentives	WITHOUT incentives
SIMPLE problem	increased performance	reduced performance
COMPLEX problem	reduced performance	increased performance

THE HAWTHORNE EFFECT

One of the oldest sources used in my dissertation literature review came from the 1939 book *Management and the worker*, by Fritz Roethlisberger and Elton Mayo. The authors conducted productivity studies in the 1920s and documented them in that book. This book, and the *Hawthorne Experiments*[34] it described, became a classic case of employee motivation, but also a story of an experiment gone wrong.

Among other things, Roethlisberger and Mayo intended to study the impact that environmental working conditions, specifically lighting, had on productivity. For that purpose they used two groups of production workers at the Western Electric Company Hawthorne Plant, who were assembling relays. They removed one group from the main production hall to a side room that had much dimmer lighting.

---

[34] https://www.boundless.com/management/textbooks/boundless-management-textbook/organizational-theory-3/behavioral-perspectives-30/the-human-side-hawthorne-170-8381/

They expected the workers in the less lit room to produce less. They just didn't know how much less. Much to their surprise, the result was opposite to their hypothesis. The workers in the less lit room produced *more* than those in the main room. Significantly more. The natural conclusion could have been that increased lighting reduces productivity, while reduced lighting increases productivity. Fortunately, they explored the results further, to find what would later be known as the *Hawthorne Effect*. The members of the team that worked in the well-lit room didn't know that they were being observed. For them, this was just another day at the factory. Their production levels were consistent with those in every other day. The other team, though, noticing the observer in the room, worked harder simply because they knew they were being observed, and they wanted to appear at their best. They were *intrinsically* motivated.

The researchers studied other social-psychological factors that affected workplace productivity, including financial incentives, and concluded that—

> "None of the results... gave the slightest substantiation to the theory that the worker is primarily motivated by economic interests."

So what type of motivation affects employee creativity, positively and negatively? While few researchers studied the topic, Teresa Amabile is the most prominent one. She used three methodologies to develop her organizational climate measurement instrument, KEYS'[35]: experiments, interviews, and surveys. Out of those, several themes emerged, and as a result she developed the KEYS creativity assessment instrument. I used KEYS at Interphase, and can attest to how easy it was to administer and to interpret the results from. More about KEYS in chapter 14. Here are the six intrinsic organizational climate factors

---

[35] KEYS is a registered trademark owned by the Center for Creative Leadership. See www.ccl.org/KEYS

affecting employee creativity, as presented by Teresa Amabile. Later they will be refined based on my own study.

Challenge: matching people with jobs for which they have the required expertise and skills, in a way that would challenge them to be creative. Managers must pay attention to what makes their employees excited, and thus intrinsically motivated. "You have to do this because I said so" is no way to motivate employees to be creative. Letting employees gravitate towards areas of the job that they like would. Kelly Johnson of Lockheed, the creator of the Skunk Works, said that "people challenged to perform at their best will do so."[36] More on Johnson and Skunk Works later in the book.

Freedom: allowing employees to choose *how* they do their job, or meet their challenge. Not *which* challenge to tackle. In Amabile's words:

> "... give them freedom to decide how to climb a particular mountain. You needn't let them choose which mountain to climb."

Employees need to know what the goal is. Very clearly. But they should be allowed to choose their own path and process to get there. Managers' intervention in choosing the path (otherwise known as micro-management) reduces creativity. I know. I've done it many times. But then again, I'm trying to help *you*. Not myself...

Resources: typically, the two most important resources in a company are *time* and *money*. Those have to be allocated carefully. Time pressure can drive creativity, but only if it is real and *externally* imposed. "Cushioning" and fake deadlines could hurt trust, motivation, and creativity, and cause employee burnout. Sometimes, creativity simply takes time. Time is needed for the individual idea generation process, in which procrastination is not all bad. But I'll talk about that later. Other, more tangible resources (money, equipment,

---

[36] Kelly: More Than My Share of It All by Clarence L. Johnson, Maggie Smith, 1989.

materials) should be allocated appropriately. No organization I know has an unlimited abundance of such resources. Keeping resources too tight might have an adverse impact on creativity. Amabile claimed that beyond a certain level of resources, the law of diminishing returns comes into play, and adding resources would not increase creativity. When this point is discussed in greater detail later, you would see that beyond a certain amount of resources, creativity actually *declines*.

Workgroup features: the construction of the team is very important to creativity. Teams must be diverse (in experience and skills), team members must share excitement over the team's goal, willingness to support each other when times are tough, and must respect each other's unique perspectives. Managers are tempted to create homogeneous teams, but that practice may eliminate the diversity of perspectives required for the team to be truly creative. "[If] everyone comes to the table with a similar mind-set, [t]hey leave with the same," said Amabile. To me, the team factors should be discussed separately from organizational climate, simply because once the team is formed, it could be more autonomous and less controlled or influenced by the organization and its executive management, unlike the organizational climate, which would still be under their control.

Supervisory encouragement: creative people don't need a pat on the back all the time. They can find their intrinsic motivation within the project. However, sustaining the level of enthusiasm requires the manager to encourage them every now and then. Managers should celebrate successes, but also support unsuccessful attempts. "Not every new idea is worthy of consideration," said Amabile, but overly criticizing new ideas and the people who brought them forward, and imposing cumbersome, multi-layer evaluation processes could discourage the presentation of new ideas. Negativity for the sake of showing depth and authority is not constructive. Punishment for failure is yet another way to kill creativity by discouraging employees from trying, due to the fear of failure and moreover—its consequences. One other form of management encouragement, as I learned during my service in the Israeli Defense Forces, is *leading by example*. This happens when managers, supervisors, or commanders lead the way themselves. Employees have much more respect *to* their leader, and appreciate the support they get *from* a leader who leads by example, more than from a controlling micro-manager who leads from behind.

Organizational support: to be creative, employees must feel that they are supported by more than their teammates and immediate team leader. They must feel that the entire organization is supportive of their goal and efforts. The organization should have values that support creativity, and procedures that reflect that. Extrinsic monetary rewards, and especially contingency rewards hurt creativity more than support it. Financial rewards make people feel *controlled* rather than encouraged. Infighting and internal politics should be eliminated, since they harm creativity significantly. Bureaucracy should be minimized, and open communication encouraged.

8.

WHO IS RESPONSIBLE FOR INNOVATION?

In the last chapter of Part 1, I gave you hope that organic innovation is possible in large, mature companies. In the last chapter, I explained that innovation is achieved through creativity that, in turn, is achieved through motivation, and specifically *intrinsic* motivation.

But whose job is it in the organization to motivate employees to be creative? In a word—*everyone's!* Through my research of creativity in startup and mature companies and from research done before that, three levels in the organization were found to have impact on employee creativity: the organizational level (through organizational climate), the team level (through team dynamics), and the individual level. Yes, employees are responsible for their own creativity as well!

THE ORGANIZATION'S ROLE

Early on I defined innovation (organizational function) as the implementation (also an organizational function) of a creative idea (individual function). The organization serves a dual role in innovation, in the beginning and at the end of the process. First, the organization has to create a climate conducive to employee creativity. The overwhelming majority of participants in my study reported much stronger presence of the positive organizational climate factors in startups, and stronger presence of the negative organizational climate factors in mature companies. Few of those organizational climate factors showed a *significant* impact on employees experiencing creativity in my study. As a reminder, the positive factors included autonomy, external challenges (market, competition, technology), exposure to the big picture, and the knowledge of the impact they had on their company's' success. The negative factors included the level of internal challenges, company politics, formalization, and processes within the company. The higher the bureaucracy in the company was—the fewer employees felt creative. When processes were used as whips instead of as guidelines—employees felt less creative.

But all is not lost. Companies, even mature ones, can work on each one of those factors in order to create a climate in which employees would experience creativity. The beauty of it—it hardly costs anything to implement! Prior research showed a positive relationship between availability (read: abundance) of resources and creativity, but my later research showed that beyond a certain level of resource availability—more resources meant *less* creativity. Employees didn't need to try as much when they had an abundance of resources, but when they had fewer resources at their disposal—they had to be more creative. My research thus concluded that additional resources were not necessary. More on that in chapter 9.

The company plays another important role once a creative idea was generated by employees (or a team): *implementing* it. The company's willingness to assume risk and try new things, its willingness to trust employees and let them experiment, prototype, and finally launch a major development effort is key to turning employee creativity into company innovation. Over time I found that the strongest motivation affecting a company's willingness to assume such risk, and trust its employees is a fear for the company's survival.

THE TEAM'S ROLE

My research also showed a strong relationship between team dynamics and the creativity level of individual members of that team. The willingness and ability to argue and debate without developing personal conflict or competition had a very positive impact on individual creativity. The ability to argue and debate is what turned team creativity from 1+1=0 into 1+1=3. Team member diversity (different backgrounds, experiences, skills, expertise, and not only demographic) led to better team ideas.

The team leader plays an important role in the team's creativity, more than any manager or supervisor in the company. A good team leader protects the team from the organizational bureaucracy and formalization, facilitates positive, creativity-supporting dynamics, encourages experimentation, risk-taking, trust, debate, humor, and playfulness.

The team leader also played a role in the implementation process. The leader had to be chosen such that he or she were also trusted and respected by upper management, when the time came to share the idea (and the prototype) and ask for permission to proceed with a major project and product launch[37]. A more substantial discussion of team dynamics is provided in chapter 10.

THE INDIVIDUAL ROLE

Finally, individuals play a role in creating an environment for themselves in which they could be more creative. They cannot solely depend on upper management, or the team and team leader in providing such environment. While the moment of invention might appear accidental, it is the result of certain actions taken by the individual to increase the likelihood of such "accidents." Those actions include consuming large amounts of multi-disciplinary information, recording it, thinking about it, and creating situations in which the "collision" of ideas is triggered. The role of the individual in creating a personal context for creativity is covered in chapter 12. It will show what *you* can do every day to increase your own creativity level. Not only at work.

---

[37] *Implementing radical innovation in mature firms: the role of hubs.* Leifer, O'Connor, and Rice, in the Academy of Management Executive Journal, 2001

ARE 2 OUT OF 3 ENOUGH?

In summary, all three levels (company, team, and individual) must participate in motivating employees to produce creative ideas and implementing them to generate consistent innovation for the company, and are equally responsible for its success. Creativity and innovation practitioners often focus on one of them, and sometimes two. Personal coaches tend to focus on individual creativity, and sometimes on team dynamics. Organizational development professionals may focus on the organizational factors. Very few practitioners would address all three.

However, the results of any effort to increase the level of innovation and creativity in a company would yield less than optimal results if not all three receive full attention. In fact, missing even one of the three would significantly hurt creativity (and thus innovation) results. Here is how:

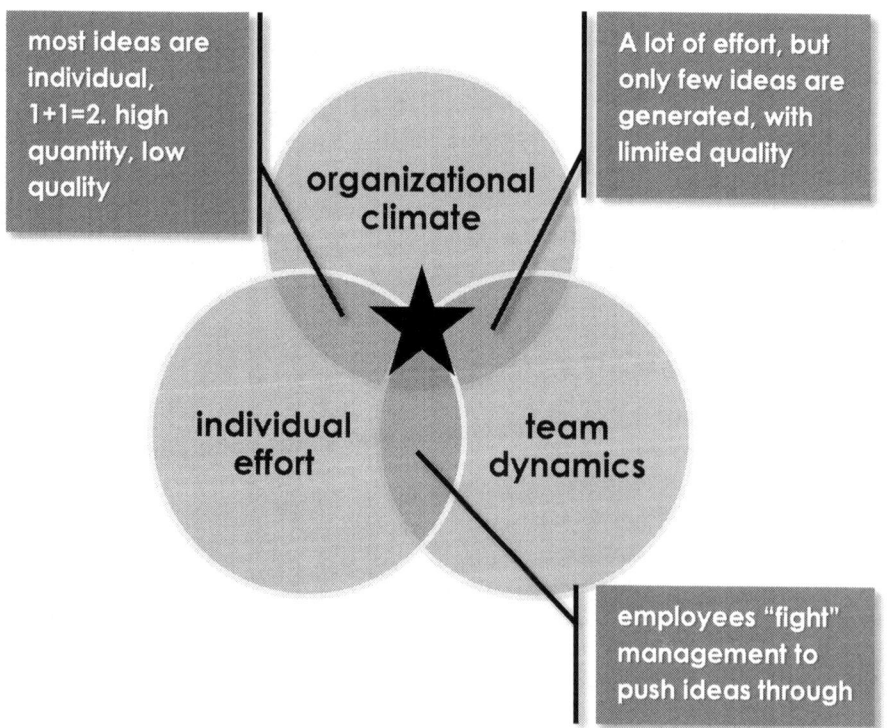

Ignoring the Organizational Climate factors would hamper creative idea generation when employees don't feel empowered or encouraged to do so. Employees might be afraid to try new things, fearing the consequences of failure. Those who never try would never fail. But they would never succeed, either. Employees would have to "fight" management to get things done, as management would not allocate resources to new initiatives. Implementation would suffer, and so would creativity and innovation.

Ignoring team dynamics would allow the generation of only individual ideas. Only ideas fully conceived within one person's brain would be presented to management. The company would not benefit from the diverse experiences and knowledge of its employees, as poor team dynamics would prevent effective ideation, and would never reach 1+1=3. "Every man for himself" would be the order of the day. Internal competition and strife would prevail, and creativity would get a lower priority.

Ignoring individual creativity would be characterized by low quality and quantity of ideas. A lot of effort would be placed on innovation. The company would likely give employees time and space to create, and would celebrate every mediocre success, but no great ideas would emerge. There could be a lot of pressure to create, and the company might implement mediocre ideas and fail to produce strong return on investment.

All three areas must be supported to achieve a high quantity of high-quality ideas, and to have those implemented. Employees should be trained to be creative, and take the appropriate steps for generating ideas with high fluency, flexibility, elaboration, and originality. Team dynamics must have low internal competition, high levels of trust, open and passionate debate, where team members build on each other's ideas. Finally, the organization must create an environment that *allows* creativity, allows employees to fail without severe consequences, and applies adequate resources to implement ideas.

un-kill creativity

9. CORPORATE CLIMATE STARTS WITH YOU

Corporate climate is one of those three areas that affect individual creativity, alongside team dynamics and individual actions. The purpose of this book is to show you what *you* could do to increase that level of creativity, through influencing all three. This chapter focuses on the organizational climate and how it influences creativity.

But before I tell you *how* mature, established companies could motivate their employees to be creative, I should tell you *why*. Why would *companies* be motivated to do whatever it takes to increase the levels of creativity and innovation, and how could you tell if they are motivated enough?

FEAR & HUNGER

Teresa Amabile explained that employee autonomy is one of the most deciding factors affecting their creativity. "People will be more creative... if you give them freedom to decide how to climb a particular mountain," she wrote in her 1998 article *How to Kill Creativity*. When I realized in the early 1990s that I was a micro-manager, I tried to understand why. I realized that giving my employees autonomy was risky. I had to trust them. I had to know how to let go of absolute control, and accept not knowing how things may develop. After all, I was placing my career success at the hands of my employees, and that was a bit too risky for me.

Having a strong creative idea flow is not enough, though. Innovative companies must be willing to take risk with radical and highly unorthodox ideas, and to place bets even with less-than-perfect odds of success, which puts their executives' careers at risk as well.

And how are these related to fear?

Aviation always fascinated me, ever since I was a child. I could identify every plane that flew overhead, jet or prop, civilian or military. It was only natural that later in life I became a pilot, and later start building and flying radio controlled model airplanes, too. When you look at the progress made in aviation technology, you could observe periods of relatively slow and incremental innovation, and periods of very fast and radical innovation. The first real manned, controlled, powered, heavier-than-air flight took place on December 17, 1903, in *Kill Devil Hills* and *Kitty Hawk* in North Carolina by Orville and Wilbur Wright, with their Wright Flyer I. Four flights took place that date, with the longest one covering 852 feet at the amazing altitude of 10 feet... The plane crashed after that last flight, and was never restored to flying condition. The Wright brothers referred to the experiences of that day as "partial success."[38] However, that day was considered the beginning of modern aviation. From that moment on, some incremental progress had been made, but on the eve of World War I, the airplane was still not a fighting machine. It was not reliable enough, nor could it carry machine guns or bombs, and therefore saw very limited use. The airplane essentially looked a lot like the original 1903 Wright Flyer I biplane, albeit slightly modified. During World War I, and as soon as both sides saw the potential use of airplanes as war machines—significant innovation began to improve aviation. Bigger and better engines were created especially for airplanes (as opposed to the adoption of non-aviation

---

[38] http://www.thewrightbrothers.org/fivefirstflights.html

engines before the war), machine guns and bombs were added, flight instrumentation has evolved, and the overall structure, maneuverability, and performance of the airplane have significantly improved.

And then WWI ended. Aviation innovation continued in the era between the two world wars (1919-1939), but not at such rapid pace as it did in the short period during WWI (1914-1919). The five years of WWI saw significantly more aviation innovation than the twenty years that followed. Some of the allied warplanes on the eve of World War II were still biplanes, not much different than those used at the end of WWI, twenty years earlier. In fact, it was the Axis countries that made the most improvement to their fleets, as they were preparing for a new war.

WWII arguably saw the most dramatic rate of aviation innovation. Entering the war with some biplanes, non-supercharged piston engines, the war ended just as the jet engine was put to use in airplanes. The jet engine was actually invented long before WWII, dating back to 1200 AD with the advent of the rocket in China[39]. The modern jet engine invention was attributed to Hans von Ohain in Germany and Frank Whittle in England, both in the 1930s. However, it wasn't until near the end of WWII that governments invested enough resources in turning those underpowered inventions into engines that could provide higher speeds to war planes. WWII saw one more dramatic innovation: the harnessing of the Atom energy and unleashing of its destructive power, in the form of two atom bombs dropped on Japan in August 1945, attributed with ending the war.

Although the rate of aviation innovation slowed down somewhat after WWII, it was still faster than during the period between the two wars. The reason was that there was actually another war taking place at that time—the cold war. The Soviet Union and the United States

---

[39] http://www.facstaff.bucknell.edu/mvigeant/therm_1/je2/history.htm

were locked in an arms race, each fearing complete destruction by the other side. While no global war was taking place, this conflict did spawn the Korean War and the Vietnam War. Other local "incidents" included the Cuban Missile Crisis. The effect on aviation innovation was very apparent. Long-range bombers were developed, air-to-air (and air-to-ground) missiles were created, and even the space race could be interpreted as a military race (providing the winner with strategic advantages such as the ability to monitor and harm the opponent from outer space) masqueraded as a peaceful and healthy technological competition. Once the Berlin wall was torn down in 1989, followed by the separation of the Soviet Union, which began in 1990, the rate of aviation innovation (and space exploration) slowed down once again. One example was the cancellation of the ultrasonic, swept wing B-1 strategic bomber program in 1988. Ending this program symbolized the end of the cold war, and was followed by the fall of the Berlin Wall and the Soviet Union, one year later.

Although the same could probably be said for many technologies and industries, I know more about aviation than any other military and civil engineering discipline. Using aviation technology as a benchmark, there was no doubt that the war effort had a very important and powerful impact on innovation in that industry than any peace time period.

IRON DOME

On April 7, 2001, the residents of the Southern Israeli city of Ashkelon were alerted, once again, to short range rockets incoming from the Gaza Strip. Three of the rockets landed in open areas and caused no casualties or property damage. The fourth one, heading directly towards a populated area in the city, surprisingly exploded in mid-air. It was not a malfunction. The short range rocket was intercepted by a new anti-missile and shell system named "iron dome"[40], which was developed in Israel. Israel is known worldwide as a hot bed for new and disruptive technologies. Most of those came out of defense manufacturers and military advanced research units. Most of the technologists used by Israel's leading technology companies came out of the research and development arm of the Israeli Defense Forces, adapting technologies previously used for military purposes to civilian use. *Check Point* (the first commercial firewall technology company) was one such example. What made Israel a source for so much innovation?

One final point. Often when someone is presented with two options: go work for a startup or go work for a mature company (especially a large one), you hear about the "stability" or "job security" associated with the large company. There is no doubt that a large company has a dampening effect on employment. In a large company, bad businesses exist on the coattails of strong businesses. Bad talent exists in the shadow of good talent. Until the 1990s, tenure was very acceptable in a company. Job security was almost guaranteed in mature companies, while the failure rate of startups offered anything *but* job security. People stayed with large and mature companies such as AT&T, General Motors, Boeing, and others like those. The dot-com bubble burst in 2000 did not challenge the job security myth, because it affected mainly technology companies, most of which were young themselves. However, the recent 2007 recession hit mature businesses hard, causing their employees to challenge that myth. But until now, employees in mature companies did not feel the risk to the survival of their companies in most cases. And they had no reason to, because neither did their management. Top management never communicated a survival fear to their employees. It would have looked bad.

---

[40] http://www.haaretz.com/news/diplomacy-defense/iron-dome-successfully-intercepts-gaza-rocket-for-first-time-1.354696

YOU HAVE NOTHING TO LOSE

It's really quite simple. Two years ago, to illustrate that point, I asked someone I had just met in a chamber of commerce reception in Houston if he would give me the keys to his brand new Mercedes E-class car so I could test-drive it. He looked at me, somewhat annoyed, and said "no!"

"Why?" I asked, and he replied: "because I don't know you, and I don't *trust* you with my car!" Makes sense, doesn't it? Letting me drive his car was a risk that he had no *reason* to take, and therefore was not willing to take.

"Let me change the scenario a bit to make my point," I added: "what if you were hurt, needing to be taken to a hospital, and this was really not where you want to leave your brand new car parked overnight. Would you give me the keys and let me drive it to your home then?" He didn't have to think twice and immediately said "of course!"

"How is that different?" I pressed. He had to think about that for a moment, realizing he gave me two opposite answers to the same question in less than a minute. He finally replied, triumphantly: "Because I didn't have a choice this time!"

Companies "think" and act the same way. When the company's financials and prospects are positive, protected, and safe (or, at least, are *perceived* as such by its top executives), it doesn't take risks. It doesn't have to trust employees enough to let them make mistakes, and it doesn't have to apply resources to crazy ideas. The "safe" projects are enough. However, when the company is *fearful* for its survival, when it is one mistake away from bankruptcy, or under attack by predatory competitors or changing market dynamics (or, at least, is *perceived* to be so)—its executives feel they have no choice.

They have nothing to lose. Under this perception they are willing to assume more risk (what alternatives do they really have?), trust their employees, provide them with the freedom so critically needed to be creative, and implement "crazy" ideas. Their decisions are driven by a sense of urgency. They feel that taking a risk with a crazy idea is better than doing nothing at all, and see the company fail. You hear the words "Hail Mary" more often.

My two-year study connected the higher level of startup creativity to the *fear* that those companies felt, which caused them to entrust employees with freedom. On the other hand, it showed a correlation between lower innovation levels of mature companies and the lack of fear perceived by leaders, which caused them to deploy "command and control" management, unsupportive of employee creativity.

How could this explain why Apple, with more than $40 in assets for every person on this planet, and which two weeks before the US had reached its debt limit in 2011 held more money in the bank than the US government, be so innovative? Surely this company could not be fearful for its survival enough to feel that it "doesn't have a choice but to trust the employees and take risks on their crazy ideas." The answer was that the late Steve Jobs, as described through articles and his biography, believed that the company was on the brink of collapse many times during his two tenures as CEO. It didn't really matter whether the company was at risk or not in reality. What mattered was that he *thought* it was.

Yes, in many cases when executives perceive that their companies are at risk—they really are. In many cases when they perceive their companies are safe—they really are. Unfortunately, more often than not, executives perceive that their companies are safe, when in fact they are at risk. Rarely, such as in Apple's case, executives fear for the future of their companies when, in fact, their companies are in great shape. The *perception* is more important than reality. This paranoia is healthy[41]. It causes executives to take risks and trust employees with autonomy, and to implement the craziest of ideas. Executives who do not fear for the future of their companies, whether justified or not, would prevent autonomy and creativity.

However, you should consider that sometimes, under pressure, CEOs and other top executives, instead of developing a willingness to trust employees and give them the autonomy required to be creative, would go to the opposite end. They would hunker down, and go to extreme levels of command and control. They would entrench the company in their current business and stop investment in anything new. Instead of taking chances with innovative products—they would resort to reductions in force until the company reached its bare bones, capable of supporting only its legacy business, which had already matured and was most likely not profitable enough to support even the minimal level of overhead the company is maintaining. I've seen that happen too. More than once.

When I interviewed at Interphase in 2008, I felt the company's fear for survival. The CEO had it, the executive team had it, and the board of directors had it. They may not have admitted to it or communicated it, but they had fear, and I felt it. Others might have been reluctant to join the company at that stage. The company, while successful to that point, had the biggest market share in a shrinking market. As Danny DeVito, playing *Lawrence Garfield*, "Larry the Liquidator," in the 1991 movie *Other People's Money*, said—

> "You know, at one time there must've been dozens of companies making buggy whips. And I'll bet the last company around was the one that made the best goddamn buggy whip you ever saw. Now how would you have liked to have been a stockholder in that company?"

---

[41] Andrew Grove, Intel's CEO, wrote more about that in his 1996 book, *Only the Paranoid Survive*.

So before you attempt to work on how your company could motivate employees to be creative, ask yourself *why*. Why would this company take risks with crazy new initiatives? Why would it give employees the freedom to do things the way they feel is right? Why would executives give up total control? The company itself has to be motivated, and the strongest motivator is the fear for survival. Without it, significant innovation initiatives would fail.

But as long as the motivator for the *company* exists, here is how the company could motivate its employees to be creative.

AUTONOMY

Autonomy was found to be one of the strongest factors affecting employee creativity as identified by Amabile, Ekvall, Burgelman, and many more (including my own study). Autonomy in the context of organizations is the freedom to try things without having to ask permission, and without fearing the consequences of failure. The more autonomy you give employees, the more they try to solve problems themselves, and the more creative and productive they become. The freedom is not to choose your project or goal—the freedom is to choose *how* you get there. General Patton said "Never tell people how to do things. Tell them what to do and they will surprise you with their ingenuity." Teresa Amabile said "… give them freedom to decide how to climb a particular mountain. You needn't let them choose which mountain to climb."

On the other hand, when you restrict employee autonomy, they become less creative and less productive. They would come to you with every little question and obstacle and expect you to solve it for them. You may not want to restrict employee creativity intentionally, but sometimes the way you *behave* when an employee fails would deter them from ever attempting anything autonomous, and effectively restrict their freedom.

OK, I explained *why* autonomy is such an important motivator, but how do you give employees autonomy?

THE BIG PICTURE

First, you give autonomy by sharing the *big picture*. Companies typically break large projects into smaller chunks and assign them to individuals or small teams capable of handling those chunks, but most likely incapable of handling the entire project. You never let a team of 5 develop the next fighter jet. But you may let them design the landing gear for that jet. You, of course, would be the big picture keeper, and you wouldn't share it with them because you feel it might be a distraction. Let them focus on their small piece, right? Well, the opposite is true. Individuals (and teams) are more creative when they understand not only the requirements for their own piece of the puzzle, but when they see the complete picture as well. As a pilot, whenever I navigated my plane on the ground in a complex airport, it was hard to know where I needed to turn. Sure, I had a map of the airport on my kneeboard, but I still didn't have the "feel" for the airport. Plus, I wanted to keep my eyes *outside* the plane. Soon after takeoff, reaching some reasonable altitude, and turning—that's when the airport reveals itself. That's when everything starts to make sense. That's when you know where everything is. Yet another aviation analogy: before you fly, after filing your flight plan, you are required to communicate with air traffic controllers via the "clearance delivery" channel. That's where you announce your intentions, and receive specific directions for your travel on the ground, and right after takeoff. You are told that after takeoff you should expect to "fly runway heading," to "climb and maintain 4,000 feet," and so on. All pilots are required to monitor and listen to the same channel. Why? Because when you hear the directions given to *other* pilots, you are beginning to know what to expect around you. You are not alone. You are part of a big "machine" called air traffic. You see the big picture.

The same is true for company projects. When people understand the role their parts play in the whole system, when they understand the interaction between their parts and other parts in the project, they are the most creative. They can draw *from* resources available in other areas in the project, and they can contribute *to* other areas of the project. Today's complex systems and projects are more intertwined than any single individual could grasp. Nor is a single individual expected to grasp the entire complex system and the interconnections between its parts. The modularization and compartmentalization of a large and complex system into small, manageable parts, with very clear boundaries, interfaces, and specifications was created by managers who felt the need to be in *control*, rather than by the nature of the system or good engineering and development practices.

So instead of keeping the big picture to yourself, breaking it down into pieces, defining boundaries, and letting people and teams work only on their respective parts—share the big picture with them. Let them "draw outside the lines" and interact with other teams. The autonomy you should give them is that you won't be the only person with a clear view of the big picture.

Another organizational factor found to positively affect creativity was the level of *challenge* that employees faced in their work. Here, my focus is on *external* challenges: funding, market forces, competition, technological challenges, and the like. *Not* internal ones. The more challenging the project is, the more motivated employees are to be creative in solving those challenges. Once again, your willingness to expose them to the big picture that includes those external challenges would support their creativity. Don't be the buffer between the outside world's realities and them. Let them understand the real challenges. Let them experience those firsthand. Let them meet customers. Let them be scared by those challenges, and they would address them creatively. Don't assume they cannot surmount the toughest challenges thrown their way. They would surprise you.

IMPACT ON RESULTS

Another form of autonomy and big picture view is the understanding of the impact that every person and every small part of the project has on the overall company results, specifically financial. After all, the company was formed to generate revenue, profits, and shareholder return on investment. Executives would typically shield employees from knowing the impact they have on those results, for several reasons. First of all, a small project may only have a small impact on the financial results of a large company. When I presented the business plan for USB 3.0 to a senior vice president in Texas Instruments, I realized that this project may generate "only" $500 million in sales. This might seem a lot for a startup, and may guarantee an acquisition in the billions of dollars. But for a company that already generated $14 billion in sales, $500 million was less than a 4% increase in sales and profitability. 4% was less than the company's stock price may have changed over a single trading week. However, every project still has an impact, and it is your responsibility to share that impact with your employees. Even if they are very busy (or pretend to be busy), you should spend time with them sharing the impact their project may have on the company's success. Not only the financial success. Sometimes, success could be related to the company's brand image, customer loyalty, or any other metric. Employees are motivated when they know that their project has impact on the company, even if only a small one.

TRY, TRY AGAIN

The most frequently discussed type of autonomy in the organization is the freedom to *experiment*. Don't confuse freedom to experiment with giving employees time to work on new things or a location in an innovation lab. Experimenting is not about resource allocation, but rather about disconnecting failure from consequences. In many large companies employees are discouraged from trying things through the *consequences* of failure. However, there is a recent change in attitude. Books were written about that, and to some extent promote the celebration of failure. *Fail Fast, Fail Often* is heard a lot. Executives in large companies are encouraged to *celebrate* failure, sometimes to the extreme. I'm not an advocate of failure. You really want to succeed, and you want your employees to succeed in their experiments rather than fail. However, imposing severe consequences for failure will deter your employees from trying new things. In chapter 12, one of the methods listed for generating ideas is experimentation. To be clear, I'm not an advocate for reckless and dangerous experiments that may result in harm to people or property. However, you learn things through experimentation, whether you succeed or fail. As a manager, you should make sure that:

- Your employees know that experimenting is acceptable, whether they succeed or fail;
- They understand that you value experimentation based on what they learned from it, and not based on whether they were successful of not;
- There are no severe, career-threatening consequences for failure; but at the same time—
- You value success more than failure.

They best way of knowing whether you have the right attitude towards experimentation and autonomy is by answering—

How do you react after one of your employees told you that he tried something you haven't authorized and failed?

This could be a make-or-break moment for your employee's future creativity. If your reaction was severely negative, indicating this was a bad career move, complaining about not asking permission before experimenting, or overall showing disproportional disappointment with the result—you are guaranteed that the employee would never try new things again, and you may have just crippled his creativity level.

If, on the other hand, you jump to the other extreme and *celebrate* that failure, you would have done a disservice to both the employee and the company. You would have sent the wrong message that failure is as good as success. Moreover, you don't really believe this is the case, do you? So you also sent a message that you are disingenuous. You are not there to make them feel good about themselves for failing. *Allow* them to feel bad about failing. Don't *make* them feel bad. Those are two completely different things.

Your reaction must be right there in the middle. You didn't want your employee to fail, but you do want to see what he learned from it. In fact, you want to see *that* he learned from it. You don't have to know what it was. That's part of freedom. You want to make sure that the employee realized that this was not a bad career move, but also that you value success more than failure. See if you can help him. Maybe you know someone else in the organization that could. Make the connection.

The only exception to the rule is when you know, beyond any reasonable doubt, that the experiment was done in a careless, grossly negligent, or intentionally harmful way. You should never accept that.

AUTONOMY IS NOT FOR EVERYONE

Not all employees *can*, or *want* to handle autonomy. Back in 1990 I led a team of 20 engineers developing alarm systems in Israel. I was the embodiment of a "micro-manager" at the time. I denied employee autonomy through both actions and words. I followed the quote attributed to Henry Ford: "Why is it every time I ask for a pair of hands, they come with a brain attached?" I wanted my employees to do exactly what I told them, exactly the way I told them, and I didn't give them the best feeling if they didn't do what I said. I had to have complete control over their work. But enough about me…

Two of my employees were involved in the development of a system that had to pass the French safety regulations. We submitted the system and failed the first time. At the time, I became increasingly busy with another project, so one morning I called both of them to my office and told them that from that moment on they had full responsibility for the project. We would meet once a week for a brief status update, but I wasn't going to tell them what to do anymore.

They began working. After approximately two months they submitted the system to the French authorities, and it failed again. I was too busy to take away their new autonomy, so they kept going. Four months later they submitted again, but this time it passed. We now had a system that could be (and, in fact, did) sell in France.

The entire experience puzzled me. I invited them into my office. Individually. I asked about their experiences working autonomously on this product. The first employee was thrilled. He was happy to own the success or failure of the project, and to not be told what to do anymore. He definitely felt more creative and productive, and—successful. However, the second employee said the opposite: "I felt that you *dumped* this project in our laps because you didn't want to deal with it anymore. You made it our problem and not yours."

In a study conducted at the Liverpool Hope University School of Business in 2014, 78% of employees said that work autonomy was important to them. The study showed that autonomy had a strong positive effect on creativity and productivity. However, you could infer from the results that 22% of employees did *not* perceive autonomy as important to them, or didn't want it.

Not all employees embrace autonomy. Some fear it. It doesn't make them bad employees, but you must be careful when assuming that if research showed that autonomy improves creativity and productivity, then it must be true for everyone. Before giving autonomy to an employee, you must assess whether that employee has a positive attitude towards autonomy or not. Autonomy is critical for creativity, but it's not for everyone.

At the same time, sometimes employees don't realize they could get autonomy from you. When an employee asks permission to do something she should try without asking—tell her that. "You don't need to ask permission for something like that." See how she reacts. She would either embrace it (most would) or it would scare her to death. Make sure you can tell the difference and respond accordingly.

BUREAUCRACY & FORMALIZATION

Amabile and others found that the existence of bureaucracy, internal politics, internal competition, strong formalization, and rigid processes may hurt creativity in the company. Challenges, on the other hand, were described as encouraging creativity.

When conducting my own study, I asked participants about the challenges they faced. As a reminder, my participants worked in both types of environments, startups and mature companies, and I asked them to compare the two environments along 11 dimensions. The dimension of *challenges* was one of them. Initially, most participants didn't report a significant difference in the overall level of challenges they faced in both environments. They didn't feel more challenged in one type of company over the other. I was ready to discount the impact of challenges on creativity. However, one of the participants provided additional insight. When I asked him whether he experienced more challenges in one of the companies, he asked me: "what kind of challenges are you talking about, internal or external?" I then realized that he treated those challenges differently. The external challenges, technological and market dynamics, forced him to be creative. In the startup he was "allowed" to observe those firsthand, while in the large company he was somewhat shielded from them, mainly by the sales and marketing organization. He was *told* what competitors were doing, and what customers needed, but never heard it firsthand. Therefore, in the large company he was less exposed to external challenges. He didn't experience *fewer* challenges, only *different* ones. In the large company he had to fight bureaucracy, internal politics, and cumbersome processes. Those challenges didn't make him creative, but they were, nevertheless, challenges.

He told me that he faced the same *level* of challenges, but in the large company the challenges were mostly internal, instead of external. Gaining that insight for the first time, I reached out to some of the previous participants, and asked them to distinguish between internal and external challenges. Almost unanimously, they indicated being exposed to frightening, yet exciting and creativity-motivating external challenges in the startup, and to annoying, creativity-demotivating internal challenges in the mature company. One participant compared the challenges through an example he gave me. In the startup, when he needed a printer, he had to figure out how to get the best printer for the lowest cost, and he worked creatively to solve it. In the large company, his challenge was navigating through the purchasing process…

For those reasons, throughout the book whenever I used the word *challenges*, I referred to *external* challenges that *positively* motivate creativity, while internal challenges were included under "bureaucracy, formalization, and internal politics."

The following is perhaps one of the worst stories in history that illustrates the blindness of bureaucracy[42]. Kenneth Taylor (22 years

---

[42] Sources:
Tribute to my Dad, Major George Schwartz Welch (2009), http://jaywelch70.angelfire.com/gsw/

old) and George Welch (23 years old) were both second lieutenants in the Army Air Corps (predecessor to the US Air Force), fighter pilots, and Delaware friends. They spent Saturday night, December 6, 1941, at a dance party at Wheeler field in Oahu, Hawaii, until the early hours of Sunday morning. They slept only two hours before they were awaken by the sound of bombs exploding and heavy machine gun fire. It was the beginning of the Japanese attack on Pearl Harbor. Even though the US had expected a Japanese attack, they were more worried about ground sabotage than an aerial attack. This was why the Navy ships were docked in a close formation, and the planes in Wheeler field parked in neat rows, which were easy to protect against a ground attack. Those neat rows, though, made it easy for the Japanese fighter planes to destroy them while still on the ground.

However, due to gunnery exercises, Welch and Taylor moved their P-40B "Kittyhawks" from Wheeler field to Haleiwa field. So that morning, instead of driving to the Wheeler airfield, they took Taylor's Buick, already riddled with Japanese bullets, to their planes in Haleiwa Field, 10 miles away, but not before they called the field and asked ground personnel to prepare the two P-40's. It was hard to convince the people on the other side of the line that this was not a drill, and that the Japanese were really attacking. Driving at speeds exceeding 100mph at times, they made the 10-mile drive to Haleiwa field in nine minutes, to see their planes fueled, armed, and with the engines running. The planes were armed with only the smaller 30-caliber machine guns, and not the more powerful 50-caliber machine guns,

---

Delawarean, medal or not for heroism on Dec. 7, 1941, holds place of honor (2014), http://delawarestatenews.net/editor/delawarean-medal-not-heroism-dec-7-1941-holds-place-honor/
George Welch, Pearl Harbor Hero and Ace, http://acepilots.com/usaaf_welch.html
Medal of Honor Nominees Portrayed on Film, Rejected Nominations, http://www.lylefrancispadilla.com/welch.html
HistoryNet: Michael E. Haskew, *American Aviators Aloft at Pearl Harbor* (1998), http://www.historynet.com/american-aviators-aloft-pearl-harbor.htm

because they suffered a shortage of the heavier ammunition, and because those machine guns were not tuned and could shoot the propeller if used. At that time, the Japanese pilots were already strafing the planes parked at Haleiwa field, killing some of the pilots who dared trying to take off and fight them. Somehow Welch and Taylor managed to climb into the two planes. They didn't wait for instructions and took off immediately. It was "do or die" for them, so they took the initiative. Welch shot down two Japanese planes before he ran out of ammunition and fuel, and had to land at Wheeler field. After refueling and arming their planes, they took off again, against a second wave of Japanese planes. Welch shot a total of four Japanese planes that day, with one of his machine guns jammed and his plane hit many times by Japanese bullets.

Although no documentation for this could be found, it was told that General Henry "Hap" Arnold, head of the Army Air Corps, wanted to award Lt. Welch the Congressional Medal of Honor for his actions that day. However, as the story continues, he was overruled by a commander who did not approve that medal because—Welch and Taylor took off *without proper clearance.* "Their pride evidently smarting from having been caught off guard and suffering the devastation they did, reasoned absurdly that Welch had taken off without proper authorization and could therefore not be awarded the nation's highest military award; the award was downgraded to a Distinguished Service Cross," which both Taylor and Welch received on January 8, 1942.

In efforts following WWII, as late as 2004, John Martin Meek (author of the book *The Other Pearl Harbor*) and US Senator Tom Carper of Delaware attempted to upgrade the recommendation to a Medal of Honor for both pilots. "Three times, we submitted to the Army a recommendation to upgrade the Distinguished Service Cross to the Medal of Honor," said a statement from Sen. Carper's office. "We even submitted a request to the Air Force, hoping to have the Air Force look at it seeing that Welch and Taylor were Army Air Corps.

The Air Force referred it back to the Army. Each time, the branch stated that there was not new, substantive material that was not considered before." However, there were no documents regarding Gen. Arnold's recommendation in 1941 for the Medal of Honor. "The Army states that in order to consider a new packet, the USA will need a copy of the original recommendation packet to determine if the original board made an error in their decision," said the statement from Sen. Carper's office. "With that said, once a decision is made by the original board, it is considered 'Administrative finality.' In this case, that was in the form of the General Order awarding the Distinguished Service Cross. The original recommendation has not been located to date and no one has been able to locate a copy either."

Welch and Taylor were not asked to be creative. They chose to take initiative that day, and they did. The bureaucracy of denying them the Congressional Medal of Honor hasn't deterred them from performing other heroic actions later in their military careers.

However, I want you to think about your employees, and yourself. How do *you* respond to bureaucracy? Is there a point at which you would avoid doing something useful simply because of the paperwork that comes with it? A CFO once told me that the purchasing process was created to deter employees from ordering things, and thus save money to the company. I'm sure that it worked, but was that the right way to cut costs? Wouldn't a better way have been to involve the employees in the external challenges associated with spending and financial results, rather than creating an internal challenge in the form of bureaucracy? There is a fine line between making your employee your partner, and discouraging her from being creative or productive.

PROCESSES

Are processes required for employees to be productive and creative? You probably think my answer would be no, just like my thoughts on bureaucracy. But processes are needed. In fact, this book describes processes for generating ideas. Well-structured ideation and brainstorming processes (as described in chapter 16) generate high quantity and quality of ideas. The individual process of idea generation (covered in chapter 12) is yet another process that increases creativity, and it works! What makes the difference in whether processes motivate or discourage creativity is *how they are used*. My study participants described the processes in large companies as impediments to creativity. They also had processes in startups, except that they didn't consider the latter impediments.

Why do we need processes? Processes help us perform repetitive jobs in an effective manner, utilizing past learnings. Documented processes reduce work complexity, and assure result consistency.

There is a story of a psychological experiment involving five monkeys. They story is believed to be pieced together based on experiments done by G.R. Stephenson and Wolfgang Kohler in the 1920's[43]. It probably didn't happen exactly the way it was described, but it makes a point. It was told that in that experiment, five monkeys were put in a cage with a ladder and bananas on top. Every time one of the monkeys attempted to climb up the ladder, *all* monkeys were soaked with ice-cold water, as group punishment, which they didn't enjoy nor appreciate. After a while, every time a monkey headed towards the ladder, the other four physically attacked it, preventing it from reaching the ladder, to avoid the cold shower. It didn't take long until no monkey would attempt to walk to the ladder. Then, the researchers replaced one of the monkeys with a new one, who knew nothing about the situation. The new monkey, smelling the bananas, immediately headed towards the ladder, only to be viciously attacked

---

[43] https://www.psychologytoday.com/blog/games-primates-play/201203/what-monkeys-can-teach-us-about-human-behavior-facts-fiction; and— http://www.wakingtimes.com/2016/02/06/the-famous-social-experiment-5-monkeys-and-a-ladder/

by the other four. That monkey probably attempted this a few more times, until it realized that it was better to quit. At that point, the researchers replaced one of the other "original" monkeys with yet another new one, and the process repeated itself. The other monkeys attacked the new member every time it tried to reach the ladder, until it stopped. Then the researchers replaced yet another monkey, and before long, none of the remaining monkeys had ever experienced the cold shower associated with one of them climbing up the ladder. All they knew was that no monkey should be allowed to reach the ladder. They just didn't know *why*.

Does that ever happen in your company? Have you ever heard the phrase "this is how we do things here?" And when you asked—was anyone able to tell you why are things done that way?

Here are four considerations for using processes such that they are inspiring, rather than demotivating creativity.

First, when your employees take part in *creating* the process, refining it, and modifying it, they feel that they *own* the process, and that it's there to *help* them. That's when processes are productive and helpful, and do not demotivate creativity. On the other hand, when employees are not allowed to question why a process requires them to do something, when the process doesn't make sense, and they are simply told "that's how we do things here," then processes are harmful. I'm not suggesting that you question every process, but you should make sure that you (and others) really own those processes.

Second, when the process is used with the intention of helping, expediting, and improving productivity and quality, it doesn't hurt performance or creativity. However, I've seen many instances in which a process was used as a whip to gain political power. There were compliance elements, checkpoints in product development processes, which managers used as a mechanism to insert their own ideas of what the final product should do. Product development checkpoint milestone meetings and approvals are often needed to make sure the project is on track to be delivered on time, on budget, and on specifications. However, occasionally I attended checkpoint meetings in which the marketing department presented a product marketing requirements document. The engineering manager was one of the approvers, but she didn't want to approve it because she thought a certain feature was missing from the product. It didn't help that the product marketing manager insisted that the feature was not required. She wouldn't approve it until that feature was included. Reluctantly, the product marketing manager added the feature, only to pass the checkpoint and continue the development of the product. The process was used as a whip, in a political manner, rather than to help the project. Processes, with all their steps, should be used with the intention for which they were created, and not to satisfy ulterior motives.

Third, some processes were created to comply with external regulations and restrictions. However, once again, they should be used for that purpose only. In many cases the internal processes added restrictions that were unrelated to compliance with any external requirements. The more transparency existed between the external requirements and the internal process, the more employees felt that the process was required. On the other hand, the more "cushion" existed between external requirements and their internal "translations," the fewer employees felt that those processes were there to help them. One example is when an external requirement mandates certain milestones to achieve certain performance, yet the internal process reduces that time by a week or two, "just to be on the safe side." Fake deadline do not promote trust in the company or its processes.

A Fourth consideration is the *flexibility* of process enforcement. How do deviations from the process being handled? Are processes being enforced blindly? Or would deviations be considered if they could help achieve the desired, shared goal? When no deviation from the process is allowed simply because "this is how we always did things here," or because "we don't want to make any exception, period," don't expect creativity. But if process deviations are allowed as long as they are believed to help—employees would feel more engaged, empowered, and motivated to be creative, especially around the process. Process deviation must be considered carefully. You may not know why the process is the way it is, and you may need to consult with those who are responsible for the process. "Don't ever take a fence down until you know the reason it was put up" (G.K. Chesterton). However, if you (or anyone else) proposed a deviation from the process, which would still allow it to achieve the desired goal, possibly in a better, more efficient, more effective, faster, or in any other way better than the original—it should be considered and the process modified if you want to motivate employee creativity.

RESOURCES

For a company to be innovative, and for its employees to be creative, they need resources. Everybody knows that. And it makes sense, doesn't it? The importance of resources to company success was emphasized in the *Resource Based View* theory:

> "Firms obtain sustained competitive advantages by implementing strategies that exploit their internal strengths, through responding to environmental opportunities, while neutralizing external threats and avoiding internal weaknesses."[44]

Different types of resources were described in literature: financial and budgetary, materials, time, personnel, tools, facilities, geography, and manufacturing. However, most researchers emphasized monetary

---

[44] Barney, *Firm resources and sustained competitive advantage*, 1991

funding as the main resource needed for innovation. After all, everything else can be purchased with money, if you only had enough. Since Creativity and Innovation are tied together, you may assume that if resources were required for innovation, then abundance of resources were important to creativity as well. But are they?

Samuel Pierpont Langley was always fascinated with aviation. Except that aviation didn't exist in the late years of the nineteenth century. He experimented with rubber band powered airplane models and other types. He incrementally built larger and larger models, and dreamt of piloted heavier-than-air flight (as opposed to balloons, which are lighter than air). In 1898 he was granted $50,000 from the US War Department and $20,000 from the Smithsonian to develop the first piloted airplane, a project he called "Aerodrome." On December 8, 1903, after the second take-off crash, he abandoned the project.

Only nine days later, on December 17, two bicycle makers, Orville and Wilbur, the Wright Brothers, completed the first manned heavier-than-air flight with their *Wright Flyer*, and led the way to modern aviation. They received no government funding for their project, and achieved that milestone on a budget of less than $1,000[45].

Paul Geroski, Steve Machin, and John Van Reenen (their research was covered in chapter 2) found that the profitability of companies had less to do with the *amount* of resources (specifically, money) spent on Research and Development and more with the persistent level of company-wide innovation.

In my creativity study, for every one participant who reported having more resources in the startup, eight reported having more resources available to them in the mature company, and one reported

---

[45] James Tobin, *To Conquer the Air: the Wright Brothers and the great race for flight*

having access to similar level of resources in both. This is counter-intuitive when you consider that for every participant who experienced higher *creativity* in the mature company, six reported higher creativity in startup companies. It therefore contradicted the belief that the relationship between resource availability and creativity is a positive one.

An interesting result came out of a secondary question in my interviews: "how did the lack of resources affect you?" Several of the participants felt they were more creative when fewer resources were available. One participant described:

> "... You have to be more creative when you have less resources, because you have to do more with less, and it kind of spurs the creativity process."

Another participant said:

> "The more resource-constrained you are—the more creative you end up being, and I think... when you have more resources, you come up with maybe less efficient ideas, or maybe more resource-intensive ideas, whereas when you know you have a lot more finite resources, you typically tend to be more creative."

Was the research prior to mine wrong? Does the availability of resources have an adverse impact on creativity and innovation? The answer is two-fold. When I discussed the results of my findings in this area with Dr. Joe Picken, the founder and director of the Institute for Innovation and Entrepreneurship at the University of Texas at Dallas, who was also a member of my dissertation committee, he suggested that the relationship between creativity and resources was neither strictly positive nor strictly negative. He suggested, and I agreed, that the relationship looks like an upside-down U-shape curve as illustrated in the following graph.

I then contacted a few of my research participants who confirmed: you must have a minimal level of resources to be able to do *anything*, but beyond a certain level of resources available to you, more resources meant that you didn't have to be as creative as you were when you were vying for them.

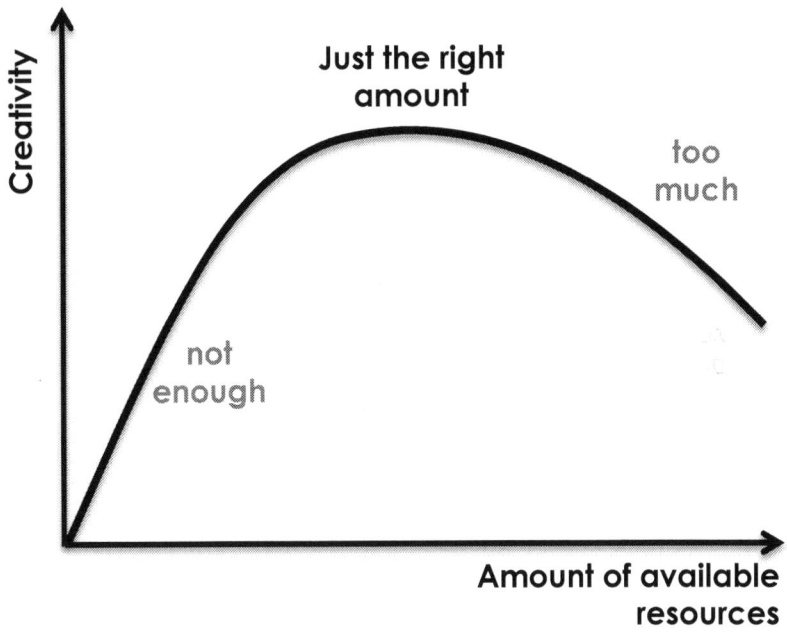

If you had access to virtually unlimited resources, you wouldn't need to "do more with less." You would have everything you needed, and you wouldn't be forced to be creative. My conclusion was that there was an optimal level of resources that would maximize the creativity of team members, and you must find that right level and keep the creative team on that specific resource "diet".

However, you should also remember that a creative idea is useless if it never gets implemented, turned into company innovation, and released to the market. The *implementation* phase of innovation may not require high levels of creativity, but requires resources for prototyping, experimenting, development, and market launch. Not all 3,000 raw ideas described in chapter 6 required resources to be conceived. Not even the 300 that were submitted. Even the 125 ideas that were allocated 1-3 man-years could be "starved" for additional resources, to increase the level of creativity. In my opinion, only the 9 projects (out of the original 3,000 raw ideas) that survived stage 4 should receive adequate (although not abundant) resources as they become major projects in the company. At that stage, the relationship between the level of resources and the probability of successful implementation and product launch is strictly positive. More resources would support better development, faster time to market, and faster adoption.

TIME

A 2016 *Business Insider* article[46] caught my eyes: *The truth about Google's famous '20% time' policy.* In their 2004 IPO letter, founders Larry Page and Sergey Brin wrote:

> "We encourage our employees, in addition to their regular projects, to spend 20% of their time working on what they think will most benefit Google… This empowers them to be more creative and innovative."

This practice by Google received a lot of attention, especially as analysts were hoping to explain the source of Google' success. Many companies followed suit and *mandated* the same. However, the article went on to describe that the process really didn't work, and was no longer in place at Google. Theoretically, it sounded like a great idea. If you gave me 20% of the time (say, Friday) away from my desk and daily work, with a single purpose of *being creative*, I should be able to generate some great ideas. So why wouldn't it work?

Giving me 20% of my time to be creative is analogous to giving me access to a race track, a great racing motorcycle (sorry, I'm a motorcycle guy, not cars…), but no gas. It wouldn't do any good. I

---

[46] http://www.businessinsider.com/google-20-percent-time-policy-2015-4

would stare at the motorcycle, then the track, then the motorcycle again... But I could not break any speed record.

20% of your time is just as a fallacy as allocating *space* for an innovation lab, where employees could go to be creative. Both are part of the company's "official" *drive* for innovation. Both are done more for public appearance and lack real substance and probability of success. Give employees 20% of their time, and they would use it to catch up on email. Give them an innovation lab, and they would catch up on email there, where nobody would bother them... The greatest ideas hardly ever come during the 20% of the time away from your "day job." They hardly ever come from the innovation lab. They come from *busy* people who had ideas *while* performing their day job, staying late, and trying things without asking permission. They didn't come from companies who *drove* innovation. They didn't come from companies who *celebrated* innovation. They came from companies that *allowed* their employees to try new things and fail without consequences. They came from companies that had the right climate for employees to be creative. They came from people who performed activities that allowed them to generate great ideas.

You see, it wouldn't matter if you told your employees (or the world) that you wanted to drive innovation. It wouldn't matter if you celebrated every little insignificant attempt at innovation they showed. They know it was not genuine. The only thing that matters is when you let your employees try things you haven't authorized and fail. Because the only way to guarantee they would never fail is by never letting them try (or making it very painful for them to fail). But those employees would never succeed, either.

MONEY

If you work in a mature, large company, and have abundance of resources, how does it motivate your creativity? I recommend to neither push resources to development teams, nor to deny them access to resources. Resources should be *available* to them, but with some (not too much) friction associated with obtaining them. The resources should be there, but not immediately available. The team must find ways to gain access to those resources. They should scheme to get them. They may take a part of one budget and move it to the "Skunk Works" area. The access to resources (whether funding, people, time, equipment) could be unofficial and "off-the-books." And as far as "beg forgiveness rather than ask permission," it is important that the organization *would* forgive, and that employees would not have to fear the devastating consequences of "borrowing" resources.

Don't get me wrong, I'm not condoning illegal, unethical, or personal misappropriation of company resources. Not one bit. But I support the appropriation of resources available in the company for new ideas that are conceived for the benefit of the company.

You see, large companies have a resource advantage over startups. If you work in a wireless startup company and need a $250,000 spectrum analyzer that could scan your frequencies, you must raise $250,000 funding from investors. There is almost no other way. However, if you are working in a company such as Texas Instruments, it is likely that such a spectrum analyzer already exists somewhere in the company. It's probably not in your department, and access to it may not be easy, but it is still much easier than when that equipment doesn't exist in your company at all. As long as the bureaucracy is not insurmountable.

INCENTIVES AND PROMOTIONS

Financial incentives, bonuses, and promotions are all common practice to reward those who deserve them in large companies. Do they help creativity?

INCENTIVES

One day, I decided that one of my employees, who worked really hard toward reaching a milestone in the project, should earn a bonus for it. In fact, he should earn a pay raise, too. But in order not to distract him from reaching the milestone, I told him that once he reached the milestone he would get both. He seemed less excited than I would have expected, but I didn't read too much into it. Two hours later, the Human Resources manager called me to her office. She told me that he came to visit her and was visibly upset, and told her he was "disgusted" with the raise and bonus that were tied to reaching the milestone. After some probing, she realized that it wasn't the *amount* of pay raise or bonus—it was the fact that they were *linked* to reaching the milestone. I met with him to understand. He believed that he had already earned those, even before meeting the milestone and, again, repeated his resentment for the milestone link. This was before I conducted my doctoral study, so I get a pass for not understanding the problem then.

This was the *Hawthorne Effect* and the *Candle Problem* all over again, and everything that Teresa Amabile and many others have said all along: employees are *intrinsically* motivated to excel in complex tasks, such as generating creative ideas. Monetary rewards don't work, and rewards tied to specific performance are the worst.

The good news is that it's going to cost you less than you thought to motivate your employees to be creative. The bad news is that everything else you must do, what this book covers, is going to require an *attitude* change by you and other executives and managers in the company, which is harder. But it's not going to cost money.

Should you completely get rid of financial incentives, or all incentive types altogether? You should definitely eliminate *contingency* bonuses. Don't offer a bonus for meeting a milestone, generating ideas, or filing patents. Those incentives are guaranteed to produce low quality patents (albeit many of them), not affect creativity, and cause the opposite effect, just like the *Candle Problem*, the Hawthorne Experiments, and my employee proved.

Remember that employees are motivated by the big picture view, and by the impact they have on their company. Therefore, the only financial incentive you should keep is company stock. Don't give *performance-based* grants. Simply give stock (or stock option) grants. You can't control the stock price. The company's performance does, and the introduction of continuous innovation through new products and services is controlled by your employees, not by you, and that would make all the difference in the world for them. You should remember, though, that the financial and stock price impact that a $100 million business has on a startup is dramatically higher than the impact it would have on a $10 billion company. The latter would have only 1% impact on stock price. Employees might be less incentivized by that.

In a 2015 Creativity Research Journal article [47], researchers revisited the relationships between financial, non-financial, tangible, intangible incentives, and creativity. For the most part they supported the known relationships described here, but they added one more element worth mentioning: the monetary incentives played a small positive role in motivation—they conveyed the sentiment that the company, executives, and managers *supported* and *allowed* creativity. The fact that there was an incentive for creativity meant that the company valued creativity. That was important for employees to know, and you should make sure they do.

---

[47] *Tangible and Intangible Rewards and Employee Creativity: The Mediating Role of Situational Extrinsic Motivation*. Hye Jung Yoon, Sun Young Sung, Jin Nam Choi, Kyungmook Lee & Seongsu Kim, Creativity Research Journal, Volume 27, Issue 4, October 2015

PROMOTION AND COMPETITION

In Corporate America, promotions are at the core of corporate aspirations. Companies use promotions to reward the best team players, and to strengthen management structure and hierarchy with better players. However, there are some significant downfalls to promotions, especially due to how they are given.

The *Peter Principle*[48] stated that "in a hierarchy every employee tends to rise to his level of incompetence." Not everyone was born to be a manager. Not everyone was trained to be a manager, and not everyone aspires to be a manager, or would be any good at it. Sometimes, taking your best individual contributor and turning him or her into a manager would eliminate one strong individual contributor and add one mediocre (or worse) manager. The promotion is typically accompanied by a significant salary and overall compensation package increases. As a result, even if the employee was not interested in the new position, she would be interested in the financial benefits from it. In an ideal world, bad promotions should be prevented through screening and assessment, which should be performed before the promotion was offered (most companies never conduct such assessment, though, and instead offer promotions based on individual contributor's performance, or entitlement, regardless of the potential dire consequences that the *Peter Principle* warns about).

However, there is another way in which a promotion could hurt the team. Promoting one team member may become a hurdle for creativity. The possibility for promotion causes internal competition within the team. Only one member of the team would be promoted, and the promotion would be based on *individual* performance. Tomorrow, one team member may become a supervisor to the others. For them, not only that they didn't get that promotion, but they would

---

[48] Lawrence J Peter, Raymond Hull. *The Peter Principle*. New Yok, W. Morrow, 1969.

now be supervised by someone who a week ago was their peer. This might feel like a demotion to them, even if that wasn't your intention.

How might team members behave when they know that one of them may get a promotion based on the team's performance? They would start blocking information from one another, as information is power[49]. They would develop internal (conflicting) agendas that would allow them to be promoted over other team members. Each one of them would develop cognitive dissonance between the need to be successful as a *team* and excelling *individually* to be promoted. Those individual agendas would not be shared publicly with other team members. Individuals would focus on "upward politics" more than productivity and creativity. As a result, the team may lose whatever trust that existed among team members. There is no simple and more direct way to put it—if you want a cohesive, effective, and creative team—you cannot offer individual compensation increases or promotions. Everything must be offered to the *team* as a whole based on team, and not individual, success, as it affects the company.

RECOGNITION

Have you ever celebrated the "employee of the month" or gave the "star of the week" award to employees just to show your appreciation for their work? If so—you are not alone. But, does it work?

It came initially as a surprise to me to find that employees were motivated by praise more than by financial incentives. I learned that while reading Teresa Amabile's research. Her questions regarding supervisory encouragement showed that employees cared about recognition more than bonuses. This was interesting enough to include in my own study. My findings were generally consistent, but

---

[49] Emerson, R. M. (1962). *Power-dependence relations.* American Sociological Review, 27(1), 31-41.

something was a little different. There is something about qualitative, exploratory research that allows you to catch details otherwise missed in a quantitative survey.

My participants didn't care very much about praise they got from the company's CEO, even when he was a Fortune 500 CEO. Even if the recognition came in front of a large group of their peers. Some of them dismissed the awards ceremony as a waste of time. They felt it was less than genuine. Especially if the CEO didn't even know their names.

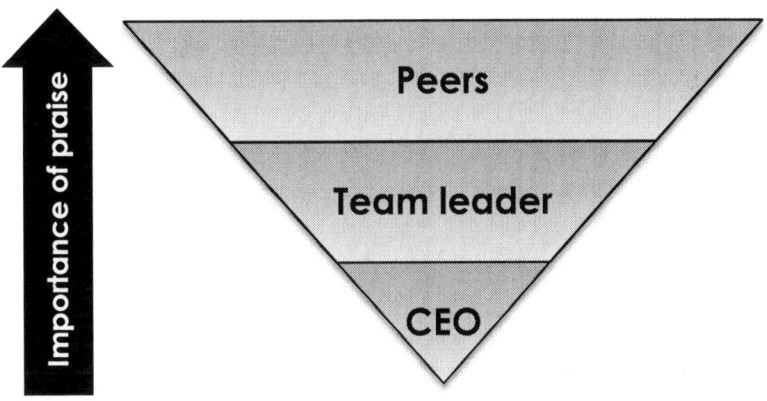

Through my interviews I found that employees cared the most about the praise they got from their *peers*. The people who knew them the most. The people with whom they spent the most time. The people alongside they fought in the trenches.

Next, they cared about kind words from their team leader. Their immediate supervisor. Another person they knew well, and who knew how hard they worked, and therefore was more genuine in her praise. Only lastly, they cared about the appreciation by top management.

So if you are considering creating an appreciation program such as "the employee of the month," the "star of the week," or any other program in which you would give an award to an employee you don't know by name—don't! You have a much smaller impact than you think on motivating them. Unless it comes with a better parking spot...

Let them do their job, and get out of their way. That's really what they need and what they want. And it will make a bigger positive impact on their creativity.

TRUST AND INNOVATION

I can't believe I'm about to do this. Don't tell anyone, but I'm going to defend *management*. Yes, the management that, according to Clayton Christensen, was not supporting the creation of radical ideas that could change markets. The same management that, according to Teresa Amabile, was not providing a climate required for employees to be creative. That management.

In 2006, while working in Texas Instruments, I flew to meet the TI team in Israel. There, one of the brilliant young engineers came to me and asked to speak privately. "I presented many great ideas to management," he started, "but they keep shooting them down." He was frustrated, and I could understand why, in such a climate, one would not want to bring up new ideas anymore.

You already know that for employees to be creative, management has to provide a creativity-supporting climate. One of the most important factors is autonomy. The willingness to try new things and fail without adverse consequences is part of it.

Until now I looked at autonomy from the employee's side. However, why should management give you that autonomy? The only circumstance in which you should get it is if management *trusts* you. How much autonomy would you give your child to try things, especially if they're dangerous? It depends on how much you trust them (and how dangerous those things are). It is easy to blame management for not trusting you enough to give you the autonomy you need, but why should they? Did you *earn* their trust?

The following diagram illustrates the circular relationship between trust and creativity. If management trusts you, they would give you the autonomy you need. They would share with you the "big picture" and allow you to try things, fail, learn from them, and then try again. They would let you decide *how* you want to execute your task to reach your goal.

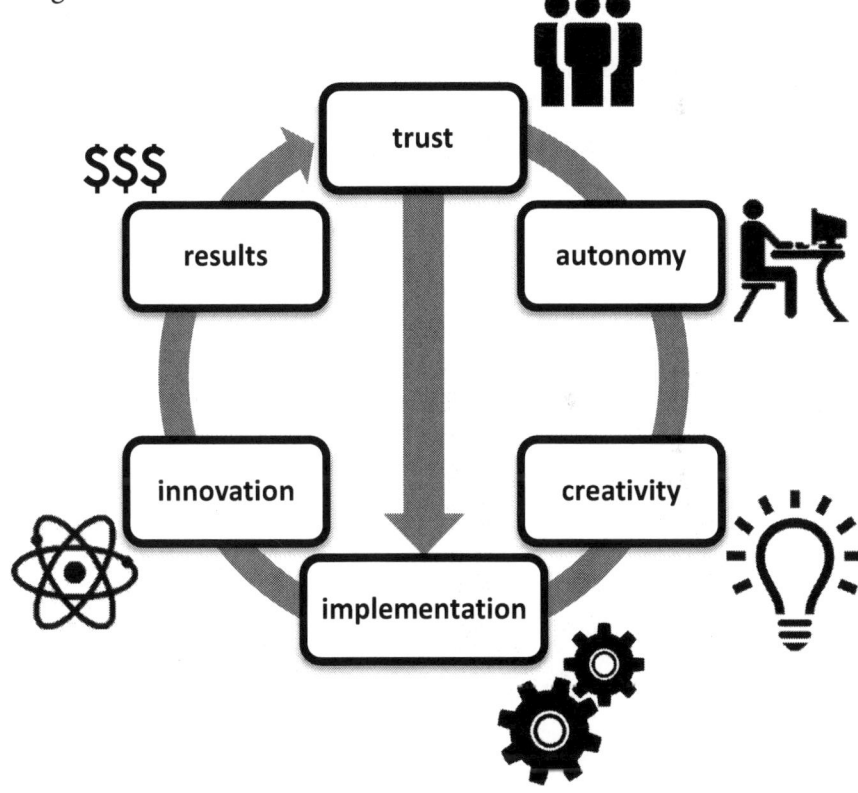

In that environment, you would get the intrinsic motivation you need to be creative. As a result, the quantity and quality of your creative ideas would increase.

Once you found that great idea, the trust that management has put in you would translate into the allocation of resources required to turn your ideas into new, innovative products, services, processes, or business models (the straight down arrow). You would not get access to those resources if management didn't trust you. And right now, they do.

As shown in chapter 2, innovative companies gain significantly higher market share, revenue, and profits than the average company. Your company's financial performance would significantly improve, because of your ideas, which were implemented.

The success of your ideas, as demonstrated by the results of their implementation, would help increase the trust that management had in you. That increase in trust would allow them to feel comfortable giving you even more autonomy, and allocate more resources to implement your best ideas, now that you've proven yourself and the quality of your ideas. It's a vicious cycle, and it works well!

But what happens if you fail to provide creative ideas that result in innovation? You would have little to no impact on improving the company's financial performance, so why should you expect management to trust you with more autonomy and implementation resources?

This cycle takes a long time to complete. From the moment management decided to put their trust in you and gave you the autonomy you needed, time would pass until your aha! Moment arrives, until your idea moves from being one of 3,000 raw ideas to an internal disclosure, a patent application, a minor project, a major project, a market launch, and finally deliver the financial results that would prove to management why trusting you was a good idea. Your new product would not be profitable during the product development or market introduction phases of the product life cycle. Only during the growth phase would your idea generate the financial performance that would close this cycle. This could take years.

It's a vicious cycle, but there is a way to break into it. I asked that engineer in Israel: "what did you do when management shot your ideas down?" "Nothing…" he said, looking at me puzzled, "what could I do?" Sometimes you have to beg, borrow, and steal resources to get your ideas out to the market, despite lack of management support. You refuse to take "no" for an answer. You don't stop with a great idea—you provide a bullet-proof (or as close to it as possible) business plan that shows how this would improve the company's financial performance. And then, again, you beg, borrow, and steal resources. When I started the USB 3.0 project in Texas Instruments[50], I had to beg engineers to work on this project and not tell anyone, but they did it. It's a risk, but it would pay off. Not only to you—to the entire company. If you are successful—this cycle would make it easier the next time around. If you were not—well, there are always other companies…

YOU DON'T DRIVE, YOU ALLOW

This is the end of chapter 9. Before I continue, I wanted to remind you how this chapter fits in context. Part 2 started with establishing that employees must be *motivated* to be creative. They cannot be *driven* to be so. There are three entities in the organization responsible for employee creativity level. The first is the organization, and the role it plays in creating a climate conducive to creativity. The organization must provide employees with the *autonomy* to decide *how* to perform the job (not to choose which job to perform), to see the big picture and the impact that an employee's ideas has on the overall success of

---

[50] See more in chapter 17 here, or read chapter 18 ("Putting it all together—the story of USB 3") in *Bowling with a Crystal Ball*, 2nd Edition.

the company, no matter how big or how small, and the knowledge that failure, although not encouraged, does not have severe consequences, if you only learned from it. The company must reduce the bureaucracy and formalization that impose unnecessary internal challenges, and let employees focus on external challenges. Management must provide the *right* level of resources. Enough, but not too much. Make resources *available* to employees, and not *given* to them. Contingent financial rewards should be avoided, and so should competition for promotions. The latter is covered again in chapter 15. Recognition, a pat on the back, is important to employees, but doesn't necessarily need to come from you.

In summary, you should avoid *driving* creativity. You should *allow* it. Remember that creativity is less like golf, and more like curling.

This chapter covered the theoretical and empirical link between organizational actions and employee creativity, as found through research and experience. Part 3 would show you the degrees of freedom that you, as a manager, have in *allowing* creativity.

The following few chapters cover the other two entities responsible for creativity in the organization: the team (and the team leader), and the individual.

10.

DYNAMICS OF A CREATIVE TEAM

As if you didn't get this already—ideas come from *people*. Not from companies. Companies can make it easy for people to generate ideas, can motivate them to do so, or can make it hard or impossible. Ideas can be generated by individuals, or by a small group of people—a *team*. Chapter 12 discusses the combinational method for idea generation, as it relates to the process of generating new ideas through combination of old ideas in one's brain. It is the single most researched idea generation method within the field of neuroscience. The effectiveness of that method could be compounded when combining new ideas from several individuals. If a creative individual with two old ideas could generate one new idea, then a team of 4 individuals, each with two old ideas, could generate 28 new ideas. This would be explained further in chapter 12. You understand what I mean, though.

Several things should be noted when forming a team, which this chapter covers in detail. The chapter begins with the understanding that not all employees in the company need to be organized into and treated as creative teams. It continues to explain the importance of diversity within the team and how it impacts the quality of ideas generated. A key factor affecting team creativity is the ability to debate a topic with passion, while avoiding competition, conflict, and political correctness. This chapter shows how to do that.

I'll start with the team *size*. When I was involved in the development of the Wi-Fi standards, the "team" was made of more than 100 members. They came from different companies, often competitors, with different business agendas, and rarely did ideas build on each other. For the most part, especially towards the development of the more advanced, higher-speed Wi-Fi derivatives such as "g", "n", and "ac", the discussion became more and more contentious, and even adversarial. Participants wanted to assure that the interests of their companies, and their protected intellectual properties were inserted into the final standard. It was a *zero-sum game*[51]. In order to conduct an effective meeting with more than 100 people, we had to use the parliamentarian deliberation rules known as *Robert's Rules of Order*. Those are highly formalized, and don't lend themselves to free-flowing, creative debates. There is simply no other way to conduct any form of debate with a team of that size. Often, especially in governing entities such as city councils and school boards, even small bodies of 7 people must use those rules of parliamentarian debate, but here mainly because those organizations are *political*, deal more with governance and oversight and less with generating creative ideas.

From what I learned, and in my experience, the optimal size of a creative team is between 5 and 8 members. It has something to do with the amount of "air time" that each member gets. If your team has 10 members, you don't get more than 10% of the time to participate. If your team has 5 members—you get 20%. For quick exchanges of ideas, that's important. Chapter 16 discusses ideation processes, where you would see this recommendation again. If you worry that 5 team members could not hold enough knowledge and experience to generate creative ideas in a complex discipline, you may extend the team. The core creative team would still be made of 5 to 8 participants, but they would rely on an extended pool of experts and workers who, while providing input, would not do so at the team meeting. Having

---

[51] More on the process of standard development, and how to be successful in it, in my book *Bowling with a Crystal Ball*.

the extended expert pool participate in brainstorming events would detract from the effectiveness of the process. Some ideation processes, though, may require more than 8 participants, but you would notice that they are typically assigned to smaller groups when it's time to generate ideas. Given the importance of keeping the team small, the selection of team members becomes a critical success factor, and would be discussed later in this chapter.

THE CREATIVITY NUCLEAR REACTOR

I often face skepticism by management teams when I explain that autonomy, low formalization, and loose processes are required for creativity. Executives have hard time imagining running their companies under those conditions. Somehow the term "creative accounting" does not instill confidence in them. Without rigid processes—manufacturing and operations would lose effectiveness and productivity. Autonomy might hurt inter-departmental coordination. Maybe as companies grow, and especially after going public, they simply cannot be creative anymore? The regulatory requirements associated with being a public company, and *liability* considerations of having "deep pockets" alone may prevent the company from building an environment that supports creativity.

But then you remember that some of the most innovative companies in the world, such as Apple, 3M, and Toyota, are large, public companies. Do those companies not have rigid processes? Are they less formalized? Do they give all their employees full autonomy to do what they want?

When I was the general manager of a semiconductor business unit in Texas Instrument, Apple was one of my clients. We made a part that was used in the iPod. We saw the iPod grow from less than a million to over 10 million units in one year. In our meetings with Apple, I didn't feel the environment that I now know is so important to creativity. I met a highly formalized team, with very strong processes in place, and not much autonomy that I could observe. In fact, it could be argued that Apple was more structured and process-driven than many other, less creative companies. So how could the same company be so innovative? And how could its employees be so creative?

The easiest way to explain this is by using the nuclear reactor analogy. I know, this sounds completely unrelated, but bear with me.

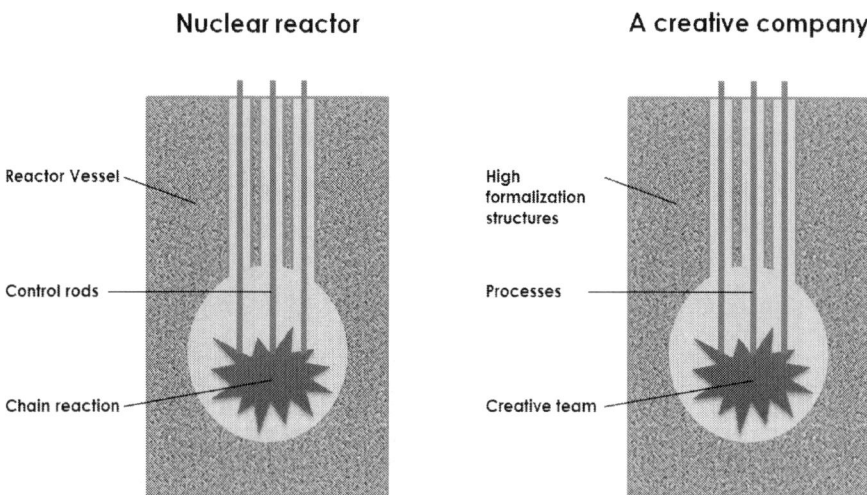

A nuclear reactor has a core, in which the atomic chain reaction occurs. Due to the huge amount of energy generated by the chain reaction—the core is embedded in a very heavy, impenetrable vessel, which can withstand that energy without letting it escape outside. Control rods are inserted inside that core, such that they absorb many of the neutrons emitted by the chain reaction and limit the amount of energy generated inside the core. As the control rods are pulled gradually out of the core—the chain reaction intensity increases, and more energy is generated and released.

The nuclear reactor core is analogous to the creative core team. Free flow of ideas (chain reaction) is enabled when the organizational impediments (bureaucracy, formalization, strict processes, lack of autonomy) are pulled out of the creative core team. However, the hard, heavy, rigid vessel is what prevents the core from exploding. The company must create an environment supportive of free flow of ideas, an environment low on formalization and processes, and high on autonomy, but needs to do so only for the *creative team*. Neither manufacturing nor accounting or administration departments could operate in the same "free flowing" environment. Those must remain rigid, formalized, with strict processes, and little autonomy.

This is how Apple and every large, innovative company work. It is not "creative," autonomous, or flexible throughout the *entire* organization. Only where it matters the most—at the product design team(s). The team I met at Apple wasn't the design team—it was the production team. But I can't leave this topic without one more example, very close to my heart.

In 1943, the legendary Clarence "Kelly" Johnson, then a young engineer at Lockheed, started a small experimental engineering department inside the company in complete secrecy. That group was tasked to develop the first US fighter jet, while World War II was still raging in all fronts. That team developed the P-80 Shooting Star. The group was known as Lockheed's "Skunk Works®" [52]. While committing to fly a prototype in 180 days, it completed its work in only 143 days. Johnson described the team with the following words:

> "The Skunk Works is a concentration of a few good people solving problems far in advance—and at a fraction of the cost—of other groups in the aircraft industry by applying the simplest, most straightforward methods possible to develop and produce new

---

[52] http://www.lockheedmartin.com/us/aeronautics/skunkworks.html

projects. All it is really is the application of common sense to some pretty tough problems."[53]

Johnson developed 14 rules[54] that are still in use today by the Skunk Works team. Very few people outside of that organization knew what was being developed. As a result, the team was given complete autonomy to develop and experiment. Johnson's approach was: "We are defined not by the technologies we create but the *process* in which we create them." A strong testament to the success of his rules and this unique approach of separating one team from the rest of the company was in the form of the many design awards they received (including the National Medal of Technology), and moreover—the results of their work: the U2 and SR71 spy planes, and the world's first Stealth Fighter, F-117A. Those results were recognized in a report that the RAND Corporation submitted to the US Air Force and Advanced Research Projects Agency in 1971[55]. The report analyzed project management of the Agena-D satellite program and compared planned versus actual results. The project was estimated to cost $60 million, but was completed in $32 million. It was expected to take 18 months, but was done in 9. It took 69 Quality control people, instead of the projected 1,200. While 3,900 drawings were expected, only 350 were needed, and instead of taking 30 days to release each of them, they were released in one day. The reliability of the first twelve launches was 96.2%, higher than anything comparable at that time.

While the CEO might be skeptical about the need to create the "loose" environment for creativity—she is not concerned with the small product design team, but rather with the rest of the company.

---

[53] *Kelly: More than My Share of It All* by Clarence L. Johnson, Maggie Smith. 1989.
[54] http://lockheedmartin.com/us/aeronautics/skunkworks/14rules.html
[55] Robert Perry, Giles K. Smith, Alvin J. Harman and Susan Henrichsen. *System Acquisition Strategies*. Rand Corporation, June 1971.
https://www.rand.org/content/dam/rand/pubs/reports/2007/R733.pdf

And she is correct—the rest of the company should not foster an environment conducive to creativity. The rest of the company must support operations, while letting the creative core be, well, creative...

And like a nuclear reactor, the sustainable strength of the company originates in its creative core, but delivered through its support mechanism.

DIVERSITY

When Human Resource professionals use the word *diversity* in companies, they refer to the following definition: "the inclusion of individuals representing more than one national origin, color, religion, socioeconomic stratum, sexual orientation, etc."

Why do companies try to achieve diversity? First and foremost, to achieve the social goal of *equal opportunity* in the workplace. Employees who belong to different ethnic groups, different genders, and different social groups deserve to have equal opportunities in employment, and not be discriminated against. But there is more.

McKinsey research [56] showed that the most *gender*-diverse companies were 15% more likely to have financial returns above industry medians, and the most *ethnically* diverse companies were 35% more likely to have better financial returns. You could infer that companies that are both gender- and ethnically-diverse would be 55% more likely to have better returns.

A second reason for diversity in companies is that diverse employees better represent the diverse *customer* base for the company's products, services, business models, and processes. A truer

---

[56] *Why diversity matters*. Vivian Hunt, Dennis Layton, and Sara Prince. McKinsey & Company, 2015. http://www.mckinsey.com/business-functions/organization/our-insights/why-diversity-matters

representation of the population leads to better understanding customers and creating products that a wider cross-section of the population would use.

There is one more advantage to diversity. Having multiple points of view as represented by a diverse group of employees could also increase creativity and thus innovation.

Here are nine diversity factors required to increase the team's creativity.

DEMOGRAPHIC

Demographic diversity is what we typically mean when we use the word "diversity." It refers to gender, ethnical and cultural background, and age, for the most part. While its initial focus is *fair employment*, this type of diversity also increases the understanding of a diverse customer base, as well as increases creativity through different perspectives stemming from those different backgrounds. Men may not be able to understand women clothing (most men, that is), and baby boomers may not be able to create products that millennials would consume. And vice versa.

The next 8 factors are not included in the "classic" definition of diversity, are not monitored by the human resources department for fair employment practices, and might have only marginal impact on understanding customers. However, they would significantly increase creativity due to the different perspectives brought to the team as a whole by the sum of its parts, its members.

MULTI-DISCIPLINARY AND CROSS-FUNCTIONAL

If the team is formed for an engineering project, the selected participants are typically engineers, mainly from the specific discipline required for that project. However, expanding the scope beyond "tier 1" of disciplines would enhance creativity. The hardware design team of a product typically includes only hardware engineers. Including software engineers ("tier 2") may allow developing products that make software design easier. Including mechanical engineers (also "tier 2"') could help in assuring a compelling form factor of the final product. I experienced a general distrust between marketing and engineering people in large companies. However, including marketing people ("tier 2"), even though the product has already been defined, could help creativity. Engineers like the product to be well defined by the marketing department, and only then handed over to engineering (in writing), and not having to interact with marketing people anymore. They don't like interacting with marketing people. Nevertheless—such interaction could lead to better ideas. During an ideation workshop, engineers may see one of the features as very hard to implement. A marketing person in that meeting might then say that this is a low value-add feature (from a customer's perspective), and thus not worth the effort or the cost (in development or production). Wouldn't that help? On the other hand, an engineer may casually suggest something that is possible and easy to implement, that he wouldn't otherwise give it a second thought, that a marketing person present in the meeting might jump all over, realizing it might offer a tremendous competitive advantage to the product, if implemented. Including finance, human resources, and others ("tier 3") could provide insights from other disciplines that may further increase the quantity and quality of ideas considered.

KNOWLEDGE & EDUCATION

Even when team members come from the same discipline, they may know (or have studied) different aspects of the project at hand. Having diverse knowledge could give yet again different perspective on similar things. Sometimes, even learning the same subject by different teachers or at different schools could provide different perspectives. Being involved in the Texas education system, I am often surprised to learn how many different ways are there to reach the same answer to the same math problem.

EXPERIENCE

Much like different knowledge and education, diversified *experiences* increase team creativity. When you walk into a room to see a team of 5 who worked together in the same company and same business unit for more than 20 years—you are not likely to get diversity of ideas. Those team members think alike. When your team is made of members who worked in very different business units, possibly different companies—you are assured to increase team creativity. In fact, one of the reasons people in startups experience higher degrees of creativity is that they don't have a "history" of many shared experiences. Employees in startups didn't work there for long, because the startup company itself didn't exist for long. The diversity of experience in startups happens naturally. In mature companies you have to make sure you bring people with different experiences.

BREADTH VS. DEPTH

Some know little about a lot (generalists), while others know a lot about little (specialists). There is a limit to how much people know and have experience with, and throughout their careers they balance breadth with depth. No doubt that you need matter experts to solve a problem, but the generalists are those who bring ideas from remote disciplines and allow solutions to be disruptive and novel. The following story illustrates this point.

In an executive briefing breakfast at Stanford, Professor and Strategy Consultant Gary Hamel described arriving at a hotel earlier than check-in time. Does this ever happen to you? Of course it does! He was told to wait for the "standard" check in time (typically 2 or 3 pm) for his room to be ready. He then asked the hotel manager why the hotel couldn't adopt the car rental business model. You get your car whenever you get there, and you are charged for 24-hour periods starting that moment. If you got your car at 11:20, you would be charged for a day until tomorrow at 11:19. Why couldn't the same be implemented in the hotel industry? "You don't understand our business," said the hotel manager, to which Hamel responded: "maybe that's my competitive advantage."

I have seen companies try to innovate by putting several people from the same business unit, from the same discipline (typically, engineering) in the same room, expecting new ideas to emerge. They don't. People who are so deeply immersed in a certain market, technology, or discipline feel bound by restrictions that may not really exist (like in the monkey experiment). This is the time when outsiders' ideas are faced with "you don't understand our business."

On the other hand, I have seen companies try to be disruptively innovative by bringing ideas far away into a target industry in which they have no prior experience or knowledge, without including specialists in the field, therefore missing some basic facts that would explain why nobody else has done it before. At least not that way. That's another way to fail.

Building cross-functional teams with people who bring depth of experience in the market and technology to be disrupted on one hand (the "insiders"), and people who have very little knowledge of "the rules of the game" in this market or technology on the other hand (the "outsiders"), but that can bring knowledge from other markets, would assure creative ideas. The "outsiders" would bring up crazy ideas, which the "insiders" would ground in the realities of the target market and technology.

While this dynamic has the potential of increasing the flow of creative ideas, there are two prerequisites for success. The first is that *trust* was already built within the team. Without trust, insiders would treat outsiders' ideas as completely irrelevant, unfeasible, radical (not in a good way), and even dangerous. They would do everything in their power to stop those radical ideas from being implemented. At the same time, outsiders would think of the insiders as blockers and lacking vision, and thus discount all objections they bring as being unnecessarily conservative. If trust was already built within the team, out of mutual respect for competence and shared values, ideas would be considered seriously, and so would objections. More on building trust within the team later in this chapter.

The second prerequisite is that both "sides" should be *constructive*. Insiders should not solely play the role of antibiotics, and outsiders should not solely play the role of bacteria. When an insider sees a problem with an outsider's idea, he should point it out, and think about possible solutions. At the same time, when an insider brings an objection, or points a problem with the new idea, the outsider should not discount it, but rather think about ways around the problem.

Andrew Grove, the former Intel CEO, and Robert Burgelman co-authored a paper at Stanford University in 2007[57], explaining how Apple disrupted the music, and later the cellular phone industries (with iPod and iPhone, respectively) through *cross-boundary disruption*, which is another name for bringing disciplines from other industries to disrupt your own. Those happen through people with multi-disciplinary experiences and knowledge. Through the combination of breadth and depth.

---

[57] Robert A. Burgelman and Andrew S. Grove. (2007). *Cross-boundary disruptors: Powerful interindustry entrepreneurial change agents*. Strategic Entrepreneurship Journal. Vol. 1: 315-327.

EXTRA-CURRICULAR INTERESTS

Whether we like it or not, we bring our extra-curricular activities to work. Be it surfing, cooking, shooting, riding motorcycles—we are the sum of our experiences, and those experiences, even if not directly related to the project at hand, could help formulate unique solutions to problems. This is one of the harder areas to force diversity at. I can't think of a time in which forming a team would include a consideration of hobbies. However, in a cumulative way, it should. In the discussion of team member selection and hiring of new employees in chapter 15, this would be one of the factors considered.

COGNITIVE PREFERENCES

Different people think differently. Some are introverts and need time alone to produce ideas they could later bring to the team, while others (myself included) need other team members to be their sounding boards. The cognitive differences between introverts and extroverts would be discussed in greater detail in chapter 12.

Some prefer the "shotgun" approach for producing many ideas in many different directions, while others prefer the "rifle" approach of finding very specific solutions to very specific, well-defined problems. Including people with both cognitive preferences in the team would increase creativity. One would see the forest, and one would see the trees. It would allow different people to see different sides of the same problem, and use different mental processes to solve it.

RISK TAKING

Some people feel more comfortable taking risk than others. My study, and research done before it showed that risk-takers tend to be more creative. As chapter 14 shows, risk-takers also prefer working in startups. The willingness to take risk, or the opposite—risk aversion, could be personal or genetic characteristics of a person, but could also be the result of the personal financial situation and the attitude towards financial security. When you are the sole provider for your family, have no life savings to fall back on, and your spouse requires special and expensive medical treatments—you may prefer to avoid risk. However, if your kids graduated from college and have jobs, your mortgage is paid off, and you saved enough money during your professional career, you may feel more comfortable taking risks. Either way, those who are willing to take risk are those who push the team to try new things, to experiment, and to not rule out anything until it blows up in their faces. Others are very careful and assure that the final product is safe for the company's health. It is important for your team to have both.

VISIONARIES VS. PRAGMATISTS

Finally, some people are naturally optimistic visionaries who have the gift of seeing what *can* be done, while others balance them with more pragmatic attitudes, and see where the pitfalls might lie. As with other characteristics—both are needed. However, you should be cautious with "devil's advocates," people who only see faults in everything. Your team should see both upsides and downsides, but to be productive and creative you must avoid having members who can only see the negative, and what *cannot* be done.

Throughout the descriptions of the nine diversity factors, I hope that the following came across: for each one of those factors, one side is not better than the other. Extroverts are not better than introverts. Visionaries are no better than pragmatists. For each characteristic, both types are important, because they assure seeing an issue from all sides, creatively. The team's ability to see problems (and solutions) through different perspectives dramatically grows as diversity increases. To increase diversity, you should select team members who are as "orthogonal" and complementary to each other on as many dimensions as possible. This will be reviewed further in chapter 15.

But there is rarely good without bad. Diversity might also delay *team bonding* and the development of trust, which is so desperately needed for the ability to argue freely and build on each other's ideas. More on that later in this chapter. As hard as it may be—it is still worth it.

OPEN DEBATE AND CREATIVITY

FROM DEBATE TO CONFLICT

Two factors were found to have the strongest, and opposite effect on team creativity: the ability to conduct open *debate* (positively affecting creativity), and personal *conflict* among team members (negatively affecting creativity). Several assessment instruments and surveys measure those factors (among others), including Dr. Goran Ekvall's *Situational Outlook Questionnaire* (SOQ®), Teresa Amabile's (and the Center for Creative Leadership's) KEYS®, and Dr. Neil Anderson and Dr. Michael West's *Team Climate Inventory* (TCI®). These survey tools measure the presence of those factors, among other, as predictors of the expected level of creativity within the team.

The two terms, *debate* and *conflict*, are sometimes considered synonymous. If so, how could they have such opposite effects on creativity and productivity? The dictionary definitions of both words are:

> **Debate**: a discussion, as of a public question in an assembly, involving opposing viewpoints;
>
> **Conflict**: incompatibility or interference, as of one idea, desire, event, or activity with another; discord of action, feeling, or effect; antagonism or opposition, as of interests or principles; a fight, battle, or struggle, especially a prolonged struggle; strife.

Ekvall defined *debate* as "the occurrence of encounters and clashes between viewpoints, ideas, and differing experiences and knowledge" and conflict as "the presence of *personal* and *emotional* tensions (in contrast to conflicts between *ideas*) in the organization."

Both terms share a common starting point: different people holding opposing opinions. However, conflict is considered stronger than a debate, has a personal nature, and involves emotions. Based on the above, the distinction I use here is:

DEBATE is issue-based, while **CONFLICT** is personal and emotional.

Why does debate have a *positive* impact on creativity? During an issue-based debate that doesn't become personal or emotional you learn the flaws in your position. You benefit from different perspectives that are brought by the diversity of experiences, knowledge, and backgrounds of your team members. Then you could take what you heard and improve your original idea. When you debate, you *experiment with ideas*. Why does conflict hamper creativity? Because it brings emotions to play, it entrenches you in your own positions, and it causes you to ignore opposing opinions. Think of it as the difference between "your *argument* is wrong" and "*you* are wrong." It's a subtle difference, but the first version would not invoke emotions, while the second may.

One day I sat in a bagel shop with a friend. Two young men were arguing at another table, using their "outside voice." In fact, they were so loud that people around them started moving away. Other restaurant patrons, not understanding a word of the conversation (which was held in Hebrew), seemed to be expecting imminent violence between the two. However, since I speak Hebrew, I knew that they were passionately arguing an *issue*. This was not personal. This was purely professional, and while loud—it was not going to lead to conflict. In fact, I'm pretty sure they might have had a beer together later that evening. Or sushi. Of whatever.

I rarely see two Americans debate a topic with that level of intensity and passion without it becoming personal. Why?

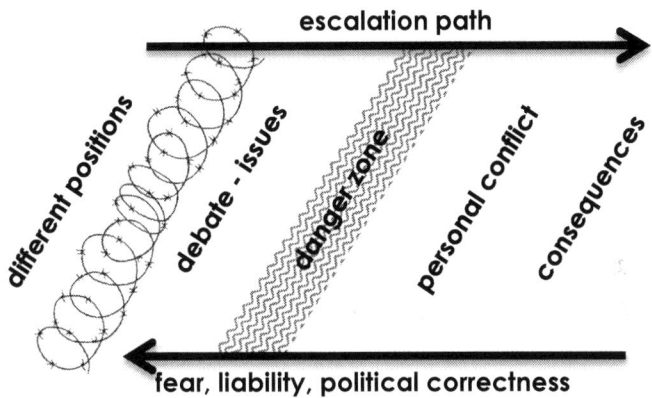

There is a continuum that begins with simply holding opposite opinions (left in the diagram), keeping them to yourself. You could then openly debate them with at least one other person. When emotions get in the way, the debate could turn into personal conflict, and possibly escalate into violence or other organizational consequences such as HR complaint, or even termination (right in the diagram). There is some distance between every two steps along this continuum. You can move from holding opposite opinions to debating them simply by starting to talk. You can move from having a personal conflict to severe consequences (such as termination of even jail time) through a complaint with the HR department or through violence. However, there is still distance between having an issue-based debate and having a personal and emotional conflict. That is the *danger zone* in the diagram. You should stay left of it, but it requires self-control, staying on issues, and keeping emotions out of it. However, the Corporate America culture (and the risk of consequences from personal conflict) forces you to stay left of the barbed wire between holding differing positions to actually debating those. That fear is fueled by Political Correctness and potential liability that became so prominent in Corporate America's culture. Say the wrong thing to someone, and you may offend them, and open yourself (and your company) to potential liability. I would even claim that we have become more afraid of the liability than about offending someone. We became a litigious society. Say the wrong thing, and you get sued. How many times did you enter a meeting in which everything was discussed except for the big "elephant in the room?" Yet once the meeting was over, participants left the room without reaching a real agreement, and told others how they disagree with the outcome? It's called "the meeting after the meeting." And it's not helping creativity or productivity.

Fearing the consequences and liability, people would prefer to stay on the left side of the barbed wire altogether. Why risk going from debate to conflict and suffer the consequences? On the left side of the barbed wire you don't passionately argue a position. On that side you would rather agree with everyone during the meeting, and come out of the meeting not at the same mind, telling others that you really disagree. You don't experiment with ideas and, as a result, you don't benefit from opinions opposite to your own. You fail to see the flaws in your positions, and therefore fail to make them better. But you avoided the potential consequences.

The value of debate is in contrasting opposing opinions. To get that value you must—

- Listen with intent;
- Speak with respect;
- Communicate clearly; and—
- Keep an open mind to the possibility that, heaven forbid, you might be wrong.

What causes conflict in the team? The following pages describe a model showing how *trust* leads to open *debate*, and how you develop that trust, since you cannot *force* it. But for now, here are a few structural factors that may cause conflict and prevent trust and debate.

The first factor is *promotions*. The negative effects of promotions were discussed in chapter 9. In general, promotions would cause internal competition, and as you can see in the following pages—internal competition would prevent the development of trust. If two employees are vying to be promoted, "whose idea was it?" would be more important than the results. Post-promotion tensions could also destroy trust that may have already been built.

The second factor is a "pre-existing condition." There may be pre-existing "baggage" between team members, which has nothing to do with the company or the job. It may not be as dramatic as one of them "stealing" the other's wife (or husband), but could be something bad that happened between the two in the past. This has to either be resolved, or these two would be at each other's throats instead of cooperating. Any idea that one of them may bring up would be attacked by the other, regardless of how good or bad it really was. Mostly because the other person is stupid. No other reason.

Having people from different hierarchical levels in the organization is a third factor that prevents open debate. If you include a supervisor and her subordinate in the same team, the subordinate may refrain from suggesting his own ideas or criticizing hers out of fear of consequences, or out of respect for her position in the company. Even if the higher level employee is from one group and the lower level (hierarchically, nothing else) employees is from another group, the result might be equally negative. As a line employee, you may avoid speaking up when there is a vice president in the group, and would definitely never criticize her ideas. Who are *you* to do so? She might actually verbalize that last question in her communications, tone of voice, or body language, intentionally or not.

Somehow you see less of that in Israel, but for a different reason, as was described in Dan Senor and Saul Singer's 2011 book *Startup Nation*, and from my personal experience. The fact that you may be my boss in our company while I may be your commanding officer next week in our joint reserve military service may equalize our positions in the team. I'm not proposing that hierarchical gaps can never be bridged and lead to good discussion and debate within a team. I've seen that happen. All I'm suggesting is that without *trust* between members at different hierarchical levels, open debate will never take place, and you must be aware of that. Bridging the trust and openness gap between people from different hierarchical levels is harder than bridging it between people at the same level.

Finally, you may have individualists in the team that simply don't like or want to cooperate, and would rather focus on claiming credit. It has nothing to do with being introverts or extroverts. It's just an individual characteristic, and you should remove such people from your team, or from the company altogether.

DEBATE AND TRUST

"Trust" is a loaded word. The definition that resonated with me the most was created by Ekvall in 1996: "the emotional safety in relationships." Where does this safety originate from? When do you begin to trust someone? One of my research participants helped me understand the answers to those questions.

John worked in a startup on the West coast, which was later acquired by one of the largest semiconductor companies. Three years later he left that company to be one of the founders of yet another startup. There was no doubt—startup was in John's blood. During my study of team dynamics, I asked him about the trust he had (or didn't have) in the team in the large company. He described severe distrust and internal competition. He described the others as "a bunch of people trying to pull themselves out of the pack and get recognition so they can move up the organization." Pretty strong words to describe the team he was part of at the time. He also described ideological debates based on different technical approaches, but not in a positive way: people were entrenched in their positions, turning ideological debates into personal conflicts. I wasn't surprised—most of my study participants described the existence of internal competition in mature companies. There was lack of trust across the board.

Sure enough, when I asked him about the environment in the second startup, he described a strong feeling of mutual trust between him and the rest of the team. Although a startup company, it was a global one. The development team resided in Israel, while John headed their North American sales and marketing efforts. "You really cannot have such a long-distance operation if there is no trust," he described. John proved my hypothesis. Large companies lack trust among team members, promote internal competition, secret keeping, and internal political "games." At the same time, startups show strong trust that supports open communications and genuine technical debate, without team members worrying about consequences of a technical debate. True "emotional safety in relationships."

But I was in for a surprise. John had described the *same* team in both stories! The team he joined after the acquisition of his first startup, which lacked trust, especially towards him, was the same team who later left the large company with him to start the second startup. The harsh words he used to describe distrust in the large company and the kind words he used to describe strong trust in the second startup were describing the same group of people!

I was lost. How could he have described the relationships with the same team using such opposite terms? The answer was not incomprehensible. When John joined the team after the acquisition he was *new* to them, and they were new to him. Something happened during those three years of working together that caused both sides to develop strong trust. The kind that allows you to leave the mythical safety of large company employment and take on the biggest business challenge—start a new company with that other person. The type of trust that can only be described by "I've got your back, and you've got mine."

Digging deeper into John's story, I realized several things. The "safety in relationships" originated in the *predictability* of their relationships. Nobody is perfect. When you don't know someone, the lack of predictability eliminates safety in relationships. If you don't know how that person might react in different circumstances, events, and things you do or say—you wouldn't feel safe, and you couldn't trust that person. However, when you can predict how that person would react to things—you know what to expect. You know how far you can push that person, and you know where to stop. You naturally learn when you *can* rely on that person, and when you *cannot*. And when you know that—you only ask them to do what you know you could trust them to do, and they do it. And then you trust them even more. My interim conclusion was therefore that trust originated in *predictability*. When John joined the team after the acquisition, he didn't know them, and they didn't know him. There was no predictability, hence no safety, and hence no trust.

What caused predictability to emerge? From John's story I found three sources: personal relationships, competence, and simply put—time together. The longer they worked together, the more they knew each other. The longer they worked together, the more they developed personal relationships that continued outside the office. Last, but not least—they each felt that the others were *competent* in what they did. You couldn't trust anyone you felt was incompetent. Perceived competence is a prerequisite for trust. It is enhanced by the time they spent together and the personal relationships they developed. Over a three-year period, John got to know the team, and the team got to know John. They developed friendships. They got to know each other's families, helped each other outside of work, and developed the kind of predictability that created the safety in relationships—*trust*. In fact, the trust they felt towards each other after three years was instrumental to their joint decision to make the bold move: leave the large company and start another startup.

Their friendship was not necessarily part of trust or predictability. It helped, but was not required. The *time* spent together created enough predictability to instill trust even without friendship. So, how long do you need to spend with another person to create trust? One year? Three years? Ten years? Obviously, in John's case, three years were enough. Or were they? One element that could accelerate trust building and shorten the time required is the *intensity* of team-building events that took place during that time. When the team goes through an unusually tough challenge together and comes through on the other side, trust becomes stronger. A startup, struggling for survival every day, provides such challenging environment. Intense events tend to expose team members to each other's limitations as well as strengths, and thus develop predictability faster. And when predictability develops, so does trust.

One day in July, Lynn, an engineer external to my penveu team wanted to see me. She felt it was urgent that she spoke with me. She told me that my team had a growing problem. Apparently, two team members got into an argument, which quickly became personal, and escalated to a point in which they stopped speaking with one another. Kind of childish, and unacceptable in a company. Now I had a problem. I started thinking about the link between the time they spent together and their ability to conduct an open technical debate (good) without turning it into a personal conflict (bad). I asked Lynn, who knew all four team members, how she would rank the trust levels between every pair of team members.

	Ken	Joe	Roger	Terry
Ken		14 / High	9 / Mod	5 / Low
Joe	14 / high		9 / Mod	5 / Low
Roger	9 / Mod	9 / Mod		5 / Low
Terry	5 / Low	5 / Low	5 / Low	

(months together / level of mutual trust)

Ken and Joe had been working together in the lab for over a year. They were hired together in May, and were the team's "founding members." They developed a special bond. They went through the toughest early challenges together. Roger joined the team in October, and Terry joined in February of the following year. The fight broke between Ken and Terry. Lynn estimated that the best relationship and trust existed between Ken and Joe. Both had spent more than a year together. The lowest trust level existed between Ken and Terry, as well as between Joe and Terry, but also between Roger and Terry. In fact, Terry was the least trusted member of the team. It would have been so easy to jump to the conclusion that Terry had a personality problem, but in fact it was something else: Terry had spent less than six months in the lab with the other team members. He did not spend enough time with them to develop predictability (in either direction), and thus trust. With no trust, technical debates turned quickly into personal conflicts. Not surprising was the fact that Ken and Joe trusted Roger more than they did Terry, but not as much as they trusted each other. The table above clearly illustrated the correlation between time spent together (of every paid of team members) and the level of trust they felt towards each other.

I later asked each one of them, individually, to rank the level of trust between himself and every other team member, and the findings were identical. The more time team members spent together, the more they trusted each other, and the more they could conduct an open technical debate without letting it escalate into a personal conflict.

FROM RESPECT TO CREATIVITY: THE MODEL

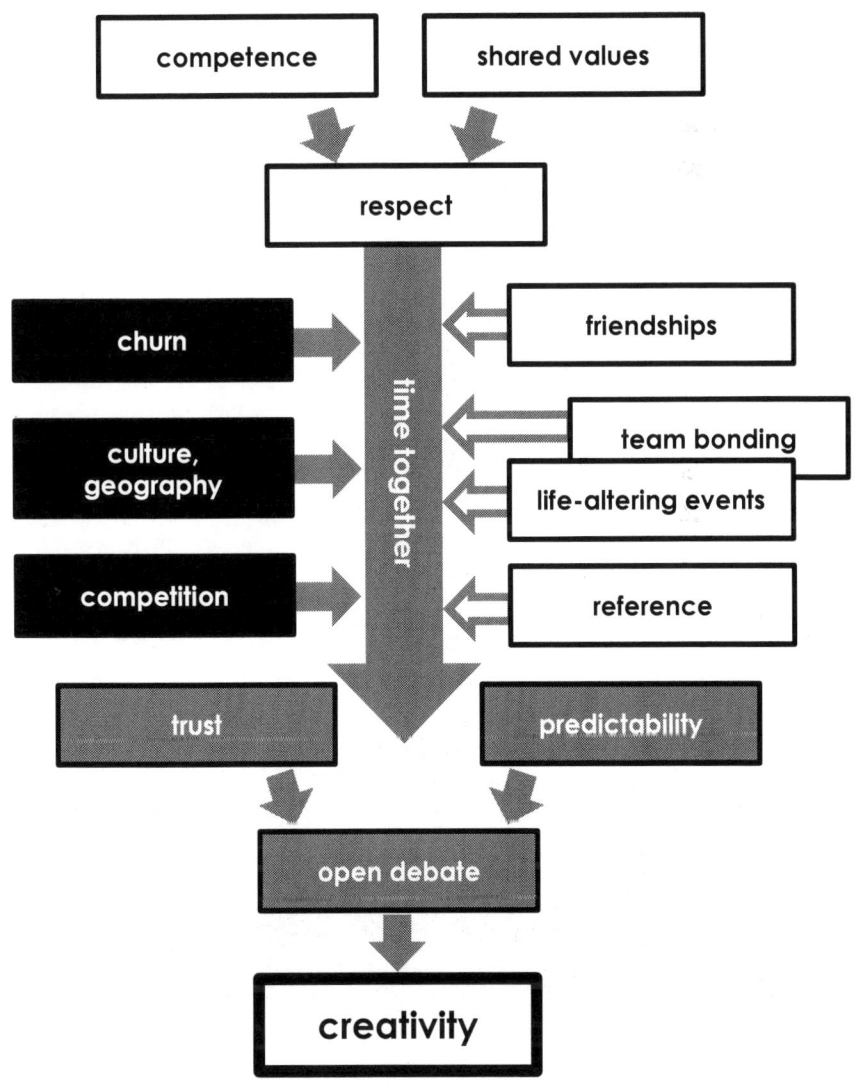

Armed with that knowledge and experience, I began developing the *From Respect to Creativity* model illustrated in the previous page. At the bottom you could see the final desired goal: *team creativity*. As research showed, creativity is strongly supported by the ability to conduct an open debate. As described in the last few pages, open debate could take place only when both *trust* and *predictability* exist among team members. Trust develops from *respect*, but would only develop over time, although certain factors could accelerate it, while other factors could slow it down or even block it from developing. The next pages discuss each one.

RESPECT

One of the most fundamental building blocks for trust is mutual *respect* for two things: the other person's professional *competence* in what they do, and sharing similar *values* with that other person. Lacking one of those would prevent the level of respect required for trust and creativity. You could learn whether this respect exists or not through interviewing individual team members or conducting anonymous surveys, but you must assure that each team member respects all other members on both accounts. Let me be clear: this respect either exists or it doesn't. You cannot force it, no matter how hard you try. Instructing team members to respect each other is futile and naïve. It is nothing more than a politically correct request, at best. As team members get to know each other, this respect may develop, or it won't. You should continuously monitor whether team members respect each other, and if they don't—address it. It is better to remove a team member who is not respected by the others (either because they think he is incompetent, or they feel that he doesn't share their values) than to keep him on the team, and risk losing trust, open debate, and team creativity. One "bad apple" on the team can eliminate the entire team's ability to debate, and so goes creativity.

As it turns out, the link between respect and trust is not completely new. Stephen R. Covey (the son of the *7 Habits of Highly Effective People's* Stephen Covey) described in *The Speed of Trust*[58] a key prerequisite for trust: *credibility*. He offered 4 "cores" of that credibility: Integrity, Intent, Capabilities, and Results. *Integrity* is "walking the talk," being congruent, inside and out. *Intent* includes motives, agendas, and the behaviors that result from it. *Capabilities* are the talents, attitudes, skills, knowledge, and style. Finally, *results* are the track record, performance, and the ability to get things done.

Covey's *integrity* and *intent* constitute *shared values*, while *capabilities* and *results* constitute *competence*. Those terms are not absolute. Here are a few examples.

What does the word *results* mean to you? For a marketing or sales person, the word means sales and dollars. Market success. To an engineer the word means technological breakthrough. An engineer often (albeit not always) cares less about financial results, but is fascinated by technical breakthroughs. A marketer couldn't care less about technical breakthrough, if it doesn't generate value to the customer. Different definitions of results could explain the typical lack of trust between business and technical people. It's a gap that is hard to bridge, but should be.

Some people are never late to meetings. I'm one of those people. I hate being late. Not only that I don't want everybody to turn their heads towards me when I make my entrance after the meeting had already started, but I just think it is disrespectful to be late. So I always arrive early. "Early is on time; on time is late," to me. Others don't mind being late. They don't consider it disrespectful. They consider it natural. They are more laid-back, and less stressed over a minor thing such as this. What's the big deal? There is no right or wrong here. But

---

[58] Stephen M.R. Covey, Rebecca R Merrill. *The speed of trust: the one thing that changes everything*. New York: Free Press, 2006.

imagine having the two opposites on the same team. One would always be upset that the other is late to meetings, and the other would be upset that his teammate is making such a big deal out of it. None of them is right, and none of them is wrong. They simply don't share that *value*. Trust is less likely to develop between them. My wife, Anat, is just like me. We both hate being late, and so we are never upset with each other. Not over this, anyway… We share that value. And that's one reason why we have been married for 23 years so far…

TIME TOGETHER

Having initial respect to one another does not immediately and automatically generate trust among team members. Trust develops over *time*. John's story described a team that initially lacked trust, but had gained it over 3 years of working together. He reported low trust and creativity initially, and high trust and creativity 3 years later.

Jenny worked in a Fortune 500 company, which reorganized teams every 18 months in order to increase diversity. This way, they believed, members would bring different perspectives to different teams. While increasing team diversity, they prevented teams from developing the level of trust needed for them to be creative. Jenny described the team environment as highly competitive. "Right before we could start to trust each other, they would reorganize us into different groups," she told me. Eighteen months are not enough to develop trust. You must let the team work together for a longer time. Let them develop trust. It would not happen overnight.

The more time team members spent together, the more friendships they develop, more often than not. Both time and friendships increase predictability among team members, and predictability creates trust.

How much time is needed for a team to spend together such that respect would turn into trust? That amount of time depends on two factors: the *intensity* of the time together, and the *polarity* of shared experiences.

The intensity of time together depends on *location*, communications *media*, and number of people in the team. A team that is geographically distributed would have a lower intensity relationship. You cannot be on the phone with the rest of the team all the time. Besides, phone can only convey words and tone of voice, which represent only 30% of communications, and lacks the 70% delivered through body language. Even if you could keep a video conferencing link open between the teams 24 hours a day, it would not provide the immediate accessibility of being co-located on the same office floor. Therefore, I rank the intensity of time together the highest when team members are co-located in the same office, and live in the same town. A lower intensity level would exist when team members are located on different floors of the same building, or in an adjacent building. Below that would be team members who reside in facilities in different *cities*, followed by facilities in different *states*, different *time zones*, and different *continents*. Even if you started your day at 8am in Silicon Valley, it is already 6pm in Israel. The work-day overlap is minimal. Add the fact that in Israel the work week starts on Sunday and ends Thursday, while in the US it starts Monday and ends Friday, and you are left with only 4 overlapping work days a week.

Quite a few books were written about global teamwork, teaching you how to bridge operations over multiple locations, states, countries, or even continents. It could be done, but with two harmful side effects. The first is that trust would take much longer to develop, and as a result team creativity would be significantly lower. The second is that, due to the low level of interaction, a recommended practice for long-distance teams would be to set clear *boundaries* and well defined interfaces and specifications between the groups—the opposite of providing the big picture view, and cross-functional interaction that are so essential for autonomy and creativity.

Don't get me wrong. I didn't say that geographically distributed teams *cannot* work together. They can. I merely suggested that it would take much longer for such a team to turn respect into trust, and thus develop the safety in relationships that would allow them to hold passionate debates, avoid conflicts, and be creative.

The second factor affecting the amount of time required to turn respect into trust is the *polarity* of shared experiences. When team members share time together—are their shared experiences positive, or negative? Are they productive, or destructive? The polarity of those shared experiences is affected by the pressure that the team is subject to, and, obviously, the respect they have (or don't have) for one another. Some of those experiences could be affected by you, the team leader. You could be a divisive supervisor who causes almost every exchange to be negative, or a bridge-builder who gets people together (inside and outside work) and helps building positive relationships.

In general, the amount of time spent together required for turning respect into trust and creativity t depends on the sum of the products of intensity i of interactions by the polarity p of them. The higher those products are, the less time is required for respect to turn into trust.

$$t \propto \sum (i \times p)^{-1}$$

Too much math for you? Don't worry. You got the point.

ACCELERATING TRUST

The good news is that there are 3 things you could do to *accelerate* turning respect into trust within the team: promote out-of-work friendships, use pre-existing credibility and references, and actively drive team-building activities.

Teammates who go to movies together, hang out, drink beer together (I'm not advocating alcohol consumption), would turn respect into trust faster. Specifically, out-of-work friendship allows them to *explore* whether they share the same values. If they are not willing to spend time together, they either don't share values (which would prevent trust from ever developing), or it would take longer to develop trust. You cannot force friendships. But you should do whatever you can to encourage it. You could be the person who invites everyone to an informal lunch on Friday. I did that. I can't quantify how effective it was in accelerating trust building, but I can tell you with confidence that it did. Just make sure that: participation in those activities should not be mandatory, the company (or you) should not be paying (you don't want them to come because lunch is free), invite everyone, and never discuss work there. Believe it or not—some managers discourage out-of-work friendships. They are afraid that any conflict outside the company would be brought in, and they are afraid of losing control. Don't be that manager.

As I explained above, a geographically distributed team would have harder time to bond outside work. Living in a different city, a different state, or a different continent altogether makes it practically impossible. The ability to knock on someone's door to ask if they are free for lunch is much preferable.

The second accelerating factor is *pre-existing credibility*. Imagine that a new member was introduced to your team. However, this member was not introduced by an executive or the human resources department, but rather by one (or more) of the other team members, who you already trust, who said: "I worked with her before, and she is really great. I'm so happy she will be joining us!" What would you think about her? You don't know her, but somehow she had just been pre-qualified by someone you trust. When a team member you *trust* introduces a new team member new with a glowing recommendation—it could shorten the time needed to start trusting the new person. The new member would still need to *earn* your respect and trust herself, but she is starting at a better place than others who were not introduced this way. Try adding members to the team by asking current team members to help you find members they know, respect, and trust. This would accelerate trust building. Remember that all it takes is one member that the others don't trust for the entire team dynamics to spoil. Don't offer referral incentives. Referral is one of those activities motivated intrinsically. Employees are more interested in bringing good people into the team than the potential financial rewards.

Finally, the third factor that could shorten the transformation of respect into trust results from sharing *life-altering events*. Life-altering events bond people more than anything. They allow them to get to know each other, and explore the values they may share (or find out they don't) very quickly and intensely. However, life-altering events (such as being in an accident or a tornado together or serving side-by-side in battle) are not within your control. Team-building activities, on the other hand, are. Most companies consider team-building activities as boondoggles, much like strategy planning. A waste of time and money, that does not yield any *immediate* performance improvement. They are wrong.

The more intense the team-building activities are, the more effective they are in accelerating trust-building. Do them on a regular basis, and make sure they are effective. Explore bad feelings resulting from a team-building activity. Are those indications of lack of respect? Lack of shared values? If so—consider yourself lucky to have discovered those early, and make personnel changes in the team. Team building events are not boondoggles. They are needed to shorten the time from respect to trust and creativity. I know what you are about to say. You are about to remind me that they cost money and that I promised you that increasing creativity would hardly cost anything. But I didn't suggest you take the team on a cruise to Alaska. There are many things you can do for much less that would have stronger impact. You just need to make sure you embark on team-building activities that are *intense*, and which lend themselves to trust-building. Make sure that all team members can participate in those events. Do not attempt rock climbing if one of your team members is in a wheelchair, and another is afraid of heights. And in case you wonder—golf if *not* an intense, trust-building activity.

DELAYING TRUST

Much like some activities could *accelerate* the time required for respect to develop into trust (and team creativity), other activities can *delay*, or altogether prevent it. Four of those are: constant churn, "bad" diversity, company politics, and internal competition.

Jenny's story, brought earlier in this chapter, is one example for constant churn. Her company was trying to increase creativity by reshuffling all teams every 12 to 18 months, and thought that taking people from different groups and putting them together in a new group would offer the much needed team diversity. However, diversity has to be more fundamental and bring experiences from different companies and industries, and not only from different business units within the same company. In fact, this constant reshuffling of people prevented Jenny's team members from spending enough time together or developing personal relationships. As a result they couldn't develop predictability or trust. Jenny described that "every time we were close to develop trust, the team got shuffled again and we had to start from scratch".

As described earlier in this chapter, diversity provides equal employment opportunity to all, provides better representation of the diverse customer base, and adds to team creativity. All good things.

How many times did an HR representative ask you to integrate people in the team *because* of diversity? I know I was asked to do so. Now, don't get me wrong—I am not favoring discrimination of any kind. I believe in equal opportunity. However, sometimes trying too hard to achieve diversity could cause more harm than good. If you force people who are so different from one another to the point that they cannot get along together in a team, you are not doing them a favor, and you are certainly not establishing a more creative environment for the team. There needs to be diversity in the team, but of the "good" kind. The kind that brings different experiences, different domain knowledge, different perspectives, and different levels of depth. This type of diversity allows "collisions" of ideas and creates new and innovative ones. However, when "bad" type of diversity, the one that cannot be bridged to create friendships, predictability, and trust, is forced upon the team, it becomes more detrimental than helpful. Some cultural differences cannot be bridged, or are very hard to. Some differences between people are just too vast. While it might be politically correct to implement diversity for diversity's sake, my main concern in this book is to help you build a brilliantly creative team, and not to be politically correct. There are different ways to assure equal employment opportunities than to force people who could not be effective, productive, or creative together to be on the same team.

The best explanation I read for internal politics came from Richard Emerson's 1962 theory of power in organizations[59]. Emerson defined *power* as being in a position to grant or deny another person's gratification—

> "It would appear that the power to control or influence the other resides in control over the things he values, which may range all the

---

[59] Emerson, R. M. (1962). *Power-dependence relations.* American Sociological Review, 27(1), 31-41

way from oil resources to ego-support... power resides implicitly in the other's dependency."

When my study participants felt that other groups or individuals in the company were blocking progress, not releasing resources, or delaying meetings—they experienced how others were exercising their *power* through using the dependence that my participants had on those resources. Employees use internal politics to gain power.

In a 2016 Harvard Business Review article[60], Jay Parikh, the global head of engineering and infrastructure at Facebook, described how Facebook attempted to prevent office politics. He believed that politics were inevitable due to our human nature and the feelings we hold. But to reduce it to a minimum, he suggested several tactics. Facebook refrains from hiring "empire-builders, self-servers, and whiners." During the hiring process, Facebook recruiters include interview questions that would help identify those. The company legitimizes *escalation*. Managers are trained not to take measures against employees who escalate "over their heads." The company often holds Q&A sessions with leadership, and regularly conducts engagement surveys. Facebook makes everyone accountable to prevent personal bias from creeping into decision making. If you are accountable for the overall result, your focus shifts from your own agenda to that of the team, and the company. The company also trains leaders to effectively manage politics out of conversations.

Finally, competition for promotions, pay raises, bonuses, or any other extrinsic value among team members has catastrophic effect on team creativity. Team members would try to promote their own ideas. Sometimes they would rather share their ideas *outside* the team with the team leader, or upper management. They share ideas with whoever controls the promotion. You must prevent such competition from taking place inside the team. This could be tricky when members

---

[60] https://hbr.org/2016/06/how-facebook-tries-to-prevent-office-politics

come from different groups in the company, which are not within your control. In that case, you must talk with managers of those groups. No internal competition among team members should exist.

ASK STUPID QUESTIONS

There is one more reason why political correctness hurts team creativity. Historically, brainstorming required you to initially defer judgment (during the *divergent* phase of brainstorming). Later, it was determined that early judgment could help in formulating great ideas within a team. However, when the team is overly *politically correct*, it avoids judging ideas altogether. Members would accept all ideas as "wonderful" ideas, even if in their hearts and minds they know some of those are pretty stupid. Here, I said it: some ideas are stupid. As a result, the team may end up with a large number of ideas, but very few, if any, that are really good, or of any value whatsoever.

"There is no such thing as a stupid question!" is one incarnation of political correctness. You are about to ask a question, knowing it might be a stupid one. You are not sure whether you should ask it or not, so you prefix it with "well, this might be a stupid question," to which you receive the automatic response: "there is no such thing as a stupid question." Sounds familiar? And there lies the problem. You are about to ask your question, which, by the way, might very well be a stupid one. 50% of mine are. However, nobody would now tell you that your question was stupid. They couldn't. Not after the assurance they gave you that your question cannot be stupid in any way, shape, of form. Now the team has to treat your question (or idea) as a good one, and settle for mediocrity in the process.

For the team to be creative, it must use true and honest judgment. Some ideas are stupid. Some questions are stupid. Some of them may appear stupid at the time, but would reveal themselves as smart later on, in a different context. How should you fight this urge to be politically correct, then?

First of all, be willing to ask stupid questions, propose stupid ideas, and be told that they are stupid. You must feel comfortable enough in your own skin to do that. Nobody expects you to only have great questions and brilliant ideas. I don't. Besides, you might find that what sounded stupid in your head gave someone else a better idea. Don't hold back. Share, and be willing to accept criticism. After all, what's the worst thing that could happen if you ask a stupid question?

Second, when someone is reluctant from sharing an idea or asking a question because they are afraid you might think it's stupid, don't assure them that "there is no such thing as a stupid question." You may be wrong. You should respond with "what's the worst thing that can happen if you ask a stupid question?" Minimize the fear of proposing less-than-perfect ideas. You can also ask "what if we find that this was a *great* question?" Encourage your team members to ask questions and propose ideas. No matter how stupid they might think they are.

Third, when you judge, attack the *idea*, not the *person*. When another team member asked a question or proposed an idea that was, in fact, stupid, don't sugar-coat it. Don't say it was a great idea if it was mediocre at best. Say it was a bad idea. Say why. Don't tell your teammate he (or she) is stupid. Don't force them to be defensive, but offer direct and honest feedback. "Say what you mean, mean what you say, and *don't be mean when you say it...*"

Fourth, build trust first. A team member's willingness to be vulnerable and ask stupid questions or propose stupid ideas comes out of trust, "the safety in relationships." Before you ask team members to feel comfortable asking stupid questions, they need to know that you would not make fun of them *personally*. They need to know that what you say is what you mean. Trust takes time to build, but without it—you never get over the fear of asking stupid questions. Very few people ever will.

Fifth, maintain the "what happens in Vegas, stays in Vegas" attitude. I would feel much safer to ask a stupid question or proposed a stupid idea if I know it stays here, between us, and I will not hear about it from someone else, who was not part of the team. And I need to trust you with that.

SET GROUND RULES

As a facilitator of high-power creative teams, I use ground rules at the beginning of every meeting. Those typically include:

- Nothing is off the table;
- In this debate, we are all equal;
- Nobody gets to monopolize the discussion;
- Nobody gets to sit quietly and only observe;
- Nothing is personal;
- What happens here stays here;
- We don't leave the discussion without reaching a conclusion;
- Once we made a decision—we all support it outside the team.

Corporate America's cultural fear of crossing the "danger zone" between debate and conflict adversely affects team creativity and productivity. The word "argument" has a negative meaning. However, if you stated (and stuck to) ground rules for discussion–you could hold a productive issue-based debate, strengthen your positions, increase your creativity, and reach better results. You have to stop being afraid of debate!

Setting the ground rules at the beginning of the meeting helps a lot. You could use the list of the rules I proposed above, and add more of your own before you start the meeting, and then let the team develop the final list of rules. Some of the rules above may not apply to them. Some may be modified by them. Make sure you have a list of rules that would support a productive meeting for *your* team. Not all teams are alike, and therefore not all ground rules should be the same. If the team participated in setting the rules, they would *own* those rules and adhere to them much more than if you forced those rules on them. The rule "nothing is off the table" assures that team members would not avoid controversial topics. The rule "what happens here, stays here" could calm the fear that your stupid questions may end up on display outside the team. Even a rule such as "stupid questions/ideas are welcome" could help. Use your imagination (and the team's) to put together a set of ground rules that would assure team members would be willing to share whatever potentially stupid idea or question they have with the rest.

I was surprised by how often this simple tool of setting ground rules changed the dynamics. Will you allow using computers and phones in the meeting (hint: do you want their full attention or not?) Ahead of an off-site event I drove to the facility to check it out. One of the participants asked me about Wi-Fi access. Already a bad sign. I checked, and then informed everyone that I would not allow the use of laptop computers of any kind in the conference room. However, I added, there are good news and bad news regarding cellular phones. The good news was that I would allow the use of cellular phones in the conference room. The bad news was that there was no cellular coverage within a 10-mile radius of the facility… Don't let participants split their attention. We cannot really multi-task. We only think we can. For the same fundamental reason you must never text and drive, you should never text and try to be creative. It doesn't work. If team members cannot disconnect from their daily activities—remove them from the team. You must be very vigilant about it. Concessions here cost dearly, and can empty the value of your ideation workshop.

As a final note, make sure you keep a "parking lot" list so you don't forget any idea. Make sure that regardless of whoever captures the ideas (whether it's you or someone else)—be truthful to what was said. People don't like their words being twisted in any way. When you capture something—make sure you ask the idea originator if this was what she meant. If not—modify it. If you had an idea as a result—write hers first, and then yours, but don't replace hers with yours.

HUMOR AND SARCASM

And just when you thought you heard it all…

In a study conducted at Northwestern University[61], Karuna Subramaniam asked two participant groups to watch two different movies. One group watched a comedy and the other watched a horror movie (*The Shining*). Immediately thereafter, she gave both groups a word association puzzle to solve, and found that those who watched the comedy were more creatively solving the puzzle than those who watched *The Shining*. She confirmed her results with MRI scans that showed increased activity in the area associated with creativity (the anterior cingulate cortex) in those people who watched the comedy.

In another study conducted at MIT[62], two groups of participants (professional designers and improv comedians) were asked to brainstorm ideas. Improv artists generated 20% more ideas than the designers (showing fluency). Those ideas were also 25% more creative (showing flexibility). The study also found that using improv warmup

---

[61] *The Power of Humor in Ideation and Creativity.* 2014. https://www.psychologytoday.com/blog/the-tao-innovation/201406/the-power-humor-in-ideation-and-creativity#_ftn1

[62] *Haha and aha!: Creativity, idea generation, improvisational humor, and product design.* 2010. http://dspace.mit.edu/handle/1721.1/61610

games improved the creative output of the product designers in brainstorming sessions by 37%.

The scientific field of *gelotology* studies the psychological and physiological effects of humor and laughter on the brain, and researchers in this field found through EEG brain scans that humor and laughter are very complex cognitive functions that involve the entire brain. The left brain hemisphere "sets up" the joke, while the right one helps in "getting" the joke.

Moving from psychology and neuroscience to sociology, a sense of humor (especially when you laugh *with* other people and not *at* them) can create friendships, and could therefore bond and build a team, such that team creativity would grow.

But it doesn't end with humor. In comes sarcasm. Francesca Gino, Adam Galinsky, and Li Huang of Harvard University found that sarcasm can be a catalyst for creativity[63]. They defined sarcasm as: "often used to humorously convey thinly veiled disapproval or scorn." Sarcasm is prevalent in organizations, and not necessarily for good reasons. Where trust is missing, especially in a newly formed group, introducing sarcasm increases conflict, and therefore reduces creativity. However, when trust exists, expressing and receiving sarcasm could both increase creativity, without causing conflicts. The reason sarcasm enhances creativity, according to Gino and her co-researchers, was that creating a sarcastic comment and interpreting the hidden meaning of one require more creative thinking, and exercises the exact same parts of the brain that would later participate in creative idea generation.

---

[63] *The highest form of intelligence: Sarcasm increases creativity for both expressers and recipients*. Organizational Behavior and Human Decision Processes, November 2015. http://dspace.mit.edu/handle/1721.1/61610

Based on the above, here are 3 simple and practical ways to increase team creativity through the use of humor and sarcasm:

> ***Use humor.*** The more humor you use, the more creative you are (while the more you complain—the less creative you would be). The more you use humor, the better you would be at it...
>
> ***Use sarcasm appropriately.*** Sarcasm could have a positive impact on your creativity, but only if you use it in a group of people who trust each other. If you exercise it on someone who does not trust you—you could have a negative impact on them, and create conflict. When among people you trust (and who trust you)—use sarcasm freely.
>
> ***Take improv classes.*** I took improv classes at the *Dallas Comedy House*. Improv is hard. Believe me. It makes you think non-stop. You get on a stage, already occupied by someone else, and try to figure out who she is, who you are, where you are, and what are you both doing there. You both build on each other's cues. At the end of a 3-hour training session I was sweating. Literally. But even if you don't take improv classes, there are scores of improv exercises you can use to develop those skills.

THE ROLE OF THE TEAM LEADER

REALITY DISTORTION FIELD AND BHAG

Steve Jobs was said to have something similar to Star Trek's *reality distortion field*. "In his presence, reality is malleable. He can convince anyone of practically anything. It wears off when he's not around". Through Walter Isaacson's biography of Jobs this is one of the most used phrases. When I read it, I was reminded of several incidents in my own past. When I became the general manager of Texas Instruments' consumer electronics connectivity business unit in 2003, I took my leadership team to an off-site strategy development workshop. I asked an organizational development professional in TI to conduct a *Myers Briggs* (MBTI) assessment for all team members, including myself, and share it during the workshop. I scheduled the session in one of TI's less known facilities—the corporate jet hangar at the McKinney airport in North Texas. The team expected us to be spending the time around a make-shift table in a smoldering hangar (September in Texas), next to some planes, spilled oil, and open toolboxes. As it turned out, TI has a very nice, spotless, air-conditioned facility to hangar the corporate jets, with a nicely equipped conference room, overlooking the runway. Never in my life have I seen airplanes treated so nicely.

When the facilitator shared the MBTI results, it became very apparent how different I was from the rest of the team. My preferences were ENTJ (Extrovert, iNtuitive, Thinking, and Judging), while all other team members grouped around what, according to the facilitator, were the TI "standard" preferences—ISTP (Introvert, Sensing, Thinking, and Perceiving). I had only one preference in common with my entire team (and the "TI standard", for that matter)—Thinking. I was an extrovert while others were introverted. I relied on intuition, while others relied on their senses and hard facts. I was making decisions using judgment, while other team members considered the perceived impact on other people first.

Given those results and the differences in our preferences, I asked the team to give me some constructive feedback. One element of feedback remained stuck in my head to this day. My systems architecture manager complained: "you only look *outside* of our organization. You don't really understand our issues inside." That helped me realize something important: TI was a company that looked *inside* more than outside. Rather than considering the market, the competition, and differentiation—engineers in the company were used to consider their own issues, scheduled, limitations, budgets and all other inward-looking things.

When it was time to start developing our Ultra-Wideband (UWB) solution, the team simply said that it couldn't be done. However, this did not prevent me from launching the program anyway. The group used to meet every Friday morning to review the progress in different projects. Once a month we added a review of the *risks* associated with each project. Most projects had three to five identified risk items. Most, if not all, were highlighted in green, indicating low risk with a mitigation plan in place. Few, if any, were highlighted in yellow, indicating moderate risk, but with a mitigation plan in place. Never have I seen a risk line highlighted in red when we launched a new product development effort. Red would mean that the risk is high, and that there is no mitigation plan for it. All of our projects to this time were pretty incremental, and well understood.

Until we launched the UWB program. In the first review the team presented me with 12 to 15 identified risk lines. Two were yellow. The rest were red. The development team was sending me a very clear message: this project involves things we don't know. We would have to move outside of our comfort zone. We would like to stay in our comfort zone. We don't like this project. We don't want to do it, but we will force *you* to make that decision. All we have to do is show most of the risks in red. At that meeting, I listened very carefully, and asked clarifying questions (without challenging the risk assessment). At the end, the team expected me to cancel the project. My reaction surprised them, to say the least. I said: "well, I see that there is a lot of risk here. You didn't tell me that it couldn't be done. You only told me that there is risk, and there are unknown things that still need to be investigated. You were very thorough in finding all those risks and uncertainties. That is very encouraging!" They looked puzzled. The last thing they expected was for me to say that this was *encouraging*. I then moved to ask them to develop a contingency plan for every risk, a learning plan for every item that was unknown, and come back with those plans. I told them: "you didn't tell me that there was no way in hell to develop this project. You told me that you identified all the roadblocks, and if we navigate around them, we will be successful!" Again, not the reaction they expected.

Fast forward almost seven years. In February 2010, I conceived the penveu idea at Interphase. Even before writing the business plan, I hired the first two engineers to start developing a prototype. Throughout 2010 and 2011, I implemented a unique hiring practice. Due to the confidentiality of the project prior to its official launch in April 2012, I couldn't share with applicants what was the project they would work on once hired. Only after they accepted the position, started to work at the company, on the second half of their first day, once all paperwork was done and the employment and confidentiality agreements were signed, I told them what the project was. I had to convince them to join the company (and in some cases leave another company) to work on something they know nothing about. It was like asking them to join Lockheed's Skunk Works, but without the brand recognition. They still joined. When I finally told them what penveu was, and how it could change the educational technology market, they got excited. It worked every time. Except in May 2010, when I hired the first two engineers. No doubt, they were excited about the prospects of the product. However, there was a technological challenge that, while I defended it with patents, was not easy to solve. We had to generate an invisible target on a computer or projector screen, and while human eyes could not see it—the pen camera would. I explained how I thought this should be done, but it was still not clear it could be done at all. The two new engineers became increasingly nervous. "It couldn't be done," I heard. The good news was that one of them was without a job at the time, and the other was still a PhD student, so they really had nothing to lose when they joined. Maybe this story would have ended differently if they did, but I honestly don't think so. I asked them to try.

Two months later, on July 21st, we had a board meeting. After presenting the product idea and the business plan to the members of the board, I invited them to the lab for a brief demonstration. On one computer screens there were several open windows. I told board members that there was a target hidden in that screen. I even drew on the whiteboard what it looked like. They got their faces really close to the screen to try and see that target, but couldn't. We then took a simple webcam, connected it to the same computer, with an algorithm my two team members have developed, and showed in a different window what the camera was seeing. The target image appeared very clearly. Not all board members were convinced, so they ran their hands in front of the camera to see if the camera was providing a live feed. It was. The camera window showed their hands moving. It also showed the target, but they couldn't see it with their own eyes.

Many people (mainly engineers) tend to want to stick to what they know and their past experiences. They don't like uncertainty. If my vision was too far-fetched, they would refer to it as "impossible" and strongly object to pursuing it. However, once they conquered that challenge, they felt like pioneers.

In *Build to Last*, authors Jim Collins and Jerry Porras coined the term *BHAG:* a Big, Hairy, Audacious Goal. They claimed that visionary companies were distinguished by having BHAGs: "powerful mechanism for stimulating progress… a huge, daunting challenge". They further described that: "A BHAG *engages* people—it reaches out and grabs them in the gut. It is tangible, energizing, highly focused. People 'get it' right away; it takes little or no explanation."

The creative team leader must be "infected" with Jobs' reality distortion field. This was true for President Kennedy in his September 1962 speech at Rice University in Houston:

> "We choose to go to the moon in this decade and do the other things, not because they are easy, but because they are hard, because that goal will serve to organize and measure the best of our energies and skills, because that challenge is one that we are willing to accept, one we are unwilling to postpone, and one which we intend to win."

It was true when Henry Ford wanted to create an automobile that everyone can own, and when in 1945 Sam Walton wanted to create "the best, most profitable variety store in Arkansas." It was true with every project that Kelly Johnson launched at Lockheed's Skunk Works, and it was true with almost every product that Steve Jobs conceived at Apple. There was always something in those products that was never done before, and it was always Steve Jobs' reality distortion field that could make the development team "feel" the ability to achieve this goal, although they always said initially that it was impossible: Squeezing a thousand songs into a battery powered, hand-held, pocket-size device (the first iPod); Putting a color touch screen, speaker, microphone, camera, and camcorder in a 1"x1" device (iPod nano), and many more. The creative team leader's vision should not be trivial. The test is the response of the product development team. If the engineers agree that this could be possible—the vision is not far-fetched enough. The goal would not be inspiring, and the resulting product would not be significantly innovative. Only when the engineers initially reject the feasibility of the goal, but stop short of calling it completely impossible, will the team leader know that the vision was far-fetched *enough*. Some of the engineers might quit. Some would complain. Some would go around the leader's head to the human resources manager or even to top management to complain. God know this happened to me more than once. But as long as the company's top management trusted this leader, the vision would remain in effect. That's how it was with Kelly Johnson in Lockheed, and Steve Jobs in Apple.

However, it is not enough to have the vision stated and for the leader to step out of the way. The leader must continue to encourage the team to meet the audacious goal. He or she must continue telling the story of the impending success. The story of the product's disruptive nature once it hits the market. Of what it would do to the market and customers. Of what it would do to competitors (crush them!) Of what it would do to the company, and what it would do to the employees. The leader must continue reiterating the impact that those employees have on the company's success.

WHAT CREATIVE TEAM LEADERS DO

Beyond inspiring "unrealistic" vision, a creative team leader motivates creativity in the following ways:

CREATIVE LEADERS DON'T DRIVE CREATIVITY.

I've already established that creativity is more like curling and less like golf. You don't drive the ball—you make room for it to slightly change direction, with very little control over it. Creative leaders don't *force* their employees to be creative. It doesn't work. They don't give employees 20% of their time to be creative, or build an innovation lab, because those don't work either. Instead, creative leaders *allow* their employees to innovate naturally and individually.

CREATIVE LEADERS ACCEPT (ALBEIT NOT EMBRACE) YOUR FAILURES.

Some of the best ideas came out of trial and error. The Marshmallow Challenge lesson was that you should experiment as *early* as possible. IDEO's *Design Thinking* encourages the same. While you could argue with the virtue of praising failure, "*Fail Fast, Fail Often*" suggests experimenting as *much* as possible. Sometimes you may not have the perfect formula, but once you experiment, you could improve and reach the desired outcome. So what separates a creative leader from a not-so-much one? The way they respond when you go to them and tell them: "I tried something you haven't authorized and failed." The uncreative leader would make it clear that you had just committed a career crime. He promises personal consequences for you. This might go in your personnel file. And a creative leader? In contrast, she would ask: "so, what have you learned from it?" or: "what's your next move?" or suggest a few people in the organization you could consult with that could help you. She would not celebrate failure, but would rather make it clear that failure is an unavoidable part of success, and as your leader—she has your back when you fail.

CREATIVE LEADERS ASK: WHAT DO YOU NEED TO MAKE IT HAPPEN?

What happens when you come to your boss with a great idea for a new product? A mediocre leader would "take it from here." Often they would put it in a stack. Or under a stack. They are not as passionate as you are about your idea, and that's OK, as long as they still let you pursue it. One of my worst experiences was when I came to see my boss with what I believed was a great idea for a next product and he, although not dismissing it, told me he would pass it on to the team that will (or will not) continue the development. I was completely out of the loop because that "wasn't my job." A creative leader would ask: "what do you need to make this happen?" It doesn't matter whether it's part of your day job or not. It doesn't have to come at the expense of your day job. He would let *you* figure out yourself how good your idea really was. He would put you to the test and see if you're passionate enough to make it happen.

CREATIVE LEADERS TELL YOU WHAT WOULD MAKE THEM SAY YES.

A creative leader would give you a list of what you need to bring so she could say "yes" and turn your idea into a funded project. As stated before, one of the most powerful employee creativity motivators is the visibility to the "big picture." Mediocre leaders tend to believe that their world is past the comprehension of the "simple" people. Well, it is not. Letting you "walk a mile in their shoes" and sharing how they make decisions and what constraints they are subject to would not only empower you, but would also make you understand the impact of your own project on the company—yet another positive impact on your creativity. Once, as a general manager for a $100m business unit at Texas Instruments, I worked with Theresa, a sales account manager for one of our biggest customers (Apple.) It was a well-established practice that general managers don't share cost and profit margin numbers with sales people. The standard practice was to give your sales manager a price to hold. Once the customer pushed back, they would call you, and you would make the final decision, which would typically be a lower price than what you gave your sales manager initially as your "final." Obviously, your final price wasn't really final. Everybody knew that, including the sales manager and the customer, and they all played the game. But I trusted Theresa, and instead of giving her a price (knowing I could afford a lower price), I told her exactly what my cost was, what my cost reduction plan was, and what was the gross profit margin at which my own boss would make my life miserable. She negotiated with the customer and settled on a price that guaranteed a better margin than I gave her. All I had to do is give here the constraints I have to live by, and trust her. She didn't disappoint.

TEAM LEADER AS A FACILITATOR

Ideation workshops generate great ideas, and solve the biggest problems, when done well. They are far more than "brainstorming." Chapter 16 describes six of those in some level of detail. Those processes must be facilitated, and most organizations turn to *external* facilitators. These are experts in ideation, and are very skillful in the art of facilitation. So why not get one of those?

Approximately a month after I joined Texas Instruments in 2002, I flew over to the headquarters in Dallas to meet my boss for the first time. Yes, he hired me as the Director of Strategy over the phone. Of course, I was interviewed by his entire team, but he wasn't available, so he trusted them and his phone interview. After a relatively short meeting (it was my last meeting before heading to the airport to fly home to Silicon Valley), I asked a potentially career-limiting question. "We don't really have a strategy, do we?" In a hindsight that really wasn't the smartest question I could have asked, and there were so many bad ways in which he could take it. Instead, he said: "I think you are right. What do you suggest we do about it?" "Let me think about it, and I'll send you a proposal within the next week," I replied. I didn't need a week. I worked through the 3-hour flight home, and by the time I landed I had a 4-page proposal for him, which I sent the following day. I proposed holding a *Scenario Planning* workshop. I facilitated one of those in the past, so I felt pretty comfortable I could do it again. However, I gave him two options: hire an external facilitator, or use me. The latter was my preference, but I didn't want to sound too eager.

At the time I joined, the business unit was developing and selling components for Wi-Fi systems. Specifically, for access points and personal computers. Although Wi-Fi had only started significant adoption a year or two ago, there were several competitors already, and profits were eroding quickly. We needed to figure out how to be differentiated and competitive. The general manager decided to bet on me as the facilitator. Maybe he didn't want to hire a consultant, or spend the money. After all, I was already paid for… Whatever his reasons were—I was going to facilitate it. Was it a good idea? The biggest question in my head was: could I be *objective* enough to facilitate a process in a business unit that I'm a part of?

The *Scenario Planning* process begins with identifying two critical uncertainties that could have significant impact on the answer to the main question: how could TI be successful in the Wi-Fi market? I invited 30 participants to the workshop, which took three days in a TI facility in Plano, 30 minutes away from our Dallas headquarters. We began by reviewing 12 presentations given by different subject matter experts. After that, we started brainstorming the driving forces that could affect our success in the market. We identified more than 20, which we pared down to 8. It was now time to vote which two were the most *critical* and most *uncertain*. Every participant had to cast his or her vote. Two driving forces surfaced as the biggest *critical uncertainties*.

And this is where we were lucky that I was an *insider*. An outside facilitator would have taken those two and use them to define four plausible future scenarios. We would not have reached the conclusion we did if we did that. But, knowing our industry, there was one driving force that I thought should have ranked much higher on the uncertainty scale but, instead, ranked almost the lowest. Thus far, I executed the process by the book. What went wrong? I wondered. Does everyone else believe that they know how this factor would develop in the future with so much certainty? I decided to try one more thing. Initially, I asked the participants to vote on each of the 8 driving forces based on their perceived certainty. Put a sticker next to that line if you thought it was uncertain. That driving force had very few "uncertainty stickers" next to it. I asked them to vote again, but this time I asked them to put their voting stickers in one of three places next to each description: on the left, if they believed this driving force would develop to one extreme over time; on the right, if they believed this force would develop to the other extreme; or in the middle, if they really didn't know. Consistent with the previous low ranking of uncertainty, very few participants placed their stickers in the middle. However, the split between those who were certain it would develop to one extreme and those who were sure it would develop to the opposite extreme was almost perfect! While individually they ranked that driving force as very certain, as a group they were almost perfectly split. As a result, this driving force immediately jumped to the top of the *critical uncertainties* list, and became one of the two driving forces that allowed us to define four possible future scenarios to plan for.

Being an insider and knowing the industry well enough allowed me to challenge the process, change it, and reach a better result. The outcome of that *Scenario Planning* workshop led the business unit to change direction and focus on developing Wi-Fi components for *mobile* phones. While this may sound obvious today—it was nothing *but* obvious in 2002, and our business unit became one of the first to develop such components in 2003, commanding 60% market share, and became a $500 million business.

In several different occasions I found that my position as an *insider* helped me facilitate the process to better results and catch things that an external facilitator might have missed. It requires a significant effort on your side to maintain objectivity, while serving not only as the facilitator, but also as a reality checker for the process and the results.

A strong, creative leader has a toolbox of ideation and facilitation tools that he or she can draw from, and can facilitate idea generation, while maintaining objectivity and semi-neutrality in the process or, at least, have someone on the team that can do that.

TEAM LEADER AS A TRAINER

The next chapter shows that individual creativity can be *learned*, and needs to be *exercised* constantly. Hiring outside trainers is one option, but the logistics and costs associated with it could often get in the way of implementing it.

The best time to conduct training is when you have the team together and undistracted, which would typically be during an ideation workshop, or right before it starts. Individual and team creativity exercises achieve more than make the idea-generation process vivid and real—they also serve as great ice-breakers, great breaks, and even great team-building exercises.

Beyond an ideation process toolbox, team leaders should also have a *creativity training* toolbox, and train their teams (as individuals and in groups) how to generate ideas.

TEAM LEADER AS IMMUNE SYSTEM

In 2010 I experienced firsthand another, very important trait of a good team leader.

I led the penveu team at Interphase. I had just finished my PhD dissertation, and knew that for the team to be creative, I had to protect them from bureaucracy and strict processes, and give them more autonomy. Just then, the company considered adopting time-keeping software called *CrossPoint*. It was going to let the company track how employees (specifically engineers) spent their time at work. It would provide us with statistics of their effectiveness on different tasks, and allow "charging" their time to different projects, although all this meant was moving money from one pocket to the other and nothing more. Needless to say, knowing that this was one more thing that could reduce employee creativity, and as a vice president in the company and member of the executive team, I objected. Vehemently. But it was to no avail. It didn't matter what argument I brought up—there was always a counter argument. Finally, the CEO got tired of arguing with me, and decided that we would implement *CrossPoint*, and that's it!

I lost the war, but I thought I could still hold my ground in one front, so I argued to exempt the employees in *my* team from using that tool. "They only work on one project, so why does it matter that we track their time?" I asked. It didn't help either. My team was forced to use *CrossPoint* as well. I lost that battle too.

Once a month thereafter, the company's budget manager would join our executive staff meetings and provide the *CrossPoint* time allocation report for all employees, by groups. Often he complained that some of the employees didn't enter their time to the system in one group or another before deadline for the report to be generated. As if they had nothing better to do...

One time, right after he completed his report and complaints, he turned to me and said:

"I don't get it. *You* were the one person who fought fearlessly against using *CrossPoint*. I would have expected that *your* team would be the worst in entering their time into the system. Instead, your team is always the first to enter their time. How come? Did you change your mind about *CrossPoint*? How are you forcing your employees to do it on time?"

"Well," I said, "if you check carefully, you would notice that not only did my team enter their time promptly, but that they all entered their time within the same 30 minutes..."

He confirmed, but seemed even more confused than before.

"Let me save you the time," I added, "If you asked them how come they all entered their time into *CrossPoint* within the same half hour, I bet their answer would be: 'what's *CrossPoint*?'"

He then got it. My team never entered their time into the system. I did. I knew exactly what they all worked on, so I spent 30 minutes a week entering their time, not bothering them with this extra step of process and bureaucracy. I met the company's requirements, but managed to keep bureaucracy away from my team.

I modeled the protection I provided my team after Kelly Johnson's "SkunkWorks" group, as described by Ben Rich and Leo Janos in *Skunk Works: A Personal Memoir of My Years of Lockheed*:

> "Our relations with the Air Force blue-suiters were love-hate—depending on whose heads Kelly was knocking together at any given time to keep the Skunk Works as free as possible from bureaucratic interlopers or the imperious wills of overbearing generals. To his credit Kelly never wavered in his battle for our independence from outside interference, and although more than one Air Force chief of staff over the years had to act as peacemaker between Kelly and some generals on the Air Staff, the proof of our success was that the airplanes we built operated under tight secrecy for eight to ten years before the government even acknowledged their existence."

It was also described by Kelly Johnson himself in his autobiography *Kelly: More Than My Share of It All*:

> "For some time I had been pestering Gross and Hibbard to let me set up an experimental department where the designers and shop artisans could work together closely in development of airplanes without the delays and complications of intermediate departments to handle administration, purchasing, and all the other support functions. I wanted a direct relationship between design engineer and mechanic and manufacturing. I decided to handle this new project just that way."

He also added that:

> "The ability to make immediate decisions and put them into rapid effect is basic to our successful operation. Working with a limited number of especially capable and responsible people is another requirement. Reducing reports and other paperwork to a minimum, and including the entire force in the project, stage by stage, for an overall high morale are other basics. With small groups of good people you can work quickly and keep close control over every aspect of the project."

And hence another role of the creative leader: you have to operate like an immune system. You have to stop the bacteria that can hurt employee creativity from entering the internal organs (your team). See the following diagram.

Block the requirement to fill timesheets and expense reports. Don't ask for weekly reports. If you don't know what your team is working on, then you are not really part of the team. If you are a true leader—you know exactly what everyone is working on without asking them to report. Fill every bureaucratic form for them. Don't let them waste their time with the purchasing and procurement processes. If they need something, and it's in your budget—get it for them. If it's outside the budget—go get the budget and then get it for them. If they have IT problems—fill the IT ticket for them. As a leader, you only let 3 things "penetrate" into the team: funding, resources, and praise. Block everything else. Like a good immune system would.

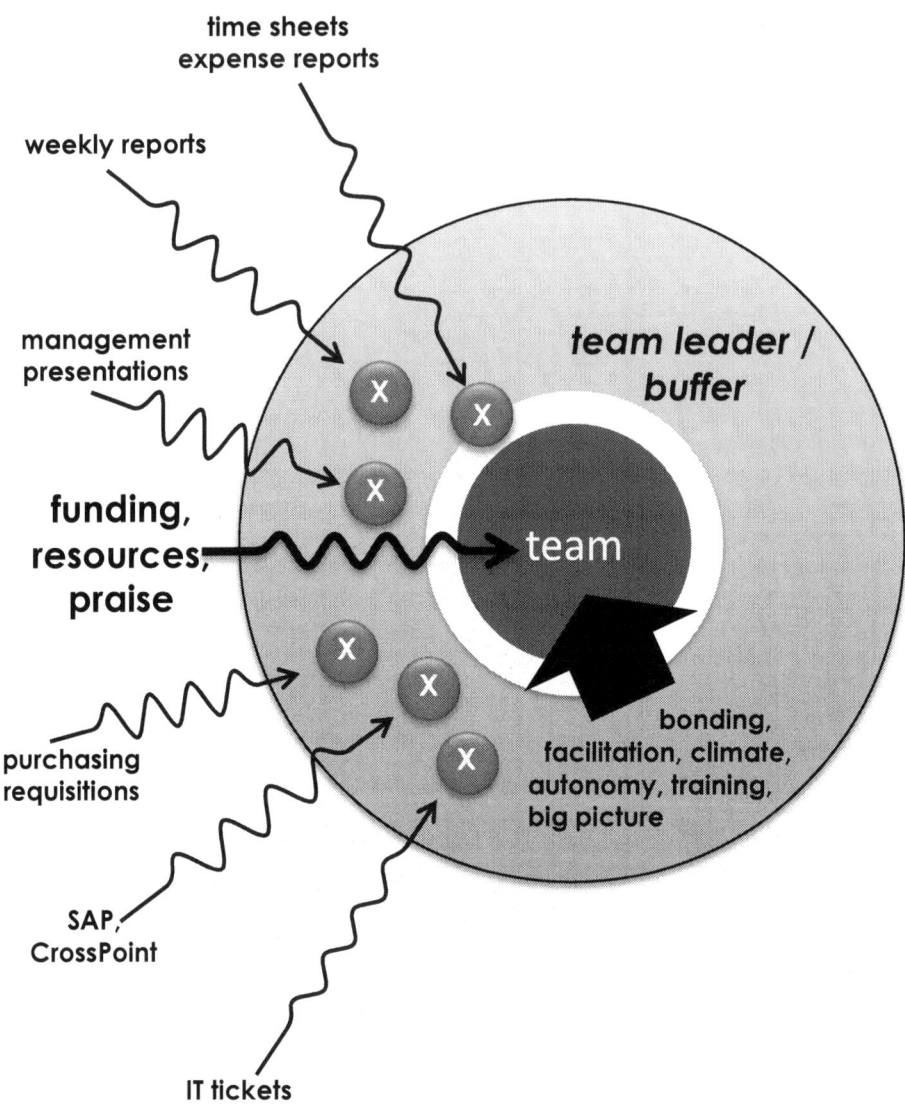

12.

WHY DO WE GET THE BEST IDEAS IN THE SHOWER

For a company to be innovative it needs creative teams. Creative teams need creative people. What makes one person more creative than others? How do you increase your own creativity?

This chapter is filled with the number 4. It begins with the 4 categories of factors affecting individual creativity. It continues with 4 methods for generating ideas, and then offers 4 steps to generate combinational ideas. It is a pure coincidence.

WHAT MAKES YOU CREATIVE

The 4 elements that made you as creative as you are today are: genetics, biography, environment, and your actions. You can affect most of them.

GENETICS

Not all people were created equal. Some are good at certain things, and others are good at other things. Some people were born with higher IQ than others. Some are "left brained" and some are "right brained" (Don't get too hung-up on that one.) Some are more visual, and others more literal. Some are introverts, and others are extroverts. Some people are more creative and others less so. Many people I spoke with resigned to that fact. Many times I heard the statement: "I wasn't born creative, and there is *nothing* I can do about it." On the other hand, some said "I was born creative. There is nothing I can do to improve it, and I will never lose it." *Neither is true.* You may have been born more creative than average, but throughout your life experiences, you could lose that creativity while another person who may have been born less creative than you would gain it. Saying that some people were born more creative than others is almost meaningless. The other three factors have a much bigger impact on your creativity, and—you can control them.

In 1921, Lewis Terman started the longest-running psychological study, which continued by his successors long after his passing in 1956. This study was covered in 5 books[64][65][66][67][68]. Terman started with 1,528 gifted elementary and high school students from San Francisco, Los Angeles, and Oakland. He used the Stanford-Binet IQ test, the National Intelligence test, and the Army Alpha test to find students with IQ higher than 135. Once the test group was finalized in 1928, Terman begand collecting data about the participants every 5 years or so through questionnaires to parents, teachers, and the students themselves. He collected medical data, and administered tests. The goal of the study was to find how different gifted students were from all the rest. His last data collection was in 1955, a year before he passed. However, his study continued by Melita Oden, Robert Richardson Sears, Less Chronbach, and more. The last publication was

---

[64] Terman, Lewis M. (1925). *Mental and Physical Traits of a Thousand Gifted Children. Genetic Studies of Genius Volume 1*. Stanford (CA): Stanford University Press.
[65] Burks, Barbara S.; Jensen, Dortha W.; Terman, Lewis M. (1930). *The Promise of Youth: Follow-up Studies of a Thousand Gifted Children*. Genetic Studies of Genius Volume 3. Stanford (CA): Stanford University Press.
[66] Terman, Lewis M.; Oden, Melita (1947). *The Gifted Child Grows Up: Twenty-five Years' Follow-up of a Superior Group*. Genetic Studies of Genius Volume 4. Stanford (CA): Stanford University Press.
[67] Terman, Lewis M.; Oden, Melita (1959). *The Gifted Group at Mid-Life: Thirty-Five Years' Follow-Up of the Superior Child*. Genetic Studies of Genius Volume V. Stanford (CA): Stanford University Press.
[68] Holahan, C. K., & Sears, R. R. (1995) *The Gifted Group in Later Maturity*. Stanford University Press: Stanford, CA.

in 1995, when some of the participants were in their 90's. The study was criticized for not being generalizable enough, for the biased selection method, and because Terman sent recommendation letters to the participants. While many lessons were learned from this research, Terman could not find that genius children had any significant impact on society. In his own words: "At any rate, we have seen that intellect and achievement are far from perfectly correlated." This conclusion was reported by others, as well. Peter Drucker[69], the business guru, claimed that—

> "Above all, innovation is *work* rather than *genius*. It requires knowledge, it often requires ingenuity, and it requires focus. There are clearly people who are more talented as innovators than others but their talents lie in well-defined areas."

James Farr[70] claimed that all individuals are capable of being innovative in their work roles. Richard Ripple[71] added that "the potential for creative thinking and behavior exists to a greater or lesser degree in everyone" and that creativity occurred on a daily basis, calling it "ordinary creativity." Farr and Michael West[72] stated that—

> "Far from being an isolated indication of genius, creative expression in the world of work is manifested by almost everyone, given the appropriate facilitating environmental conditions."

Different researchers agreed that appropriate training had a positive impact on individual creativity and that creativity could be learned and practiced. Nigel King[73] found that training could enhance

---

[69] Drucker, P. F. (1985b). *The discipline of innovation*. Harvard Business Review, 63(3), 67-72.
[70] Farr, J. L. (1990). *Facilitating individual role innovation*. In M. A. West & I. L. Farr (Eds.), *Innovation and creativity at work* (pp. 207-230). New York: Wiley.
[71] Ripple, R. E. (1989). *Ordinary creativity*. Contemporary Educational Psychology, 14(3), 189-202.
[72] West, M. A., & Farr, J. L. (1990a). *Innovation and creativity at work: Psychological and organizational strategies*. New York: Wiley.
[73] King, N. (1990). *Innovation at work: The research literature*. In M. A. West & I. L. Farr (Eds.), *Innovation and creativity at work* (pp. 15-59). New York: Wiley.

creativity. Farr focused on creativity *enhancing* techniques such as brainstorming, morphological analysis, and lateral and divergent thinking. Finally, Scott, Leritz, and Mumford[74] conducted a meta-analysis of studies addressing the effectiveness of creativity training and reached the following conclusions. Since they represented an overall consensus, I "adopted" them here:

1. Creativity training is effective, mostly on divergent thinking and problem solving;
2. Creativity training has different effect on different people;
3. The strongest and most effective element of creativity training is cognitive processing activities;
4. The cognitive capabilities that have the biggest impact on the effectiveness of training are: problem finding, conceptual combination, and idea generation;
5. Training techniques that work the best are: critical thinking, convergent thinking, constraint identification, and use of analogies;
6. Lecture-based instruction is the most effective on divergent thinking; and—
7. Training effectiveness improves when it includes an explanation of the cognitive processes that occur, and when training is lengthy and challenging.

In summary, while there was still debate on whether personal creativity characteristics are born or acquired, the majority of research done to this point suggested that whatever differences in "born creativity" were, they could be completely overturned through training, exercises, or lack thereof.

Do other cognitive and psychological characteristics play a role in creativity? For example: are extroverts more creative than introverts?

---

[74] Scott, G., Leritz, L. E., & Mumford, M. D. (2004). The effectiveness of creativity training: A quantitative review. *Creativity Research Journal, 16*(4), 361-388.

A 2016 article in Quartz[75] suggested that in order to be more creative, you must feel comfortable being *alone*. A 2012 study concluded that spending 4 days immersed in *nature* would improve creative problem solving by 50%(!) Apple founder Steve Wozniak was quoted saying that inventors and engineers work like artists, and therefore need to be alone, outside of their companies, where they can invent peacefully without others affecting them. Reflecting on my days as an engineer—I would have to agree.

However, as the article stated, one had to feel comfortable being alone, which is hard. The article described another study in which participants were asked to spend up to 15 minutes in a room with no stimulation. After a while, many of them started zapping themselves with electric shocks just to avoid feeling lonely and bored, and to avoid thoughts they wanted to suppress.

Does that mean that introverts are more creative? Brainstorming is based on combining ideas from multiple people. Ideas from one person are enhanced by another, leading to a product that none of the participants could have envisioned individually. Many of my best ideas came when I was with other people. Even if others didn't consciously contributed to them, the mere fact that I had to explain my ideas to other people made my original ideas better. Group brainstorming is hard for introverts, though. They would rather be left alone to think, and thus would not benefit from other people's thoughts. A 1982 study of the correlation between the Myers Briggs type Indicator (MBTI) and individual creativity found that creative people are significantly more intuitive, perceiving, and moderately more extroverted[76]. Does that mean that extroverts are more creative? According to researcher Mihaly Csikszentmihalyi:

---

[75] *What creative people understand about the importance of being alone.* Belle Beth Cooper, March 30, 2016. http://qz.com/649771/what-creative-people-understand-about-the-importance-of-being-alone/

[76] Carne, J. C. & Kirton, M. J. (1982). *Styles of creativity: Test score correlations between the Kirton Adaption-Innovation Inventory and the Myers-Briggs Type*

"If there is one word that makes creative people different from others, it is the word *complexity*. Instead of being an individual, they are a multitude."

Creative people are both introverted and extroverted, but at different times. They need and use the companion of others to build better ideas, but they also use solitude to let ideas incubate, and they use triggering activities to force combination of those incubated ideas. In other words—being introverted or extroverted, long believed to be related to creativity, is not.

BIOGRAPHY

The second category of factors affecting individual creativity is biography. Two people may have been born with the same IQ, and with the same "born creativity." However, as Malcolm Gladwell described in *Outliers*—those who spent their summers learning did better in tests than those who spent their summers getting in trouble. Gladwell claimed that Steve Jobs, Bill Gates, Steve Ballmer, and Bill Joy were simply born at the right time (all born in the late 1950s) and therefore were exposed to the early days of computing, which led them to greatness in that area.

The research described a few pages ago concluded that creativity was affected by exercise more than by genetics. Some people, throughout their lives, exercised their creativity more than others. Some went to school and took classes that forced them to think differently. In one of his most inspiring speeches, at the 2005 graduation ceremony in Stanford, Steve Jobs (who never completed more than six months of college) described how influential was the moment he dropped out of the "formal program" and started auditing calligraphy classes on his success, the ideas he produced, and his

---

Indicator. Psychological Reports, 50, 31-36.

obsession with design. The experiences you have, the diversity of those experiences, the education you received, and other life-changing events affected your level of creativity. Some of those were decided for you by your parents, by the part of society you were born into, by the location you were born at, and by the era you were born into. Other factors were decided by you. You have to take responsibility for the choices you made, and how they affected your creativity (and will affect it in the future).

In my own study I reviewed 43 years of research that yielded the following list of individual characteristics found to have had a positive effect on creativity. Some of them were supported by only a single or few studies, while others were supported by many. Note how many of those are not characteristics you were born with, but rather ones that you developed throughout life (and could still develop):

- Being a hobbyist;
- Persistence;
- Curiosity;
- Broad interests;
- Attraction to complexity;
- Intuition;
- High energy;
- Proactivity;
- Openness to experiences;
- Unconventionality;
- Originality;
- Outcome driven;
- Honesty;
- Self-motivation;
- Self-confidence;
- Creative self-image;
- Cognitive abilities (genius, brilliance, general intellect, divergent thinking style, ideational fluency, ability to find problems, associational, analogical and metaphorical, imaginative);
- Risk orientation;
- Ambiguity tolerance;
- Prior relevant job experience (including startup experience);
- Expertise;
- Education;
- Domain knowledge (and being at the forefront of technology);
- Practicality;
- Independence;
- Resourcefulness;
- Opportunistic;
- Being an achiever;
- Passion;
- Strong will;
- Joyfulness;
- Strength;
- Compassion;
- Irreverence for the status quo;
- Explanatory style;
- Social skills;
- Naiveté (being new to the field);
- Commitment to the project, the organization, and ownership;
- Strong desire to innovate.

Don't consider this a complete list of the individual characteristics of creative people. First, because not all researchers agreed on all items. Second, what makes a person creative is a *cumulative* list of characteristics, and not only one. The more items on the list you could check—the more creative you might be. Most important is that, for the most part, those characteristics, although developing over time, are *learned, acquired,* and within *your* control.

CLIMATE FOR CREATIVITY

This chapter focuses on what *you* could do to increase your own creativity. As a manager, leader, or executive in the company, there are two things you could do to affect the creativity of others. The first is to provide appropriate training. The second is to provide the right climate. You control the organizational and team factors that were covered in greater detail in chapters 9, 10, and 11. In the company setting, the employees are a captive audience, allowing you to affect their creativity the most. You must create the right climate. After all, eggs will not hatch if the right temperature doesn't consistently exist in the incubator…

GREAT IDEAS ARE *NOT* ACCIDENTAL

The fourth category includes actions *you* could take to improve your own creativity. After I had the idea for penveu, I had put together a business plan and presented it to the Interphase CEO. A week later I presented it to the board of directors. My presentation was received very well, and the directors described the product as very innovative and life-changing for the company. After the board meeting was over, one board member followed me to my office and stated decisively: "an idea like this comes to a person only once in a lifetime."

"Why do you think that?" I asked, to which he replied: "because innovation is *accidental!* You cannot control when an idea like this will come to you."

I had to think about that for a while. He believed that innovation was purely accidental. His position was supported by the glory of great "accidental ideas" that preceded my penveu. Newton's apple, Archimedes' Eureka! and others. However, were those really accidental? Or was there an event that was merely the stimulus to launch this idea into their consciousness?

I took the analogy further. Say I was riding my bike, and wanted to have an accident (I told this story once to an audience that included my two daughters, Maya and Shira. They had a terrified look on their faces when I said that, so I immediately explained that this was a hypothetical scenario. Then I had to explain what a hypothetical scenario was…). If I was riding my bike on the bike trails in the park, the probability of an accident is minimal, if at all. Cars don't drive in parks trails. However, if I was riding my bike South on the Dallas Tollway[77] at 8AM—I *would* have an accident. Guaranteed! And the analogy: The *aha!* moment may be accidental, but you can put yourself in situations where those accidents are more likely to happen. In other words—you can act in ways, and do things that would allow you to be more creative. The following pages describe what actions you could take to increase the probability of such "accidents."

---

[77] The Dallas Tollway is an infamously jammed highway in the Dallas area.

4 METHODS FOR GENERATING IDEAS

In her article *Creativity as a Neuroscientific Mystery*[78], Researcher Margaret Boden described 3 types of creative idea generation processes, and I added a fourth one here. Due to the seemingly "accidental" nature of idea generation described above, creativity is often treated as *unpredictable*. However, scientific studies were conducted to understand the processes leading to creativity, and offered neuroscientific explanation to one of them. The main three, distinguished by the sorts of psychological, cognitive processes that took place to generate ideas, are: *combinational, exploratory,* and *transformational* creativity. The fourth that I added was *team*-based combinational creativity.

COMBINATIONAL CREATIVITY

Of the four methods, combinational creativity was studied the most by neuroscientists. There are several explanations to the cognitive and brain functions that take place when generating combinational ideas. It was defined as the generation of *new* ideas through combining *old* ideas. Since it was researched the most, it is the method that offers the most control mechanisms. The next section in this chapter describes it in greater detail. The premise of combinational idea generation is that old ideas are *already* in your brain, and neuroscientific research focused on the *brain activity* that led to making those connections.

EXPLORATORY CREATIVITY

While still supported by old ideas in your brain, the *exploratory* method suggested exploring beyond what you know. Experimentation

---

[78] In the book *Neuroscience of Creativity*, MIT Press, 2013.

without knowing what the outcome might be and curiosity for the unexpected both lead to ideas that could not have been generated through simple combinations of old ideas. Unlike combinational creativity, the area of exploratory creativity was not researched by neuroscience as much. This method is not discussed in greater detail in this book, other than emphasizing the importance of allowing employee to explore, experiment, and prototype.

TRANSFORMATIONAL CREATIVITY

Margaret Boden defined ideas generated through transformational creativity as "impossibilist[79] surprise." The process begins by changing "the rules of the game." You must take one (or more) of the *rules* that prevented you from generating radically new ideas and ask yourself what would happen, or what would be possible if that rule did not exist. One example that Boden provided was the 1985 hypothesis that some carbon molecules could be hollow spheres, contrary to common wisdom at the time. Pursuing that hypothesis led to the development of carbon nanotubes and the entire field of nanotechnology, and to winning a Nobel Prize in 1996. Boden believed that transformational creativity generated the most *radical* ideas—the kind that had a higher likelihood of winning a Nobel Prize. Unfortunately, those are also very rare (transformational ideas, as well as winning a Nobel Prize). Like exploratory creativity, neuroscience is in its very early days of understanding and explaining transformational creativity.

The discussion of the IDEA ideation workshop process in chapter 16 includes a question that follows this type of thinking: What could I do if restriction X didn't exist?

---

[79] Don't bother looking it up, it's not a real word...

COMBINATIONS OF THE METHODS

Each of the first three methods described above could lead to the *individual* generation of new creative ideas. However, Boden suggested that in reality you would most likely be using a combination of all three methods. You would typically start with the higher-order methods (such as *transformational* or *exploratory* creativity), and could then complement them by using the lower-order methods (*combinational* creativity). The difference is in the questions that you may ask.

TEAM CREATIVITY

A fourth method not discussed by Boden is the *team*-based combinational creativity. The 3 processes described above relied on creative ideas generated by *one* person. However, ideas can also be generated by a team of creative people, as described in chapter 10, with the right diversity and the right dynamics, by which old ideas, pieces of the new idea, reside with multiple people, and the team, through debate and communications, would generate those combinations. This method of idea generation is not the focus of neuroscience, as it occurs in multiple brains, and is more within the focus of the field of communications and social studies.

THE 4 STEPS OF IDEA CREATION

For the most part, the focus of this book was on increasing the level of creativity of employees in your company, mainly through changing the organizational climate and affecting team dynamics. This section could apply not only to your employees. It applies to *you*, and not only at work—it applies to you at home. The following will teach you how to be creative. It doesn't matter whether you think you were born creative or not. This works for everyone.

The combinational idea generation technique was, as described before, the one most researched by neuroscientists, mainly because it deals with old ideas already in your head, combined into new ideas, and for the most part does not involve any experimentation, changing rules, or communications with other people. The following is a description of how to make it work in an *intentional* and *consistent* manner. You use the combinational method every day, whether you know it or not. You might as well know how it works, and make it work better.

In 1939, James Webb Young worked at an advertising agency (think *Mad Men*, but before TV…), when a co-worker walked into his office and said:

"You have produced a lot of advertising ideas. Just how do you get them?"

James initially thought this was a joke, but quickly realized it wasn't. The man standing in front of him was serious, really wanted to know the answer, and the agency was waiting to learn how to generate *more* and *better* ideas.

This was similar to what happened to me 71 years later, in 2010, when one of the company's directors followed me to my office after I presented my latest idea and flat out told me that my idea was accidental!

Both Young and I reacted the same way—we wanted to understand *why* and *how* we generated great ideas, and after much research and thinking, we reached relatively similar conclusions.

James Young's conclusions were published in his 59-page classic book, *A Technique for Producing Ideas: the five-step model anyone can use to be more creative in business and in life!*

My model, bearing some resemblance to Young's, is described as a four-step formula, is illustrated in the following figure.

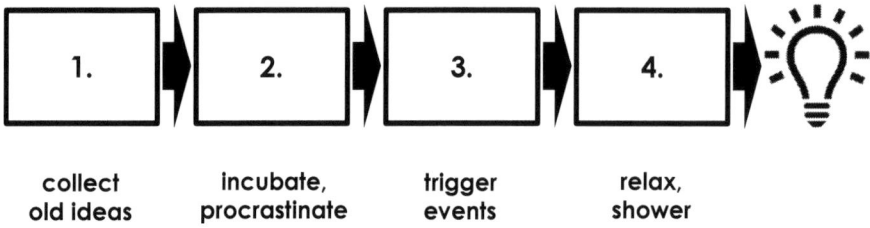

STEP 1: COLLECT OLD IDEAS

James Young suggested that the first step for producing *new* ideas was to fill your head with *old* ideas. I agree. Collect as many ideas as possible. Broad and narrow, superficial and deep, generic and specialized. Write important ideas down, or record them using a voice recorder. This would help you remember them. Even the fact that they were important enough for you to capture would help. I read *Popular Science, Popular Mechanics,* and more. I watch TED and other interesting videos I can find on YouTube while on my treadmill every morning. Some of the ideas you would capture are *problems.* Some are *solutions.* Always remember that one man's problem is another man's solution, so you don't have to categorize them as such.

In my creativity workshops I often ask for two volunteers and throw them plastic balls. I then explain that one ball represents an *old* idea that resides in the left side of your brain, and the other represents an old idea in the right side of your brain ("left brain-right brain" don't have any special meaning here). I then stand in the middle, representing the medial prefrontal cortex (the area of the brain where old ideas connect to form new ones). Finally, I ask them to throw the balls at each other and aim such that they would meet in the air right above me. They try it. I've done this more times than I care to remember, but I have yet to see the first time the balls would actually meet in the air. If the balls would meet above my head—a new idea would be generated.

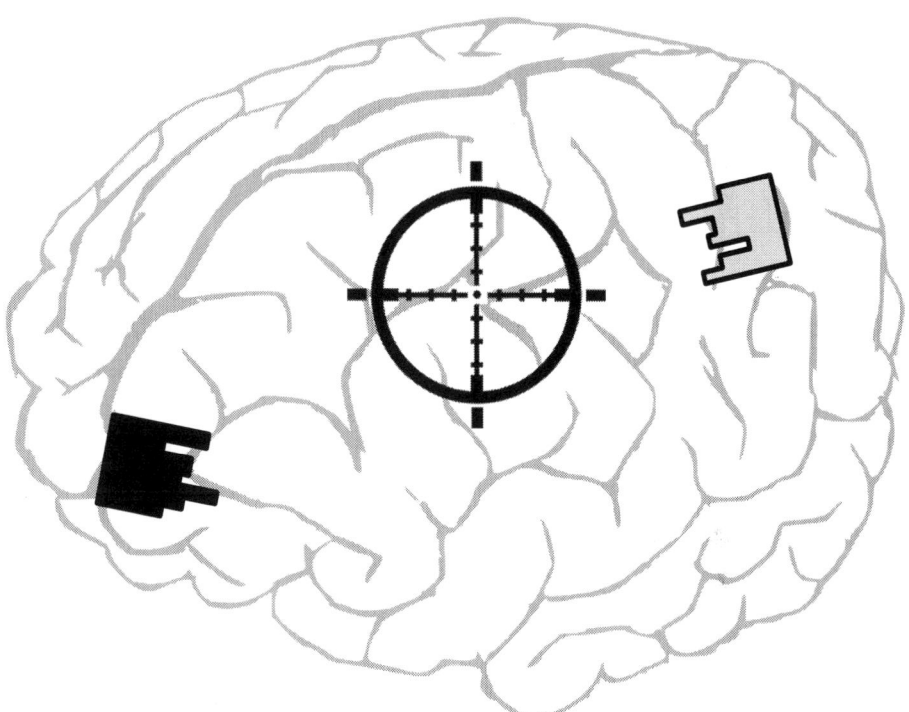

The figure above illustrates this analogy. There are two ideas in my head. One is a problem (the black one) and the other is a solution (the grey one). They have to meet right there in the medial prefrontal cortex, where the crosshairs are. What are the odds?

Disappointed, I then ask my participants what could they do to increase those odds? They are not allowed to come any closer. The connection must occur above me. The best solution—instead of throwing only one ball each, how about if they threw dozens of balls at the same time? What is the probability that two would meet then?

The following figure represents a brain full of old ideas. Problems and solutions. What are the odds now?

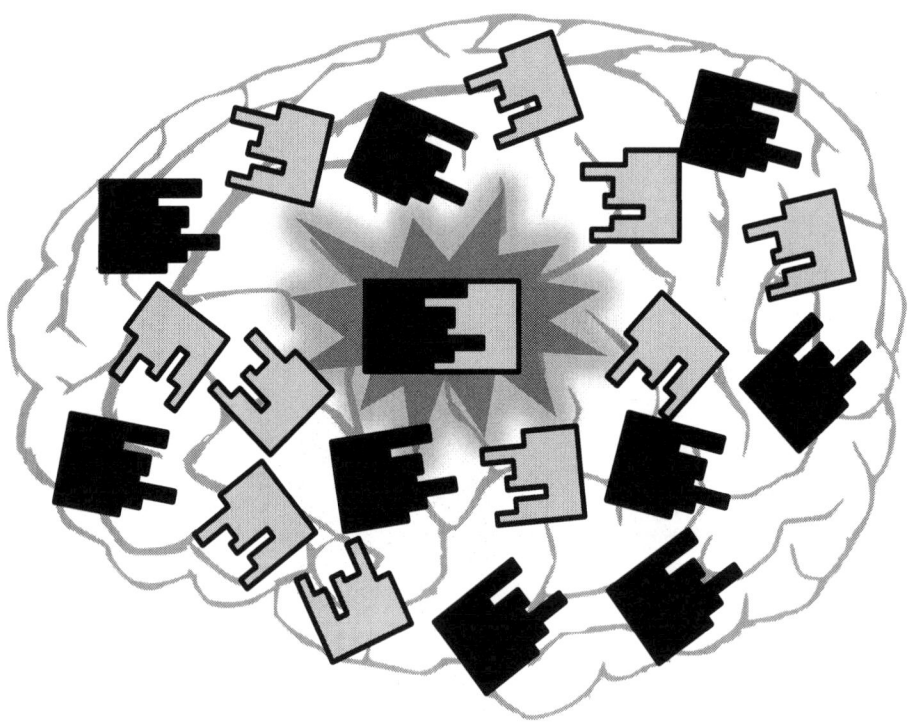

Mathematically, two ideas could form only one combination. Three ideas (A, B, and C) could form 3 combinations (AB, BC, and AC). The number of combinations that could form using n ideas is:

$$\frac{n(n-1)}{2}$$

The following figure illustrates this point further. Adding one more idea to n existing ideas in your head would add n possible new combinations (the new idea combined with each one of the old ideas).

You get the idea (pun intended): the more old ideas you have, the better the chances are that combinations of them would generate new ideas, and the higher the probability that some of those ideas would have higher value.

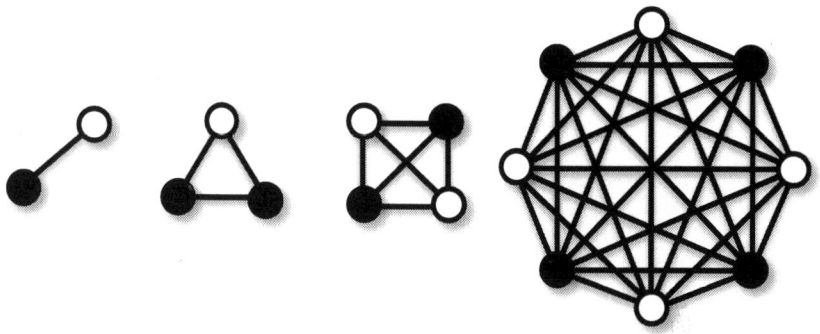

The ideas you fill your head with don't really have to be *old*. I like to think of Science fiction movies as "the art of the possible." Using camera tricks and computer graphics allowed studios to generate things that defy nature, physics, and everything we know. Here is a thought: science fiction defies what we know *today*. They show what *can* become reality *tomorrow*.

In the first episode of *Star Trek* (aired in 1966), Lieutenant Uhura, the communications officer, had a small wireless communications device in her ear, which she used to speak with the others. Little did the creators of *Star Trek* know that 33 years later, in 1999, the *Bluetooth* specifications would be published, and such devices would become a reality. Or was *Bluetooth* inspired by *Star Trek?*

Jules Verne's *Nautilus* submarine that appeared in his book *Twenty Thousand Leagues under the Sea* in 1870 inspired the modern submarines (even though the first submarine was built in 1620.)

Science Fiction is not grounded in what you know *today*, but it is a great source to what could become real tomorrow. When I facilitate ideation workshops, one of my favorite activities is to describe to a group of engineers something I saw in a science fiction movie, and ask them how they would implement it if they needed to. You'll be surprised how often they had the answer...

Watch science fiction movies and read science fiction books. Don't bother trying to figure out how everything was done. It wasn't. It's an illusion. It's just a movie, remember? But ask yourself—what could I do if that existed?

Think of the Hoverboard in *Back to the Future*. The flip-phone and the wireless ear-piece in *Star Trek*, and so many devices that appeared first in science fiction movies and became reality simply because they illustrated something that *could* be, and later someone figured out how to make it happen. Perhaps the strength of science fiction movies is in how real they make everything feel. You can envision yourself using the technology shown there. Think of Science Fiction movies as seeing how a prototype works. Your next step is to build it.

STEP 2: INCUBATE, PROCRASTINATE

One day in 1991, I was in the middle of writing a program for an electronic system I had developed for the company. It was a computer-based system, so I had to write code for it. In fact, most of the work was the development of the code that would run on that system. Up until then, I did most of my software development in assembly language, which is the most basic, structured, although very unforgiving type of coding. I was happy with that. But in 1991, I decided to develop this system in C language. This was my first ever attempt to develop in C, and I was going to learn it on the fly through hands-on experience, trial and error. My motivation was *intrinsic*. But that's not the point.

Everything was going well, and the program grew more and more complex. One morning, I added a certain feature that simply refused to work. It didn't matter what I did, I couldn't get the damn system to respond to a certain parameter. Taking full responsibility for my work, I assumed that *I* did something wrong. I spent the next 12 hours undoing almost everything I wrote and rebuilding it. I developed debug code only to find my bug, but all to no avail. I just couldn't find what I did wrong.

I would probably have worked through the night to solve it, if I wasn't supposed to meet my girlfriend (my wife for the last 23 years) to see a movie at 9:30. It was already 8, so I had to stop what I was doing. So I did. I have to admit that there was a moment when I considered calling her and blowing off that date. I know—I'm a geek. But I couldn't let this problem win. It was driving me crazy.

Eventually I left the office, and met my girlfriend to see the movie. To this day she still remembers that in the middle of the movie I whispered in excitement: "I got it!" Not sure I actually *whispered*. I don't even remember which movie it was. All I knew was that I thought I had the answer for something I struggled with for 12 hours, in the first 30 minutes of the movie.

The next morning I started the day by testing what I thought the problem was. It took me 20 minutes to realize that I was right. As much as I thought the problem was caused by something that *I* did, the problem was in the compiler—the tool used to develop software. The kind of tool that you assume was perfect and would never let you down. It took getting my mind away from what I had been working on for 12 hours straight, and into something completely different (the movie) for me to solve it.

But I wasn't the first person to encounter this phenomenon:

Arianna Huffington described in her book *The Sleep Revolution*, and told *Business Insider* that "during sleep the neurons of the brain are reorganized, so we see new patterns, we see solutions, where before we could only see obstacles."[80]

She quoted psychologists from UC San Diego and neurologists from the Harvard Medical School, who found that our ability to make connections and generate creative solutions was assisted by *sleep*, and specifically the REM (Rapid Eye Movement) part of sleep. If sleep represented up to 33% of our lives, the experts claimed that the probability of inferring connections between distant, old ideas increases by 33% if the incubation time includes sleep.

"How often have we woken up with clarity about a problem or having resolved an emotional issue? That's why dreams are so important," Huffington said. "Sleeping on it" is not just a figure of speech.

Let ideas incubate in your head. Procrastinate. You don't need (and can't) *force* old ideas to connect in your head whenever you want them to. Furthermore, the longer you wait, the more ideas you may collect before two old ideas combine into a new one.

Procrastination is often considered a bad word. However, there are times when procrastinating makes you more productive and creative. When creating a presentation, for example, I almost always wait until the last moment before I begin working on it. Here are 4 reasons why:

> (1) You get more ideas. Creativity is a process of generating new ideas from combinations of old ideas. The probability of creating combinations of old ideas increases as you gather more of those. When you procrastinate—you have more time to collect old ideas.

---

[80] http://www.inc.com/business-insider/how-to-productively-sleep-on-an-idea.html

> (2) Ideas incubate. In the creative process, once old ideas occupy your head, they need time to incubate. Procrastination gives you that time. The probability of two old ideas meeting increases the longer they both incubate in your head.
>
> (3) Better alternatives come up. Before making decisions, you should consider alternatives. The more alternatives you have, the higher the probability that you make a better decision. You may stumble upon an alternative simply because you didn't rush to make a decision early.
>
> (4) You have time to discuss your ideas with more people and get their feedback, which could result in better ideas and decisions. You won't benefit from their feedback if you make decisions too early.

However, procrastination is not *always* good. There are times when it can hurt. Here are 3 such examples:

> (1) It is the last moment and you realize that you need more information but it's too late to get it. You think you know the scope of the task at hand, the form to be filled, the report to prepare, and as you reach the deadline you discover that there is a piece of information that you don't have access to, and may not obtain until after the deadline.
>
> (2) Getting close to the deadline stresses you. It doesn't stress me, but many people get stressed when a task is not complete, and the deadline is looming. If you are one of those—procrastination is bad for your health.
>
> (3) Something else comes up. You thought you could work on it at the last moment, but then life happened. The time you allocated for that late task is now occupied by something else, likely more important, and the task you didn't complete will not be done on time.

So which is it? Procrastinate or not? Here is the wisdom you need to know the difference:

Are you a person who stresses out if you are too close to the deadline? If you are—don't procrastinate. It could have negative physiological effects on you and the quality of your work. Do it early so you can sleep better and keep your sanity. You don't stress over last minute tasks? Enjoy the benefits of procrastination.

Do you know if you have all the materials you need to complete the task? You don't have to complete the task right now, but at least glance over it to make sure you have everything you need to complete it. If there is an external piece of information or material you need—go get them now, and then procrastinate. The remaining task has to be entirely within your ability to complete without needing to find additional external information or support.

Do you expect more ideas may come up? Do you think you know enough? Sometimes you know everything there is to know about the topic. OK, maybe not everything, but very close to it. In that case—procrastination would not give you any new or useful information. On the other hand, if you know less than enough—take your time and get more ideas and information, and collect more input from other people before jumping to complete the task.

How sure are you that no new, higher priority activity could come up at the expense of the task at hand? Is your schedule generally predictable? How willing are you to take the risk that a family or personal emergency would prevent you from completing the task?

Finally—what are the consequences of missing the deadline? Can you survive them? Can the task be rescheduled for a later date? Is the deadline so rigid that missing it would mean that you lose a major opportunity in your professional life that would never present itself again?

One more advice. If this is an important task, and the deadline is non-negotiable—consider doing the "two-step." Complete the task "good enough" early on. Then procrastinate. When you get closer to the deadline, you would have collected more ideas, more alternatives, let your ideas incubate more, and would be generally in a better position to improve your work. However, if an unexpected emergency came up—you would still have something. And you would be much less stressed over it.

STEP 4: TAKE A SHOWER

After you collected old ideas as proposed in this chapter, your brain could now combine them into new ideas. Guaranteed. The question is only *when*. The final two steps in this 4-step process are required. You must allow your brain to do certain things that would cause it to start combining those old ideas, in what would appear to be a very natural way. It would seem accidental. Have you been paying attention so far? For example, have you noticed that I skipped step 3 and jumped directly to step 4? No, it wasn't a mistake. I wanted to talk about step 4 first. Step 4 is the "aha!" moment. It is your "Eureka!" Step 3 would make step 4 more powerful, and more immediate. But in order for step 3 to make sense, I must first explain step 4. OK, enough conjecture. Let's get to it.

Step 4, simply put, is: *take a shower*. No, seriously. In 2011, I held my *Great Ideas are NOT Accidental* workshop in Richardson, Texas, and asked the participants where they got their best ideas. Almost 90% of the attendees exclaimed: "in the shower!" The only way I could explain how 90% of the participants got their most creative ideas in the shower was if they spent 90% of their days in the shower. Well, do you? But seriously, have you ever thought about what was Newton doing when the apple fell on his head? That's right—he was sitting under a tree. Let's just call it relaxing. Where was Archimedes when he realized that the volume of water displaced must be equal to the volume of the part of his body he had submerged (also known as the "Archimedes Principle") and shouted "Eureka!"? That's right—he was taking a bath. Showers were not common during the third century BC.

James Young suggested that if you collected old ideas in your brain, all of a sudden, a new idea would come:

> "It will come to you when you are least expecting it—while shaving, or bathing, or most often when you are half awake in the morning. It may waken you in the middle of the night."

But he didn't explain *why*. Here is why.

In a 2016 article[81], Neil Stevenson of IDEO described how Neuroscience was helping in understanding creativity in people. He underwent a brain MRI scan (voluntarily) to help in research done by the *Imagination Institute*, which leads the charge against the "left-brain, right brain" model. The operation of the brain is much more complicated than that over-simplified left/right model. The frontal lobes are responsible for our executive, organizational functions, and in fact separate us from our ancestors (our eyebrows are higher than theirs due to the development of the frontal cortex with evolution). Whenever you exercise your organizational/executive skills, your frontal cortex "lights up."

However, the study shows, instead of searching for areas that "light up" for creative functions, the focus was on the neural networks that operate when the executive functions are *not* utilized, during daydreaming and relaxation. "Creativity is a *mode*, not an *identity*," said Stevenson. Instead of exercising your "creativity muscles" you should learn how to shut down your executive frontal cortex and let yourself daydream. This is why your best ideas occur in the shower, or while resting.

My commute from my Sunnyvale home to my Texas Instruments office in Santa Rosa, California, took an hour and forty minutes in the morning, and then two hours in the evening. Believe it or not, but I enjoyed that commute. It was beautiful and inspiring. After a while, I started driving on "autopilot." This was long before autonomous cars leaped out of science fiction movies and into reality. My brain was relaxed, and ideas kept coming.

---

[81] https://medium.com/ideo-stories/inside-the-brain-machine-neuroscience-changed-how-i-think-about-creativity-86f49503bbc8#.dkvsmscm8

Perhaps one of my best investments at the time was an Olympus digital voice recorder. I could fill it up with ideas by the time I reached my office in Santa Rosa in the morning, but not as much when I drove back home. Perhaps because of the heavier traffic Southbound in the evening, which prevented my frontal cortex executive section from going into "auto pilot" mode. One piece of unrelated advice if your commute is two hours each way—don't drink and drive. I don't mean alcoholic drinks. I mean *any* drink. I stopped drinking anything at least two hours before my commute home. It helps you make the drive without stopping...

The conclusion is that in order for your brain to make those connections between old ideas and produce new ideas, you need to *relax*. Rather than forcing your brain to work harder, let it work "in neutral."

So why did I skip step 3?

STEP 3: TRIGGER

Can you tell the difference between the colors Aqua, Cyan, Teal, and Turquoise? The answer is: hardly, if at all. They look very much alike. Even if you put them next to each other, you would still be hard-pressed to tell them apart. But put Aqua next to Maroon and you could definitely see the difference. Having your brain constantly in "neutral" would not be as effective as *changing* your brain's activity level dramatically. Your brain would generate more ideas if it's relaxing immediately following a high-intensity, high-focus brain activity.

This is why I changed the order of steps 3 and 4. You had to first understand why ideas occur when your brain is resting in step 4. Now you can learn how to enhance step 4 by inserting step 3—an *intense activity*.

Perform high-intensity, completely unrelated activities on a regular basis. For me, it was flying full-size airplanes as a pilot, riding fast motorcycles, and more recently—flying radio controlled airplanes, some of which fly faster than 130 miles per hour. James Young alluded to this step when he said:

> "Drop the problem completely and turn to whatever stimulates your imagination and emotions. Listen to music, go to the theater or movies, read poetry or a detective story."

Wasn't that exactly what happened to me when, after 12 hours of trying unsuccessfully to solve my software problem, I found the solution in 30 minutes, once I started watching a movie with my girlfriend?

When I moved from Israel to Silicon Valley in 1998, I joined a small company called *Voyager Technologies*. How small was it? We didn't have enough employees for a single football team. The CEO, Ray Shook, and I met every morning at 8AM to plan the day. It was a small wireless engineering company which, in 2000, I negotiated and sold to PCTEL for $22 million. In 1999, a year after joining Voyager, I began taking flying lessons. The airport at which I took my flying lessons was 3 miles south of the office, so I drove there once or twice a week after work. One morning, as soon as we finished our morning planning meeting, Ray asked me:

"Did you go flying yesterday?"

"Yes, I did. Why?" I asked.

"Because you seemed a lot more focused this morning. I noticed that you were more focused after every time you fly," he said. Interesting…

You see, there is a triggering mechanism that plays a role here. All those old ideas, which have no value by themselves, are in your head. They have been there for a while. It would be an unexpected moment when they combine into something new. However, you must *trigger* that moment, and intense experiences would certainly trigger it. You can watch a "triggering" movie, such as *Star Wars*. Not *It's a Wonderful Life*...

Better yet—start a dangerous hobby, like I did. The day after flying a plane, riding your motorcycle, or practicing any other dangerous, intense hobbies or experiences—you would have ideas. Many ideas. In the shower. At night. While driving on "auto-pilot." Wherever. And this is why. To me it happened often when I took a shower right after flying one of my 10-pound, 130mph radio-controlled airplanes. Sometimes it happened when I took a shower after working out on the treadmill. It became so predictable for me that I could plan for it. In fact, I stopped worrying about ideas for articles or my weekly videos. I fly my planes, or work out, take a shower, and get down to writing. The ideas just keep coming.

So, if you needed an excuse to buy a motorcycle, take flying lessons, or start building and flying radio controlled jets—now you have one!

Even if you are not ready to take on something dangerous, there are so many other things you could do. Jessica Stillman, a fellow *Inc. Magazine* contributor, reviewed the science behind the link between *walking* and creativity[82]. Jessica noted that some of the greatest minds in history, including Charles Darwin, Friedrich Nitche, William Wordworth, and Aristotle were obsessive walkers. She quoted scientific research showing that almost any type of exercise would

---

[82] *The science of why you do your best thinking while walking.*
http://www.inc.com/jessica-stillman/the-science-of-why-you-do-your-best-thinking-while-walking.html

"light up" the brain. In a 2014 *New Yorker* article, Ferris Jabr explained the link between walking and creative idea generation[83]. He first noted that when you walk (or exercise in any other way), your chemistry changes: "The heart pumps faster, circulating more blood and oxygen not just to the muscles but to all the organs—including the brain." Jabr described experiments showing the connection between exercise, memory, and attention. Not only that new ideas were generated, but the size of areas in the brain has grown too, indicating that the physical activity contributed to longer-term creativity impact. One of the more prevailing set of studies he quoted was done in 2014 by Marily Oppezzo and Daniel Schwartz at Stanford University[84]. In 4 experiments, they asked 126 students to conduct certain physical activities, and then take creativity tests. The relationship between the two was strong. He reached an interesting conclusion, though:

> "Perhaps the most profound relationship between walking, thinking, and writing reveals itself at the end of a stroll, back at the desk."

Did he mean "in the shower?"

You don't have to fly an airplane and share the air with "triple-sevens," or fly a 10-pound radio controlled jet at 130mph, or ride a racing motorcycle that reaches 60mph from a standstill in less than 3 seconds. Other intense activities would do. In a nutshell, a relaxing activity (step 4) following an intense one (step 3) is when your brain would start making those connections and generate new and better ideas. This is your serendipity moment. Make sure you have a way to capture those ideas…

---

[83] *Why walking helps us think.* Ferris Jabr, 2014, The New Yorker. http://www.inc.com/jessica-stillman/the-science-of-why-you-do-your-best-thinking-while-walking.html

[84] *Give Your Ideas Some Legs: The Positive Effect of Walking on Creative Thinking.* Journal of Experimental Psychology: Learning, Memory, and Cognition. 2014, Vol 40(4). https://www.apa.org/pubs/journals/releases/xlm-a0036577.pdf

Now you understand the process of combinational idea generation that takes place in your brain. You know how to make it work in a deliberate way. It is not as simple and as immediate as flipping a switch, but it works, and science (mainly neuroscience) explains it. I delivered on my promise to you that there were 4 simple steps to help you generate creative ideas in a consistent manner. In the next several sections I will share a few extensions to the process.

STOP DOING THESE

Once you triggered the executive part of your brain (stage 3), you should let your brain shut down (stage 4), so it could start combining old ideas into new ones. However, there are several activities that could prevent that from happening. You probably can't stop doing them altogether, so at least be aware of those, and reduce them when you can. For the most part, three things may prevent your brain from relaxing: trying hard to focus and concentrate, drinking coffee, and filling up "dead time" with *organized* activities, such as checking email.

Coffee sharpens the executive attention and prevents your brain from drifting. Let's face it—that's exactly why you drink coffee. To stay awake and alert. When you stop drinking coffee, your mind would drift more often. You would be more likely to daydream. And that's when you would be creative. I'm not suggesting you completely stop drinking coffee. If you do—don't forget the effects of coffee withdrawal. It's a real thing. All I'm suggesting is that you drink less.

Clayton Christensen, in *The Innovator's Solution* (sequel to *The Innovator's Dilemma*) realized that the RIM Blackberry's "main job" was *not* to communicate and connect, but rather to fill small snippets of time with productive activities. Those same activities would light up your frontal cortex executive area and slow down your creativity. "Our phones are a jungle gym for the executive control network," and thus prevent us from enjoying some quiet time. Think about it, how often do you really need to check emails? Facebook? Twitter? Would it be enough if you did it once an hour? Probably so. How often do you really do it? There is a reason why our best ideas occur without a phone in our hands. While walking, for example. I bet that Charles Darwin, Friedrich Nitche, William Wordworth, and Aristotle were not using their iPhones when they were walking and thinking...

Down time is when you are the most creative. Take times in the day in which you would have no responsibility. I know it's hard. There is always something to do. Don't worry—it will wait for you. Don't try to prevent it with coffee; don't try to fill "dead time" with your phone. Embrace "down time" and you would increase your creativity. For the first 10 minutes after you wake up, don't turn on the TV. Don't reach out for your iPad, iPhone, or any other device to check emails, Facebook, or your schedule. Those can wait 10 minutes. Just let yourself daydream.

ZAP YOUR BRAIN?

Researchers at the University of North Carolina[85] explained that alpha waves represent the time in which the brain is free of executive functions (planning, executing, focusing) and can make connections of old ideas into new ones, the foundation for individual combinational creativity. They believed that stimulating the brain with such alpha waves has two potential benefits to creativity. One, it could disconnect the brain from the environment, allowing it to make idea combinations without focusing on external events. The second is

---

[85] *Novel Brain Stimulation May Boost Creativity, Treat Depression.* Liam Davenport. Medscape, April 28, 2015.
http://www.medscape.com/viewarticle/843829

that it could enhance phase synchronization between the frontal areas of the brain, increasing the probability of idea combinations.

In a 2015 study, 20 participants were subjected to 5 minutes of 10Hz transcranial alternating current stimulation (10Hz-tACS) of the frontal cortex. In the next 25 minutes, the participants' creative performance were tested under the Torrance Test of Creative Thinking (TTCT), and showed a 7.4% improvement in their creativity. Stimulating the brains of a second group with a 40Hz-tACS showed no such improvement. It appeared that the stimulation worked only in the Alpha wave range (8-12 Hz). The stimulation was applied to the brain through external electrodes, using a non-invasive procedure. The primary goal of that study was not creativity-related, but rather to develop novel treatments for psychiatric illnesses, through relaxing the brain with alpha waves. The effect on creativity was only a secondary goal. While finding the interesting impact that Alpha wave stimulation had on creativity, the researchers pointed out that they did not examine whether the effect *persisted* after the intervention was over. The effect might still be temporary until further studies show otherwise.

Another study, this time by the Georgetown University Medical Center[86], claimed that the use of *direct* current (tDCS) could also positively affect creativity, and other brain functions.

Does that mean that we would soon see products that could make us more creative on Walmart shelves? Not so much. At least not in the near future. Dr. Rachel Wurzman, a postdoctoral research fellow at the Laboratory for Cognition and Neural Stimulation at the Perelman School of Medicine at the University of Pennsylvania, is one of 39 researchers who, in an open letter, warned that—

---

[86] *Electrical brain stimulation enhances creativity.* Georgetown University Medical Center. April 14, 2016.
https://www.sciencedaily.com/releases/2016/04/160414095949.htm

"Published results of these studies might lead DIY ["Do it yourself"] tDCS users to believe that they can achieve the same results if they mimic the way stimulation is delivered in research studies. However, there are many reasons why this simply isn't true… It is important for people to understand why outcomes of tDCS can be unpredictable, because we know that in some cases, the benefits that are seen after tDCS in certain mental abilities may come at the expense of others."

"We don't know how the stimulation of one brain region affects the surrounding, unstimulated regions," said a co-author of that open letter and an assistant professor of Neurology and the director of the Laboratory. "Stimulating one region could improve one's ability to perform one task but hurt the ability to perform another." Finally, they warned, different people may experience different results, some of which could potentially be adverse. In other words—don't try this at home! Not yet, anyway. Give science time to bring this technology to the masses. For now, just do what works and doesn't have adverse side effects.

PART 3: FROM CREATIVITY TO RESULTS

13.

MANAGEMENT'S DEGREES OF FREEDOM

The first part of this book covered innovation, creativity, the relationship between them, and why they are important. Innovation is the *output* of your organizations. It is the "bottom line" of why you are reading this book. The second part addressed how different factors at the organizational, team, and individual levels affect creativity. This is the third and final part, but also the practical one, since it provides you with an action plan. What do you have to do to achieve the level of innovation you want in your company? I told you *why* certain things are important to creativity. I told you *what* you need to do. Now I'll tell you *how* to do it. This is where rubber meets the road.

THE 80:20 RULE

In 2009 I helped a company administer the KEYS instrument (more in chapter 14). We sent the survey to all employees, and had a 90% return rate. The employees were definitely engaged, and wanted to take part in improving the innovation level of their company. The way KEYS works is that the surveys are sent directly to the Center for Creative Leadership (CCL). CCL analyzes the responses and sends a summary report. Once we received those reports, we held a conference call with CCL, and they explained the results. Of the 8 climate factors, we were overall "industry average," although in certain areas we were above average and in other areas we were *below* average. We were only two weeks away from the company's all-employee meeting, and had a perfect opportunity to share the results with all the employees.

At the event, the vice president of human resources took the stage and described the process. When it was time to talk about the KEYS results, she said "I'm happy to say that we did *extremely* well!" Once she came off stage I asked her why did she use the words "extremely well?" I mean, we were industry-average, at best, and in certain areas *below* average. "Well," she explained, "I expected us to do so poorly, that being industry-average to me was extremely satisfying."

I know that people don't like to hear bad news, and even more than that—they don't want to *deliver* bad news. However, the problem with calling it "extremely well" was that busy people ignore things that are not broken, and if you tell them that our climate was great, even if they knew that it wasn't, they wouldn't have to work on it. Even worse—they could think that their management was completely detached from reality, untruthful, or that the survey misrepresented reality. None of those were good outcomes, but all of those resulted from stating that we did "extremely well." By the way—using KEYS to assess the organizational climate for creativity says nothing about the employees themselves. Those results didn't mean that we had average *employees*. They meant that we had an average *climate* for creativity.

There are three important things you should do immediately with the results of the introspection-assessment phase that will be discussed in chapter 14. First of all, you have to be *honest* about the findings. Even if everything looks bad. Don't sugar-coat it, because you could lose the urgency to do anything about it.

Second, use the 80:20 rule. Don't try to fix *everything*. You can't improve everything at once. Start by identifying 20% of the areas that, once improved, would have 80% positive impact on employee creativity, and spend 100% of the effort on those. Those areas should be your initial targets.

Third, you must make hard choices. The hardest choices revolve around *personnel*. If you experienced poor team dynamics, you must intervene and change the team structure. You may have to bruise a few egos, and maybe let a few employees go. Just do it. Keeping the wrong people in the wrong place would hurt the company and hurt them more than if you kept them at the same place. I can't begin to tell you how many times I had these conversations in different companies, organizations I advised to, and board rooms. Those conversations always started with complaints about poor performance of a certain individual, but when I asked "why don't we remove this person from that position?" the answer was an excuse such as "but he has been working for us for over 10 years now." No doubt—letting someone go is hard, but you are not doing them a favor by keeping them in a place in which they don't perform well, when they might strive elsewhere.

4 PHASES

In general, you have several degrees of freedom in affecting creativity levels in your organization, which could be categorized into 4 phases: introspection, intervention, ideation, and implementation (There is no I in team, but there are two in creativity in two in innovation, so having a 4-I process only makes sense…)

The *introspection* phase establishes a baseline of where you are now, and allows you to set goals for the future. During the *intervention* phase, you should implement strategies and actions that would increase your employee creativity levels, such that they would be able to produce higher *quantity* of higher *quality* ideas. You would then facilitate *ideation* workshops to put that creativity to work and generate ideas. Finally, in the *implementation* phase, your company would turn creative ideas into successfully launched products, services, processes, and/or business models.

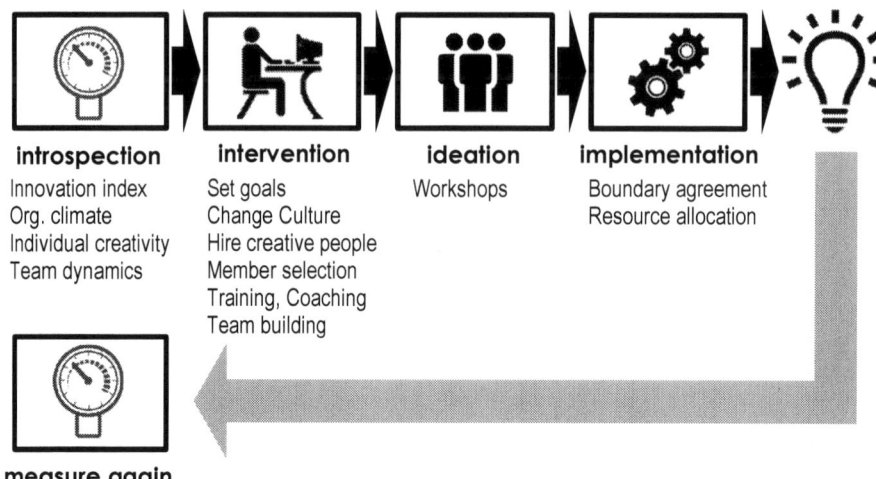

The specific steps of those four phases are:

- ***Introspection***
    - Measuring innovation level.
    - Surveying organizational climate for creativity.
    - Testing individual creativity.
    - Assessing team dynamics.
- ***Intervention***
    - Setting innovation goals.
    - Changing organizational culture, starting with you.
    - Hiring creative people.
    - Selecting the right team members and leader.
    - Training & Coaching.
    - Team building.
- ***Ideation workshops***
- ***Implementation***
    - Replacing the innovation funnel with boundary agreements.
    - Allocating resources to major projects.

And once you are done, there is one more step:

- Measuring again, and making course corrections.

The different phases take time. The introspection phase may take months, if not more. Intervention should be an ongoing effort whose effects take time to show. An ideation workshop could take a month or two to prepare for and to summarize. The first ideation session may result in ideas that cannot, and should not be implemented, and the next one would not take place for a few months. Finally, the implementation phase, beyond replacing the innovation funnel with a boundary agreement, takes time too. As you start adding those times up, you may be discouraged and believe it would take years before you start seeing the fruits of this work. However, there are two degrees of freedom that you have in implementing the process.

The first is *scope*. Implementing the process in a small company is relatively easy. However, this book, and the processes it describes, were developed for Corporate America. Fortune 500 companies have more than 200 employees. Heck, there are startups with more than 200 employees. You don't have to implement it throughout the entire company at one time. This could be an insurmountable effort. Identify the core team that must be creative (see chapter 15). This could be a small team of 5-8 people. You could work with 2 or 3 such teams, but not more. This would make it a much more manageable process. Start small. See that it works. Make course corrections, and instead of forcing it on other business units or groups in the company—advertise, socialize, and market this process to others. Let them come to you.

The second degree of freedom you have is the ability to implement the different four phases of this process in *parallel*, rather than in a sequential manner. Sure, only after you completed the assessment of the organizational culture, team dynamics, individual creativity, and the innovation index, will you know exactly what changes should be made during the implementation phase. And only after you are done implementing those changes, including personnel changes, and after months (if not years) of training and team building, and after months (if not years) until employees realize that the culture has changed, and feel free to experiment and innovate, will you have the level of creativity you wanted to achieve in the company. And only then, will you begin facilitating ideation workshops, and only after the third or fourth workshop will you have ideas that are worth implementing (although, your employees, and not you, should make that determination, as chapter 17 will show). Don't forget that once you started implementation, it could still take months (or years) until you launch the new innovative, game-changing, market-dominating, profit-making product, service, process, or business model. Overall, it could take *years* from the beginning of introspection to the launch of a new product, if you do it completely sequentially. But that's not what I recommend.

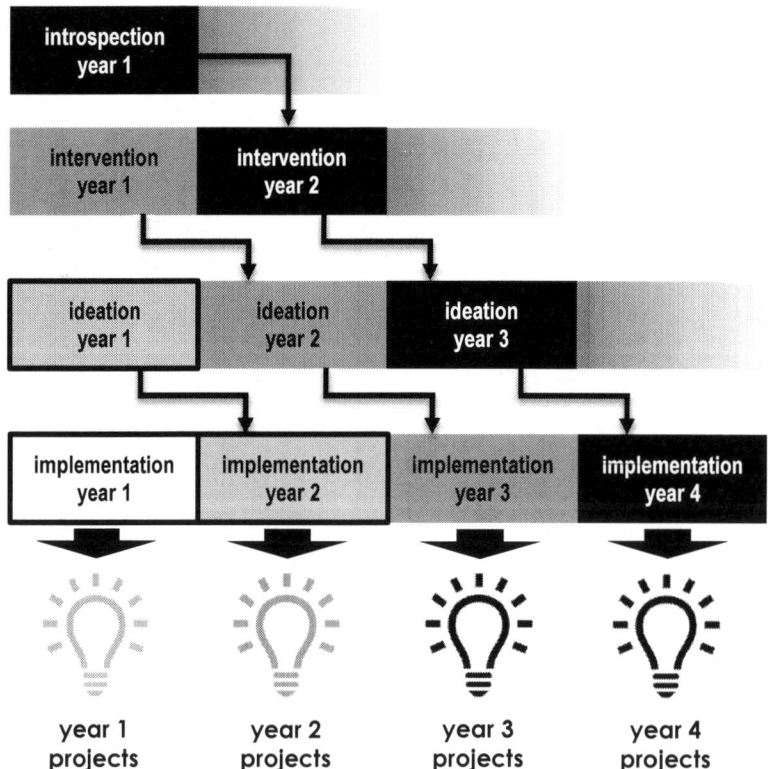

You should launch all four phases at once. Even though the introspection phase would not be done yet, start the intervention with what you already know needs to change. If you read chapters 9, 10, and 11, you would know enough about what would make an impact on employee creativity. Start the intervention phase with a few of those elements. As time goes by, and as you start seeing the results of the assessments, you could start adding elements to the intervention phase, or modify what you have already started. If you find that some of the initiatives you started were needed—keep pursuing those. If you find that others are not needed, are not as effective, or are not within the 20% activities with 80% impact—drop them. Start training and coaching your teams. They would need that either way. Meanwhile, start facilitating ideation workshops. Your employees would not have all the tools in their hands yet, and may not be as creative as they would be later, but good ideas may still result from those workshops. Finally, if those ideas feel good (to the employees, not to you. See chapter 17)—start implementing them.

Year 1 projects may not be the most innovative, and may not result from well implemented creativity and innovation processes, but that doesn't mean that they are completely useless. Year 2 projects would benefit from including what you have learned from the introspection phase in Year 1. Year 3 projects would benefit from your employees having more creativity tools in their hands, and better climate that would be more supportive of their creativity, and so on. Every year your projects would be more creative, innovative, and powerful.

After you are done with the introspection phase in year 1, don't stop assessing. You may not need as in-depth assessments as you did in year 1, but you must continuously evaluate the organizational climate, team dynamics, and the creativity of new hires. People change, and so does the organization. You should make sure that your intervention efforts are working. Keep measuring your innovation index every year, so you could see the "bottom-line" impact of your efforts. Intervention efforts should run continuously. You must adopt a new culture, and refine it as you get new assessment results. You would also continue to hold ideation workshops on a regular basis.

The more of those you hold—the more proficient you become, and the better the resulting ideas are.

IMPLEMENTATION STRATEGY

The process of developing an innovation strategy is similar to the development of any strategy. My favorite analogy is your GPS navigation system. First, it needs to know where you are. It does that through searching for (acquiring) satellites. Once satellites were acquired, it calculates exactly where it is. This process used to take hours, then minutes, and now it takes seconds. The equivalent is the innovation level measurement, along with organizational climate, team dynamics, and individual assessments. Now you know where you start. You know what areas need to be worked on. The second step is for you to choose the destination. The navigation system would not start guiding you until it knows exactly where you want to go. You cannot be vague about this. Based on the innovation metrics, you must set the goal you want to reach in your company. Based on the assessments you should decide what are the areas you must focus on (use the 80:20 rule) and what you want to achieve.

With a navigation system you typically determine the route preferences (shortest route, fastest route, scenic route, toll-free route, etc.), but you don't do that every time you start driving. The parallel is your determination of the acceptable terms and conditions to go from where you are today to where you want to be by the end of the year. What's acceptable? What's not? This is done through the boundary agreement. The fourth step is the actual determination of how to get *there* from *here*. What are the actions you are willing and committing to take to achieve your goals? Then you must execute. Put the car in gear and drive to your destination.

14.

INTROSPECTION: WHO, ME?

And so we begin with the first step of increasing innovation level in your company—*introspection*. The dictionary definition for the word is:

> **introspection**
> [in-tr*uh*-**spek**-sh*uh* n]
> noun
> 1. observation or examination of one's own mental and emotional state, mental processes, etc.; the act of looking within oneself.

But what is it that you need to observe? It's really simple. There are three things to measure. Like any system, your company has three parts: *input*, *transformation*, and *output*. This is illustrated in the following image.

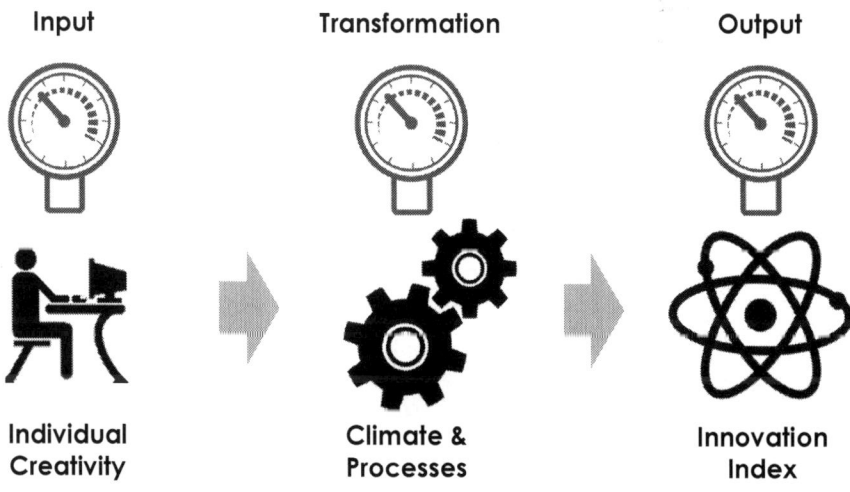

The *inputs*, the raw materials that your company uses are the people who work there. That part of the assessment is the measurement of your employees' creativity. How creative are your current employees? How creative are those you want to hire?

The *output* is the level of innovation achieved by the company. Although it sounds simple, it is rather a complex matter, and I had to develop a new innovation index to help with that. It is presented next in this chapter. Your company's level of innovation is the reason you are reading this book, and if you got this far, it is obviously important to you.

The *transformation* is what comes in between. It is what you do in your company to transform the raw inputs (your people, existing and new-hires) to increase the output innovation level. It includes the climate you create and the processes you put in place.

Theoretically, there could be an interim fourth measurement point: the quality and quantity of *ideas*. However, since having great ideas is meaningless if they are not implemented, I chose not to spend time in assessing quality and quantity of ideas, and focus on the absolute, meaningful output—the innovation index. If, somehow, you implemented a climate supportive of creativity and still can't get any good quality innovation output, it might be worthwhile to measure the quantity and quality of ideas to determine whether you have an *implementation* problem.

The three measurement areas are discussed throughout this chapter, but not necessarily in a specific order.

MEASURING INNOVATION

WORST DIET EVER

I leased my last car. When you lease a car, you must select your annual mileage "allowance" for the lease. That allowance plays a role in determining the residual value of the car when you return it at the end of the lease, and as a result—your monthly payments. If you elect a high mileage allowance, you pay more. If you elect a low allowance, you pay less. However, when it's time to return the car, if you exceeded the allowance you've elected, you would have to pay a penalty for every extra mile driven. So you should estimate the mileage you expect to drive in the next three years or so as accurately as possible.

When I leased my 2010 BMW 5-series, I estimated I would drive 12,000 miles a year. It was a conservative estimate, considering my office was less than 4 miles from home. However, when it was time to return the car after three years, I realized that I drove less than 10,000 miles a year on average. I didn't have to pay a penalty, but I obviously overpaid throughout the lease period. It was probably not too much, but still. So when I leased my 2013 BMW X3, I was smarter. I elected a 10,000 mile a year allowance. And that's when things went wrong.

Not three months after I got the car I found myself in the middle of an election campaign for the Plano School District board. I was driving all over town, accumulating more miles than I had ever driven before. After the elections, I felt that I had too many miles on the odometer, but didn't know exactly how many more. Not that the math was so difficult, but I didn't see a reason to calculate it. In early April 2014, I realized that I had more than 18,000 miles on the odometer, when I was supposed to have no more than 15,000. There was no doubt that I was going to return this car with more miles than the allowance I elected. I checked the lease agreement and found that I would have to pay 20 cents for each mile over the allowance. If I had

3,000 miles over my allowance halfway through the lease, I was going to have 6,000 miles over the allowance by the end of it. Not that paying $1,200 was the end of the world, but I didn't want to pay it.

So I've put myself on a "diet." I calculated the number of miles per week I could drive such that by the end of the lease I would have no more than 30,000 miles (I had less than 12,000 miles left to "spend" over the remaining 18 months). I then calculated and found that I was "allowed" no more than 145 miles per week to meet that goal. I started resetting the trip odometer every Monday morning and counted how many miles I drove that week. Every morning I compared my wife's planned trips with mine, and whoever had the shortest trips would drive the X3 that day. I drove 131 miles the first week of this "diet" (14 miles under "budget"). This increased my weekly allowance (to stay under 30,000 miles by the end of the lease) by just a bit. However, during the following weeks I drove 61, 67, 78, and 98 miles. Each week therefore added to my weekly allowance. By the end of the fifth week, my remaining weekly allowance was already up to 152.6 miles. By August, my weekly allowance was over 167 miles, and if I maintained the average weekly mileage—I would have returned the car with less than 25,000 miles. Well below my goal.

What does that have to do with measuring innovation, you ask? Good question! I couldn't have been on a path to meet the 30,000 mile limit if I hadn't started *measuring* my mileage on a weekly (and daily) basis. You can't be successful if you don't know when you are successful, and when you are not.

And, in case you were wondering, I won the election...

HOW DO WE MEASURE INNOVATION TODAY?

Peter Drucker wrote that "the business enterprise has two–and only two–basic functions: marketing and innovation." The executive surveys done by the major consulting firms and quoted in chapter 2 showed that the majority of senior executives perceived innovation as one of their top three priorities, if not the single top one. The 2010 McKinsey survey of 2,240 executives showed that more than 70% of corporate leaders tout innovation as a top three business priority. However, that survey also revealed that only 22% set *innovation performance metrics*.

Companies may put innovation at the top of their priorities, but without proper innovation metrics, they could not improve it. At the same time, they use a plethora of metrics for measuring everything else in the company, from profitability, inventory turnover, to return on capital and more. Nothing for measuring innovation.

The following discussion is limited mostly to *product* innovation. If your company is in the business of innovative services, processes, or business models, the following discussion may not be applicable to you, but could still help.

EXISTING PRODUCT INNOVATION METRICS

There are different product innovation metrics described (and used) today. Some are highly academic and theoretical, while others are more practical and used by companies on a regular basis. Some are very complex, while others too simplistic. Different metrics measure different aspects of product innovation, such as the *novelty* of the product itself, the *creativity* level of employees, and the effectiveness of the idea-generating *process*. In general, innovation metrics could be categorized into two groups: *input* metrics and *output* metrics. Input metrics are more *predictive* in nature, as they measure the idea generation process effectiveness and the creativity of the people who participate in it, along with the organizational culture that increases (or reduces) employee creativity. However, those do not measure actual levels of company innovation, which is an *output* metric, *descriptive* in nature. I found that the different metrics were not applied consistently by companies, and were used mainly as a public-relations tool, rather than to improve innovation in the company.

One common input metric is the amount of investment in research and development (R&D) in the company. Companies strive to have between 8% and 15% of their sales revenue invested in R&D. Engineers would always try to increase that percentage, and CFOs would try to lower it. This percentage varies by industry and by company. The effectiveness and yield of R&D dollars vary as well. This chapter later shows that sometimes higher level of resources may result in lower creativity and thus less innovation. Apple's financials show an interesting, counter-intuitive relationship between R&D expenses and profitability. Apple experienced 68.3% annual revenue growth and 373% annual profit growth in 2005 with R&D spending increase of only 9.2% in the previous year, leading to that enviable profit growth. However, in 2015, it experienced only 7% revenue growth and 7.2% profit growth, while its R&D budget grew over 30% annually in each of the last 4 years[87][88]. As my friend and mentor Dave Schaefer told me once when we saw a new pilot crashing a $30,000+ turbine-powered radio-controlled jet airplane: "having money doesn't make you a better pilot…"

Another common innovation metric is the *number of patents* filed (and issued) by the company. However, the *quality* of patents can vary dramatically, and while some patents may protect ground-breaking, "crown-jewels" innovation, others may only protect relatively minor, easy to circumvent ideas. Many companies incentivize employees to file patents. I received a $1,000 bonus whenever one of my disclosures was filed as a patent by Texas Instruments. I knew engineers who self-

---

[87] https://www.bcgperspectives.com/content/interactive/innovation_growth_most_innovative_companies_interactive_guide/
[88] It should be noted, though, that even after such growth in R&D expenditures, Apple spends only 3.4% of its revenue on R&D.

imposed "quotas" of patents to be filed every year to generate an additional income stream for themselves. This is an example of how *not* to use an extrinsic motivator. What you would get is a high *volume* of patents, but not necessarily of high *value*. If the company measures the number of patents as an indication of creativity—that metric would not be representative, although easy to manipulate with bonuses.

Yet another metric is the *number of ideas* generated at the company (again, unqualified by how novel, useful, or feasible they are). Another one is the mere number of *new products*, leaving the word "new" open for interpretation. Other metrics focus on financial results, such as the percentage of sales that are reinvested in research and development, or the *Balanced Scorecard Institute's* RoPDE (Return on Product Development Expense) metric.

Perhaps the most famous metric is 3M's NPVI (New Product Viability Index), which measures the percentage of sales generated by products that did not exist 5 years ago[89]. This metric is problematic for several reasons. First of all, it does not define what "new product" means. Was the iPhone 6S "new" in 2015 (the year in which it was introduced)? It certainly didn't exist in 2010, 5 years earlier. However, the iPhone 4 existed in 2010. How innovative was the iPhone 6S compared to the iPhone 4? Or even compared to the first iPhone, introduced in 2007? Should you look at the iPhone 6S in a binary way as an innovative product, and therefore "count" the revenue from it towards the 3M New Product Viability Index as a new product that didn't exist 5 years ago? Or as a product that was only *incrementally* improved over an 8-year period instead?

---

[89] See starting page 13 of 3M's 2015 Sustainability report. In 2015 it was 32.8%. http://multimedia.3m.com/mws/media/1064170O/3m-2015-sustainability-report.pdf

Before proposing my growth innovation index, I'll answer a critical question: What should a good innovation index measure, then?

CRITERIA FOR A GOOD INNOVATION INDEX

COMPARATIVE

A good innovation metric should let you compare your company's current innovation performance with prior years' performance, and with your competitors' performance. The ability to compare to prior years' performance would help continuous company innovation improvement. It gives you the ability to know if your improvement efforts are working or not. The ability to compare against competitors performance increases your company's competitiveness, market share, revenue, and profitability relative to its competitors.

ALLOWS SETTING TARGETS

A numeric-quantitative metric allows you to set goals. If, for example, the metric you use showed a performance of 0.17 last year, then company management could set a target of 0.24 for the following year. A subjective-qualitative metric might not help management set targets for the following years. Without the ability to set targets, you cannot measure improvement.

ACTIONABLE

A metric that details a relatively *simple* relationship between measurable and quantifiable input and output parameters allows the company to act on them. Setting the target to 0.24 for next year is not enough if there it isn't clear how the different factors affect that index. Knowing that the 0.24 is the product of two factors, one factor ranking

0.8 (out of 1.0) and the other 0.3, might indicate that there is a better opportunity for improvement of the second factor.

FEASIBLE AND PRACTICAL TO MEASURE

Some parameters are impractical or hard to measure. All parameters in a good innovation index should be readily available, already measured, or easy to measure. They should not require significant research or effort to retrieve and calculate. In order to be able to compare company innovation performance to competitors' innovation performance, those factors should also be publicly available (even if through paid sources such as D&B, although having to pay for them makes them just a bit less desirable).

TIMELY

Some of the existing metrics are *lagging* indicators. For example, measuring the financial performance of innovation, or the RoPDE™ (Return on Product Development Expense) would only show performance improvements once products passed the *growth* stage of their life cycle. The same applies to "X% of revenue from products that didn't exist Y years ago," since those products may have already been in development Y years ago, yet were not counted because they haven't started generating significant revenue yet. On the other hand, measuring the investment in Research and Development is a *leading* indicator. It may indicate how innovative the company would be in the *future*, when the current R&D effort shows results. However, remember the relationship between Apple's R&D expenditures growth and profitability growth described before. R&D expenditures as a percentage of sales are not a strong indication of the effectiveness of R&D efforts. The innovation index should show *current* innovation levels, combined with how it could support *future* growth.

COMPREHENSIVE

A good innovation index should measure the innovativeness of products along all innovation dimensions: *novelty, usefulness,* and *feasibility*. Stating that the product did not exist 5 years ago, and thus the revenue from it should be counted towards the innovation index is not enough. The iPhone 6S did not exist 5 years ago, but how different was it from the iPhone 6? 5S? 5? 4S? 4? Furthermore, is 5 years the right timeframe? Should it be 10? Or maybe only one year? The comprehensiveness of the innovation index should be balanced against the complexity of obtaining input data and calculating it.

BALANCE PAST AND FUTURE INNOVATION

"X% of revenue from products that didn't exist Y years ago" only considers revenue-generating products, and fails to show how the company positioned itself towards the future with current ongoing projects. On the other hand, R&D expense as a percentage of sales indicates only future innovation positioning, but the innovativeness of existing products. A good innovation index should include and balance the two. A company that has very innovative products currently generating revenue is not as well positioned into the future as a company that has a strong innovative product pipeline. At the same time, a company with a strong innovative product pipeline should not be considered as innovative as one that already generates impressive financial performance from innovative products.

THE GROWTH INNOVATION INDEX (GII)

As you can tell by now, I believe that the ability to measure innovation is important if you want to increase it. You can also tell that I'm not satisfied with existing metrics. Based on the above criteria, I developed the Growth Innovation Index (GII) that, while mainly aimed at *product* innovation, could be adapted to be used for service innovation. The fundamentals of this index are presented in the following pages.

THE QUESTION

The right question makes up 90% of the answer. Therefore, defining the product innovation index must start by determining the question it should answer. Typical questions addressed by existing metrics include: "Are our *current* products innovative?" and "Are we investing enough to be innovative in the *future*?"

Innovation is important to you. But why? Because you want to *grow*, and *innovative growth* is the most profitable type of growth. Therefore, the question should be:

How innovative is our growth?

Innovation that doesn't lead to growth should not be counted, since companies and their shareholders would not be interested in innovation for innovation's sake. Growth that is not the result of innovation (such as due to entering new markets with existing products) should *not* be counted (here), as it does not command the superior financial performance associated with growth resulting from true innovative products that have profound impact on their markets, and deliver very strong market shares, revenue, and profits.

The following considerations are the basis of the proposed Growth Innovation Index.

WHERE IS THE PRODUCT IN ITS LIFE CYCLE?

The question "what percentage of our revenue comes from products that did not exist 5 years ago?" is misleading. Some products have longer life cycles, while others have very short ones. The life cycle of a cellular phone is one year, before it is replaced by a newer model. No phone that sells today would have existed 5 years ago, and thus it would be a mistake to consider every phone innovative (as much as the phone manufacturers would like you to think so). At the same time, vacuum cleaners have life cycles in excess of 10 years (the term "life cycle" doesn't refer to the time a consumer uses the product, but rather to the time from product market launch to its end of life, when it's taken off the market). The real question, then, is "where is the product in its expected life cycle?"

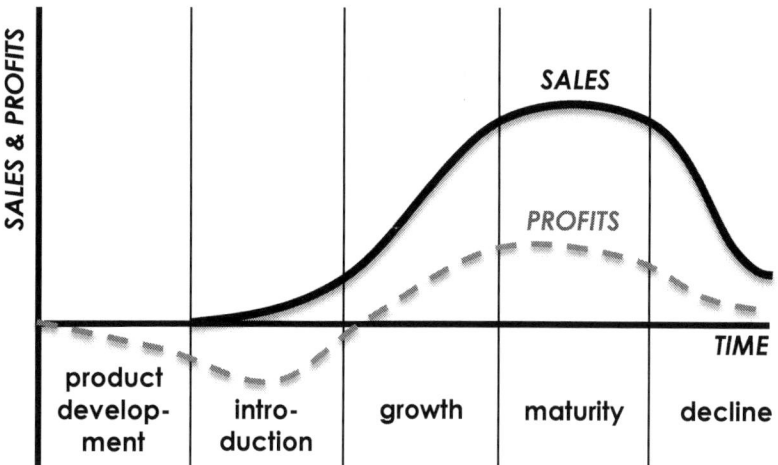

If the product is at the *late maturity* stage of its life cycle or beyond, then competition is fierce, differentiation is low, and profits are razor-thin. On the other hand, products at the *growth* or early maturity stage generate the highest profits. A product with a 5-year life cycle that was introduced 4 years ago would provide very low profitability in its last year of service, while a product with a 20-year life cycle would be driving very profitable growth 4 years after its introduction. At the same time, a product in its first year since introduction (or still in development) may have great profitability *ahead*, but no significant profitability to report in that first year, so future profitability should be discounted to its net present value.

PRODUCT DIFFERENTIATION

If *patentability* is one measure of innovation, then you should determine the innovativeness of the product based on its *novelty*, *feasibility*, and *usefulness*. Those are the same three tests applied before a patent office would issue you a patent for your invention. For the purpose of the proposed index, I considered 3 factors in determining the innovativeness of a product, one input and two outputs:

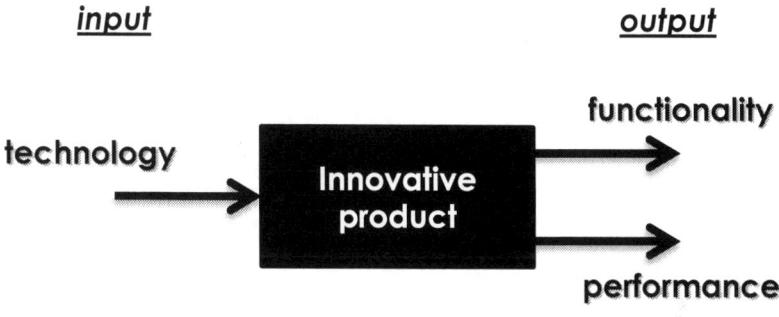

> **Technology** (input): the technological difference between this product and other products that currently exist in the market (whether made by your company or not). This should be viewed through your company's eyes;
>
> **Functionality** (output 1): the difference in functionality between this product and other products in the market, valued by customers;
>
> **Performance** (output 2): the difference in performance between this product and other products in the market, valued by customers;

These parameters are unique to every company and industry, and can be somewhat subjective. Therefore, it is important that you either develop a *rubric* to determine the level of differentiation in each of those three factors, or otherwise assure consistency (year over year) in making those determinations. The three are related, but should still be determined individually. For example, consider the introduction of the iPhone 6S again (I swear, I have nothing against the iPhone 6S. I use one). How different was it from other relatively similar products? Technologically, you can probably rank it as being 20% (0.2) different from other products. Functionality-wise, given some new functions the phone has, the size of the screen, you may determine it to be 0.3. Finally, the performance improvement (processor speed? Storage capacity?) compared to other products might be determined as 0.28. Giving an equal weight to all three differentiation factors, the average differentiation would be 0.26. Although the rankings could be linear as described in this example (any number between 0% and 100%), I recommend using 3, 4, or 5 point scales[90] with appropriate, self-developed, yet consistently used rubrics. A linear scale might be too subjective and thus unreliable.

Here is a hypothetical example. Your company makes a new vacuum cleaner. The rubrics that your company had put in place are:

Factor	1 (0%)	2 (50%)	3 (100%)
Technology (33%)			
Battery	Same or worse	10% more capacity	20%+ more capacity
Motor	Same or worse	25% more power	50%+ more power
Functionality (33%)			
Different Heads	Same or worse	More heads	More head functions
Modularity	Same or worse	1-4 parts	5+ parts
Performance (33%)			
Operating Time	Same or worse	10% longer	20%+ longer
Vacuum pressure	Same or worse	5% more	10% more

You can use scales with more than 3 points, and you can give negative numbers (if the technology, functionality, or performance are

---

[90] A 3-point scale means that each factor would have the values 0, 50%, or 100%. A 4-point scale would have the values 0, 33%, 67%, or 100%. A 5-point scale would have the values 0, 25%, 50%, 75%, or 100%.

worse than comparable, existing products.) A negative numbers could be due to a compromise you had to make to add another important feature. The sound quality of a mobile phone, for example, is worse than that of a landline phone, but it is a compromise users were willing to make to gain the added dimension of value—mobility.

The new vacuum cleaner you are about to release has the following specifications, compared to existing products (whether from your company or not):

- 20% longer battery life [100%]
- Same motor [0%]
- More head functions (cleaning toilets, for example) [100%]
- It has 3 modular parts [50%]
- Operating time is 20% longer (battery driven) [100%]
- Generates 5% more vacuum [50%]

The average innovativeness of the product is therefore 67%.

INPUT

To comply with the *measurability* requirement, the input variables of the new innovation index must be easy to obtain. Since this is a *product* innovation index, you must collect data for each product in your company, whether generating revenue or still in development. The data should include actual data, but also business plan projections:

- Expected lifecycle of the product (in years);
- Years since (or until) market introduction (a positive number if the product was already introduced, and a negative number if market introduction is in the future);
- Expected lifetime revenue from the product;
- Cumulative revenue generated by the product since market launch;
- Revenue from the product last year alone; and–
- Product differentiation (as described above).

BUSINESS PLAN ACCURACY

The innovation index should indicate innovativeness of current revenue-generating products, but also products in development that would only start generating revenue in the future. While the actual past performance of the product is known and thus accurate (one would hope...), future performance depends on the company's *forecasting accuracy*. As a result, forecasting accuracy should be tracked and used as a factor in calculating the innovation index, especially with respect to products in development that have not yet generated revenue.

GROWTH INNOVATION INDEX

I went back and forth many times before disclosing the equation and process I developed to calculate the growth innovation index, *GII*. I eventually decided against it. Not because I wanted to keep it confidential. On the contrary! I would like to keep it as public and available as possible. The reason was that I'm still making changes to it. Since I introduced it for the first time, it went through at least 3 different significant iterations. I presented it several times, and used it to help companies calculate their innovation index. Every time, I had to tweak it a little so it achieved what it was designed to do. Finally, after much deliberation, I decided to keep it *out* of this book. However, you would have access to understand, calculate, and otherwise use this index when it is available on my website: http://www.largescalecreativity.com/growth-innovation-index-gii/,
and it will likely be updated over time, as more companies use it. For now, I can only tell you that GII would give you an index such as "32% of our future revenue growth would be coming from innovative products."

MEASURING CREATIVITY

The product growth innovation index measured the *output* of your company's innovation process. It's now time to learn how to measure the *input*: the creativity of your employees, current and future.

CREATIVITY METRICS

There are different metrics and assessments available today for measuring creativity. They vary by the different fields. Creativity is a broad term that deals with creating books, poetry, music, pictures, and many more areas. However, the focus of this book is on creativity that leads to the introduction of new, useful, and feasible products, services, processes, and business models. The best measure of creativity that I found in that context is the *Torrence Test of Creative Thinking* (TTCT)[91], which uses several tests of divergent thinking and measures four scales. TTCT was developed in the 1950s, and is still in use today. One example illustrating the dimensions of TTCT, at a most simplistic way, is to ask participants to list all the uses for a paperclip (or a pen, or anything else put in front of them) they could think of in a set amount of time (5 minutes, typically). The four TTCT scales (with the acronym FFOE) are:

> **Fluency** - the number of ideas you have. When you were asked to provide ideas, how many ideas did you generate? In the activity, the more uses you have for the paper-clip, the higher you rank on the fluency scale.
>
> **Flexibility** How different are the ideas from one another? If most ideas are relatively similar to one another, they would rank low on the flexibility scale.
>
> **Originality** - How different are those ideas from the original use of the paper clip or pen? "Writing with it" would rank very low on originality. Breaking it apart into its different elements and suggesting uses for these

---

[91] Runco, M. A (1993). Cognitive and psychometric issues in creativity research. In S. G. Isaksen, M. C. Murdock, R. L. Firestien, & D. J. Treffinger (Eds.), *Understanding and recognizing creativity: The emergence of a discipline* (pp. 331-368). Norwood, NJ: Ablex.

> parts that are far from what the pen was designed for would rank high on the originality scale.
>
> *Elaboration* - the amount of detail that you provide with your descriptions. A very brief description that lacks detail and fails to explain how you could turn the product in your hand into the product (or use) you are proposing would rank low. However, providing a great amount of detail and imagination would rank high on the elaboration scale.

Administering TTCT is a pretty involved process that requires experts. But like everything in life, there's an app for that…

I met Farzad Eskafi and Dr. Kenes Beketayev, the founders of Berkeley-based *SparcIt*, at the *Crab House* in San Francisco's *Fisherman's Wharf* for the first time. They had both just "exited" their previous logistics application startup, *PINC Solutions*, and wanted to move on to create a new "sound research based" startup. The area they chose was online assessments, and specifically creativity assessment.

Eskafi told me that the idea came to him when he watched his nephew playing with Legos, ignoring the user manual, and using his natural creative instincts. They immediately started reading every piece of research on creativity, and that's when they met with Mark Runco, a researcher and an authority in the area of creativity research. Their request for an NSF (National Science Foundation) grant was initially denied, because the NSF evaluator assigned to them didn't believe that what they wanted to achieve was possible. "We convinced him over the phone that we could do it," said Eskafi, "and eventually we got the grant." That first grant was for $150,000.

"It took us less time to develop the engine than it did to test and validate it," joked Eskafi, after telling me that they spent 6 months writing code, and 12 months testing it. The online creativity assessment tool was officially launched by SparcIt in February 2015. Runco, who serves on their advisory board, referred to SparcIt as a "giant leap in creative thinking assessment." To test the efficiency of the tool, he competed with them over the assessment of 300 participants. He graded the creativity of all the participants in 3 days. SparcIt completed it in 10 seconds.

SparcIt measures the 4 elements of creativity determined by the Torrance Tests of Creative Thinking (TTCT): Fluency, Originality, Flexibility, and Elaboration.

SparcIt partnered with the State University of New York (SUNY) at Buffalo, which is offering a free online course (MOOC) to increase the level of individual creativity. SparcIt conducts the pre-, mid-, and post-testing for SUNY, and 7,000 students have already taken that combination of assessment and online class, resulting in improved creativity. Since the online assessment tool was launched in February 2015, over 35,000 people took it. The cost of taking the test is $35 per person, and it takes 20 minutes to complete online.

RISK

When I started my doctoral research, I linked innovation to creativity. I assumed (and found this to be true) that the source of greater innovation in startups (compared to mature, established companies) is a greater flow of creative ideas from *people* in the organization. I had two possible hypotheses to consider:

More creative people are in startup companies

- Or -

People are more creative in startup companies

Those two sentences use the same words, but with a slightly different order—have completely different meaning. The truth could be any one of them, both, or none of them. My research concentrated on the latter, and therefore compared the creativity levels experienced by people who worked in both types of companies. I hypothesized that there was no difference in tendencies of creative (or less creative) people to prefer to work in one kind of company over the other. Even if there was—since all my participants worked in *both* types of companies—that factor was isolated.

However, long after I finished my research, proving the latter to be correct (a person would be more creative in a startup than in a mature, large company), I decided to challenge the former. Could it be that more creative people prefer to work in startups, and less creative people prefer to work in large companies? While I didn't want to believe that (after all, I did choose to work for Texas Instruments at some point)—I found it to be the case. But why?

The link between being creative and preferring to work in a startup was not direct. A correlation between two phenomena (call them *A* and *B*) could be due to four possible reasons. One: *A caused B* (being creative caused employees to choose to work in startups.) Two: *B caused A* (working for startups made them creative.) Three: there was yet a third factor, *C*, that affected both *A* and *B* similarly. Finally, four: the correlation was completely accidental.

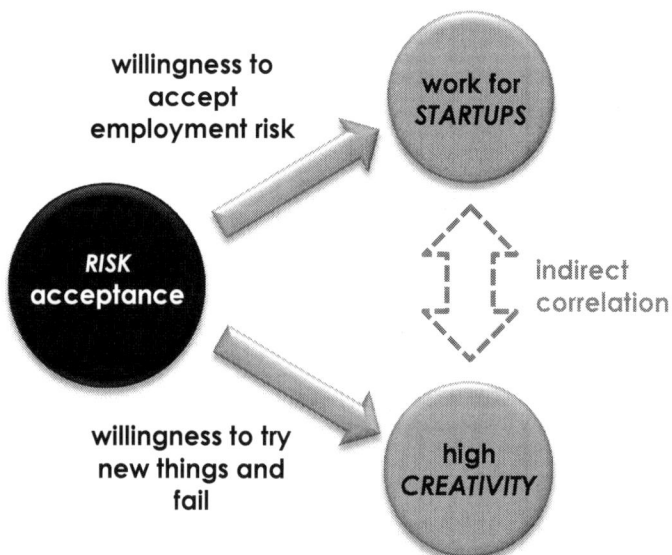

There is some truth to the first two. Creative people prefer the startup environment that allows them to continue being creative. The startup culture supports creativity, as my research proved, and creative people know that. Given that the startup environment supports creativity, then people who work there have an opportunity to develop their creativity, and thus working in a startup positively affects their creativity.

However, I also found the third to be true. There was a *third* factor, *C*, that affected *both* the attraction to work for startups *and* individual creativity. That third factor was the willingness to assume *risk*. A significant part of creativity is the tendency and curiosity that pushes people to *experiment* and accept failure as part of the learning process. When you fail, you learn from it, and you make sure you don't repeat your mistakes. When you fail, you may encounter a phenomenon that could spark a new idea. I considered Newton's apple such a mistake. He obviously sat to rest under the wrong tree, and learned something from that mistake. Creative people are willing to accept the wrath of their bosses when they fail. They are willing to take risks and try things. That willingness makes them creative.

At the same time, a startup company is not the safest place to work in. Startup failure rates are much higher than those of Fortune 500 companies. Fortune 500 companies fail too, and don't offer job security anymore, but they are definitely safer than early stage startups. Risk-takers would be more willing to work in a startup, since they focus on the potential *upside* from success (the "exit strategy") more than the downside from failure.

It's not that creative people work in startup companies *because* they are creative, or that working in a startup companies is the only factor that makes them creative. It is their willingness to assume risk that makes them more creative, *and* gives them the preference for working in startups. C (the willingness to assume risk) affects both A (creativity) and B (tendency to prefer to work in startups).

What does this mean for mature companies? This book, for the most part, shows how to increase the creativity of employees already working in the company. Nevertheless, you could get a head-start through hiring creative people. Through modifications to your corporate culture, team dynamics, and individual actions you could later increase their creativity, but why not *start* with a higher level of employee creativity?

This section suggested something simple: you could hire more creative employees if you hire employees with a history of working in startups. The longer that history, the more creative those employees are likely to be. The earlier the stage they joined startups, the higher the risk they were willing to take, and the more creative they are.

I recommend testing your employees' willingness to take risk. I reviewed a few tools that assess risk attitudes, but haven't settled on a specific, proven risk-willingness assessment tool. I can only presume that by the time the second edition of this book comes out I would have a tool recommendation for you. One such tool is the *Risk Attitudes Profiler*™[92]. It is a $4 online tool. I couldn't tell you how accurate or reliable it is. I can only suggest you check it yourself. Either way, I recommend that you include a test to assess risk willingness of your employees, current and future.

INTROVERTS, EXTROVERTS, AND MYERS BRIGGS

Through the discussion of the need for both introverts and extroverts to increase diversity in chapter 10, I quoted a study that correlated the *Myers Briggs Type Indicator* (MBTI) preferences test with creativity. That study found that creative people were significantly more intuitive, perceiving, and moderately more

---

[92] Humanmetrics, *Risk Attitudes Profiler*™, http://www.humanmetrics.com/rot/RiskGuide.htm

extroverted than less creative people. So, could you use MBTI as a hiring screening tool? The Myers & Briggs Foundation developed ethical guidelines for the use of the MBTI test. The guidelines focus on the fact that *people are different*, and that those preference differences should not be used as a screening or hiring criteria. Specifically:

> "It is unethical and in many cases illegal to require job applicants to take the Indicator if the results will be used to screen out applicants. The administrator should not counsel a person to, or away from, a particular career, personal relationship or activity based solely upon type information.[93]"

I could fiercely argue that there is nothing unethical in requiring job applicants to take any appropriate test, and to *screen* as well as *steer* them towards (or away from) a specific position. I could argue that we have become overly politically correct and hence the requirement above. However, I cannot argue that those *are* the requirements made by the creators and owners of the MBTI test, and we must respect their wishes and use their tool as they deemed appropriate. Or not use it at all.

MEASURING CLIMATE

At times I had to remind myself that this is a practical book and not another dissertation... I was about to review the history of all the tools ever developed to measure the climate for creativity in organizations. I was going to compare them, and tell you how they were developed, and how their reliability, validity, and credibility were measured and established. But this is a *practical* book, so I'll skip all of that. Besides, you can find such a review in my dissertation, *From Startup to Maturity: A Case Study of Employee Creativity Antecedents in High-Tech Companies*. But in this book I will only share that the

---

[93] https://www.capt.org/mbti-assessment/ethical-use.htm?bhcp=1

best and most relevant tool in my opinion is KEYS®[94], which is owned and administered through the Center for Creative Leadership[95] (CCL). I qualified and am certified to administer it.

KEYS is an online tool. I told you about it and a little the research behind it in chapter 3. It has 78 items, which offer some redundancy to assure that survey-takers understood the questions well. In my experience it takes 20 minutes to complete. Every item is presented as a statement, with which participants must agree or disagree at different levels (there are 5 levels). For example: "I have the freedom to decide how I am going to carry out my projects." Do you agree? The 78 items fall within 4 general categories, and 10 sub-categories. Those are:

- ***Management Practices***
   - Freedom
   - Challenging Work
   - Managerial Encouragement
   - Work Group Supports
- ***Organizational Motivation***
   - Organizational Encouragement
   - Lack of Organizational Impediments
- ***Resources***
   - Sufficient Resources
   - Realistic Workload Pressures
- ***Outcomes***
   - Creativity
   - Productivity

Three of the four general categories are *climate* categories (Management Practices, Organizational Motivation, and Resources), and one is an *outcome* category, including creativity and productivity.

---

[94] http://www.ccl.org/leadership/assessments/KEYSOverview.aspx?pageId=65
[95] www.ccl.org

The 2016 published price to administer KEYS included a base price of $2,000 for up to 100 participants. Beyond 100 participants, every additional participant costs $15, and beyond 500 participants, every one costs $12. The process is simple: once you engaged CCL directly or through a certified facilitator, the project starts. There is little customization included in the *demographics* section, to make it relevant to your specific organization. For example, you may want to separate management from line employees to see differences in the organizational climate perceptions by the two groups. You may want to separate certain business groups so you could compare them, or identify specific issues within specific groups, which would otherwise be blended together and masked. Imagine that you had a problem with business unit A. They believe they don't have enough access to resources. At the same time, business unit B, closer to headquarters and top management, has an abundance of resources. Summary results might show the average, but would hide the differences. Even worse—the low creativity and productivity levels in one group could be masked by other creative and productive groups that would average those up. Finally, remember that management does not have the same perspective as employees do, and your ability to obtain separate reports may be important to identify localized problem areas.

Beyond internal comparison within your company, CCL holds a database to compare your company to your industry's average. As different industries are expected to be different, CCL maintains a the averages of 17 industries in their database, including: automotive, chemicals, computers & office equipment, conglomerates, consumer products, electrical & electronics, food, healthcare, manufacturing, nonprofit, service, computer software & services, personal care, drug & research, government, advertising & printing, and consulting. Compare your company's climate to other companies in your industry, so you don't try to over-correct things that are normal in your industry, or ignore things that are not.

When we administered KEYS at Interphase, the entire process took less than a month, and included close to 100 participants, in our headquarters in Plano, our manufacturing facility in Carrollton, and our R&D center in France. The next chapter will tell you how to use the results.

One clarification I have to make here: I am not affiliated with the Center for Creative Leadership in any way. I participated in their "developing the strategic leader" program in 2004, I used KEYS in 2008, and was certified to administer it. But that's it. I'm not benefiting in any way, shape, or form if you decide to use KEYS or any other tool, for that matter. I just wanted to make that clear…

INTERVIEWS AND FOCUS GROUPS

I used *interviews* for my creativity climate study, due to their exploratory nature. When studying research methods in my doctoral coursework I learned about the risks with survey questions that were not well crafted. Some people would understand them differently than others, and sometimes an answer on a scale is simply not insightful enough. For example, KEYS includes the following item: "I feel little pressure to meet someone else's specifications in how I do my work." If you feel a *lot* of pressure, would you agree with the statement? After all, the statement indicates you feel *little* pressure. Not a lot. Surveys can be tricky. Furthermore, remember that *words* carry only 7% of the message. The rest is carried through tone of voice and body language. When you ask a question through a survey, you only get 7% of the answer. Not even that, because the respondent didn't write a single word, and rather checked a box. You couldn't see his discomfort when he answered the question.

Therefore, whenever I conducted an organizational creativity climate assessment I started with surveys (such as KEYS) only to identify general areas of concern. I follow the 80-20 rule: 20% of the issues generate 80% of the problems. Once the surveys were done, I would analyze the results and see where the problem areas are. I would then turn to interviews. I strongly advise *against* a company employee conducting the interviews. It's not too difficult to conduct the interview or a focus group, but it's not too simple, either. You need to have the experience and sensitivity to pick up on things that were left unsaid, and drill deeper. However, the biggest issue is confidentiality. An employee would hardly ever be willing to complain to the human resources person interviewing him, for fear of retaliation once the word gets out. In fact, is there anyone in the organization you could really trust? You need an external professional facilitator to conduct interviews and focus groups. The facilitator would make it clear that "what happens here, stays here." Even then, not everyone would believe that, but it's still a lot better than using an internal person.

You may be able to interview *all* the employees in the company, in a business unit, a group, or a team. The smaller the number of employees there are, the easier it is to get 100% interview coverage. That would be best. You would not miss anything. Each interview could take hours, if you don't focus. This is why I typically conduct those only *after* I have the initial survey results, and have identified the problem areas. Based on that, I can create a subset of questions I would use during the interviews (or focus groups). During an interview you must use all your senses to pick subtle clues. Note when the interviewee uses cynicism or sarcasm. Note discomfort when answering specific questions. You should probe, but be very gentle. It is very easy to get an interviewee to clam up, but very hard to get them to open up.

Some areas are better explored individually, whereas others are better done through focus groups. When you conduct a focus group interview, make sure you do it with a group that feels comfortable enough with each other to answer questions out loud. You may want to start with an icebreaker. The disadvantage of a focus group is that sometimes a participant would be afraid to share something in the presence of others. On the other hand, sometimes one participant may share something, which would cause the others to jump in and add detail. It also varies with individual personalities. Some feel more comfortable being interviewed in a group, while others feel the opposite.

ASSESSMENT TOOLS SUMMARY

This chapter covered different assessment tools. It is very important to start with *introspection* and know where you stand, before deciding how to intervene. The assessment tools I described measure the *input* (employee creativity), the *climate* for transformation, and the *output* (company innovation). Different tools could be more suitable for different functions. There are certain metrics that could be measured by more than one tool, and my recommendation would be to use multiple tools to gain more insight.

The following table summarizes the tools I described. The first column describes the area being measured, be it innovation, freedom, trust, fluency, etc. The second column shows the organizational level assessed by that tool: corporate, individual, or team. The third column shows whether the tool measures Input (IN), Output (OUT), or Climate (CL). The following columns reflect the applicability and effectiveness of different specific tools for the different areas. Each cell with a "+" sign indicates that the tool is applicable for this metric. In few cases I marked a "½", where the tool is only partially suitable for this metric.

Measures	Level	IOC	GII	KEYS®	SparcIt	Interview	Focus Group
Innovation	Corp	OUT	+				
Creativity	Ind.	OUT		+	+	+	
Productivity	Ind.	OUT		+			
Freedom	Corp	CL		+		+	+
Challenge	Corp	CL		+		+	+
Encouragement	Corp	CL		+		+	+
Encouragement	Team	CL		+		+	+
Group support	Team	CL		+		+	+
Impediments	Corp	CL		+		+	+
Resources	Corp	CL		½		+	+
Leadership	Team	CL				+	
Fluency	Ind.	IN			+		
Flexibility	Ind.	IN			+		
Originality	Ind.	IN			+		
Elaboration	Ind.	IN			+		
Trust	Team	IN				+	½
Respect (C+V)	Team	IN				+	½
Time together	Team	IN				+	+

A few examples from this table: individual creativity could be measured by *KEYS, SparcIt*, and through interviews. Corporate innovation level can only be measured by the *Growth Innovation Index (GII)*, and that's the only item that *GII* measures. *KEYS* provides only a partial assessment of the resource level needed, and interviews and focus groups could complement it.

The assessment stage can be overwhelming. You may quickly bury yourself in data, both quantitative and qualitative. It is also very easy to become demotivated by the number of areas that need to be "fixed." However, I'll repeat my advice from the beginning of chapter 13: First of all, you must acknowledge reality. Not everything is great, and if you tell your employees, managers, and executives that everything is perfect—they would not be willing to allocate time, effort, or resources to fix what needs to be fixed. Second, you can't (and shouldn't) try to fix everything at once. It's too much to take on, and you are bound to fail. Use the 80:20 rule. Spend 100% of the effort on fixing 20% of the items that have 80% of the impact.

Never lose sight of what your end game is: increasing your employee creativity levels, generating more (and better) ideas, implementing the best ones, increasing your company's innovation level, and enjoying the financial results from it.

15.

INTERVENTION: YOU FIRST

If you completed the introspection-assessment phase in its entirety, good for you! Hopefully, you are not waiting idle for the final assessment results. After reading Part 2 of this book, you should already have a good idea of what you must do. Some of the areas where you could affect your core teams' creativity probably already resonated with you. You already know that some changes have to be made. Start making them. Don't try to change *everything* at once. Follow the 80:20 rule. Take one team, one group, one business unit, and start there. Maybe you are the leader of one team—start with your team. Later on, your team would get noticed and other teams would want to emulate what you did.

To recap, at the intervention phase, your degrees of freedom are:

- Setting innovation goals;
- Changing the culture throughout the organization, starting with you;
- Hiring creative people;
- Team member and leader selection; and—
- Training & Coaching.

This chapter covers all of those. Most importantly is that you take action *now*, and develop new habits. You cannot start and stop. You cannot make exceptions and excuses. You need to have 100% commitment to the steps you choose to take, or you would completely lose credibility. Don't do anything you don't believe is required. Don't do anything just to show that you have an effort in place to increase innovation. Don't just "show and tell."

SETTING INNOVATION GOALS

Chapter 14 described different innovation metrics, and proposed the growth innovation index (GII). You can find more information about it in my website[96]. Whether you decide to use one innovation metric or another, it is important that you use one that is suitable and meaningful for *your* company, even if you have to develop one yourself. Look at the criteria in chapter 14. Modify them if you must. You could start by measuring the innovation level in your business unit. Unlike some of the other innovation metrics, the *Growth Innovation Index* has to be measured at least at the business unit level. You cannot use GII to measure innovation at the *team* level, since it would be missing the implementation part.

Now that you have established an innovation level baseline in your business unit (or company), you should decide what your innovation level goal is for the next year. Depending on the innovation metric you decided to use, you should consider how long it would take for you to turn the organization's "innovation machine" around.

In September 2004 I was leading the Consumer Electronics Connectivity business unit in Texas Instrument. It generated close to $100 million in sales, part of a $250 million group, responsible for all silicon components that connect consumer electronics devices to one another. We built components that connected iPods with PCs, digital camcorders with TVs, and the like. There were 89 people in my group. Every September we launched the process of setting the priorities for the following year. September 2004 was no different. The connectivity standards that our products supported were maturing and commoditizing, and as a result our gross profit margins were declining. Revenue was important, and all three general managers

---

[96] http://www.largescalecreativity.com/growth-innovation-index-gii/

were asked to include a "top-down" 2005 priority of increasing revenue by 20% over 2004. Something was missing, I felt, and it took me a few days to put my finger on it. I met with my supervisor again and said:

"I can see that we want to increase revenue 20% year-over-year, but how about a goal of increasing revenue 100% in 4 years?"

To that she replied: "it's the same thing. If you grow revenue 20% every year, then in 4 years you would have grown it by 100%."

Actually, 107%... But to me those were two completely different things. In order to grow the business unit's revenue by 20% in one year, the products you would sell should already exist. This could only be done through selling more of the same products to the same customers, or sell the same products to new customers. It could not be done through the development of new products, because this would take much more than a year. Especially in the semiconductor industry, where even minor changes to a product could take more than a year to implement. If we only focused on a one-year horizon, we would never develop new products, and with the maturity and commoditization of our existing products—growing revenue would become harder.

"I disagree" I replied to her, "growing revenue by 20% a year requires turning and pulling a completely different set of knobs and levers than growing revenue by 100% in 4 years. The latter requires us to project the future of connectivity, while the former doesn't. It allows us to start with a clean slate. And that's exactly what I want to do." To my surprise she eventually agreed, and I went on a quest to identify the future of connectivity[97], leading to the creation of USB 3.0.

Setting innovation goals for one year might preclude efforts that would only yield results in two or more years. Objectives drive

---

[97] This story was taken from my book: *Bowling with a Crystal Ball*. 2nd Edition, 2015.

behaviors. If your innovation index, whichever you chose, showed that your current innovation level is 0.2, it might not be achievable to reach 0.5 next year, but you can set a goal of 0.5 in 4 years. Innovation is a long-term game. Setting easily achievable goals would not drive your organization to be competitive. Setting impossible goals would cause burnout and turnover, and you risk losing the trust of your people. The right goals are those that are slightly beyond what you know is possible. Those are the BHAGs that Collins and Porras referred to in *Built to Last*.

CLIMATE CHANGE, YOU FIRST

I'm about to start talking about climate change. But don't worry, I'm not going to ask you to drive a hybrid car or to ride share. I'll talk about changing organizational climate to make it creativity-friendly.

It would be so much easier if I told you that all you had to do is to close a part of the building to make an innovation lab, write a few rules for the employees, hire a graphic designer to turn those into inspiring posters you could then hang all around the building, or give a few additional bonus checks for great ideas or patents. After all, it's only money. With a few short emails you could order it all done. Find a place for it in the budget, and you're done! But it doesn't work that way. The only thing that works is changing culture and attitude, and *yours* must change first. The good news is that it doesn't cost any money. Your R&D budget doesn't have to grow. The bad news is that it's hard work. But you must do it. It's just like losing weight. There is no amount of money that you could pay to lose weight without limiting what you eat and working out. You can't just pay someone to lose weight for you. There is no silver bullet. You have to do it yourself, and it's hard. Hopefully, by now I provided you with the motivation you need. Now, it's time to do the actual work.

Let's assume for a minute that during the introspection phase, through KEYS, individual interviews, and focus groups, you heard again and again that the autonomy levels that employees experienced were low. Sit down with those employees (or use an external facilitator, which could sometimes bridge the gap) and agree on what needs to be done by both sides (you and them) to change that perception. Remember that 10% might be true (that you are really limiting their autonomy), but 100% is true in their perception. Once you agreed on what should change—write down simple rules (and consequences) that you and your employees both agree to adhere to, and execute them. You may want to meet on a weekly basis to follow-up and see change. Cost so far? None! You didn't have to build an innovation lab, buy new equipment, give anyone one day a week to be creative, or write a few fat bonus checks. The biggest effort required so far was your commitment to live by the rules you have just set.

I must admit that the hardest thing about changing how you work and your attitude is to get *credibility* for it from the same team of people who know you and have worked with you the longest. They would be highly skeptical that you could really change. They can't wait to see you "go back to your old ways" just to prove that nobody can really change. It is so much easier to gain credibility for the new way you act when it is with a new group of people that never knew you before. I knew quite a few managers and executives that couldn't step out of their perceived behavior until they moved to another company, where, with a different group of people, they could act differently. I know that there will be times when you would be tempted to go back to your old ways. After all, it is in your nature. These are the habits that you had developed over many years. This behavior is your comfort zone. Especially during stressful times. I've seen CEOs do the best they could to give their teams autonomy. They had put an honest and genuine effort in changing themselves, but under pressure they caved, even if for only one meeting, and fell back to their old "command and control" ways, and immediately lost credibility for everything they tried to do differently.

No doubt, the way you acted until now became a habit for you, and became the perception of who you are. This is your brand. Would you believe me if I told you that Walmart had changed its business, and is now a high-end apparel chain? Habits and perceptions are hard to change. However, they are not impossible to change and, furthermore, if you consistently pursue new behaviors they eventually become your new habits, replacing old ones. Over time, your employees would realize that you really have changed.

Your *attitude* must change first, but your peers' and employees' attitudes must follow. Focus on the middle-management level. People who manage other people must change their attitudes as well. It doesn't matter if you decided to embrace employee autonomy and made it "the law" in the company, if between you and your front-line employees is a manager who does the opposite.

The rest of this section discusses the 4 main areas you should focus on to improve the organizational climate for creativity: *autonomy, resources, bureaucracy,* and *incentives.* Note that *team* climate is not listed here. It will be discussed separately later in the chapter. Obviously, you could start working on all areas. They all make sense. However, based on results from the introspection phase, you may find that some areas need more work, and some need much less.

AUTONOMY

Giving employees autonomy is hard, especially when you haven't done it before. As described in chapter 10, trust would not develop overnight. I'm not only talking about your employees trusting you. I'm talking about you trusting your employees. It's very easy for me to say "well, you *must* start trusting them" and leave it at that. After all, you already bought the book... But it would also be unrealistic. Your trust in your employees is part of a vicious cycle (as illustrated in chapter 9), that is constantly fed through performance and results. In other words, your employees must earn your trust. However, here are 7 things you can do to help your employees earn your trust. You have to take the first step, and let their performance earn the rest.

DON'T GO OVERBOARD

More often than not, once the case was made for the importance of autonomy for creativity—managers and executives buy into the concept and, understanding it goes against their grain, give practically *unrestricted* autonomy. It doesn't feel right to them, but they do it anyway because they understand how important it is. Science proved it to them, as this book showed. Don't go overboard. Give the autonomy employees really need. Don't give them more. Don't sign blank checks. Give autonomy for *how* the task should be done, and not *which* task should be taken. This could be negotiable, but only to a certain extent. Let employees experiment, and let them fail, but don't *celebrate* failure. *Accept* failure, don't show them the stick, but demand that they learn from their failures. Put boundaries in place, preferably after negotiating them. Once boundaries are in place, and your team adheres to them, it becomes easier for you to trust them. When you don't put boundaries in place or set expectations, misalignment of what's reasonable could prevent them from earning your trust.

NOT ALL EMPLOYEES WANT AUTONOMY

The *Liverpool Hope University School of Business* 2014 survey showed that 78% of employees perceived work autonomy as important, which means that 22% thought it was not. Remember the story from chapter 9. One of my employees did not appreciate the autonomy I gave him, while his colleague did. Before you give autonomy, make sure you give it to someone who would thrive as a result. Not to someone who would feel terrified or abandoned by you.

AUTONOMY TO SEE THE BIG PICTURE

Part of autonomy is the view of the big picture. Show your employees what it means to walk in your shoes. Explain what restrictions *you* are subject to. "Give a man a fish, and you feed him for a day. Teach a man how to fish, and you feed him for a lifetime." The more you give them the ability to see things from *your* perspective, the more you eliminate friction in the future. You could make them your partners, rather than people you have to manage. You are likely to trust your *partners* rather than people who don't understand what you are going through and keep asking for more and more. As Kelly Johnson said—

> "In the Skunk Works we put them in the experimental shop under the engineers' direction and made them a party to developing the data. That always is a good tactic: involve the employee in the whole program as much as possible to arouse his interest and inspire his best performance."

Johnson was famous for bussing all employees to the flight line to watch the first flight of a prototype they designed.

HIRE A COACH

Change is hard. Changing your habits and organizational culture is harder. You may not be able to do that all by yourself. There may be times when you might unintentionally revert to your "old ways." Hire an executive coach to work with you. I had one working with me at Texas Instruments. He helped me focus on my interactions with my team. He helped me set the expectations and improve communications. Sometimes you need an outsider for that.

PUT THE RIGHT MANAGERS IN PLACE

The management layer between you and the employees can break everything you are trying to achieve. You may insist on providing autonomy to employees, yet your middle managers counteract it. On the other hand, a good middle manager could be better at providing autonomy than you are, which would make things work. Once you have the right managers in place—give them the autonomy *they* need, and let them run their team. If you stay out of their way, and they manage the team to superior performance—you would start trusting them.

BREATHE DEEP: HOW DO YOU REACT?

No doubt, this is not going to feel comfortable. One of your employees would come to you and tell you about something he tried, something you have not authorized, and failed. This would be your test. Take a deep breath, and follow the advice I gave you before. Don't celebrate failure, but don't reprimand over it either. Your reactions and interactions have to be moderate and appropriate. Otherwise he would never try again. Sure, he would never fail again, but he would never succeed again, either.

BE CONSISTENT

The most important thing you could do is—be consistent. Your reactions and interactions must be consistent 100% of the time. Not 99% of the time. If there is 1% of the time in which you revert to the "old ways," you would lose the credibility you gained with the other 99%. It's like a diet. It doesn't matter that you were very conscious about your calorie intake in the morning and over lunch, if you completely let yourself go at dinner.

If you follow the 7 items above—you may have given your employees a little more trust than they earned (or that you were willing to give them), but they would perform, earning your trust based on their actual performance, rather than your willingness to take a chance on them. You must be the person to break out of that cycle.

RESOURCES

Your team cannot be creative without resources. That's pretty obvious. Pushing them too hard to produce without giving them adequate resources would put too much pressure on them, and they might fail to deliver. I'm not telling you anything you don't already know, but that's not my point. I want to make sure that you don't give them *too many* resources. As the chart in chapter 9 showed—the relationship between resource availability and creativity resembles an upside-down U-shaped curve. Give the team too many resources—and they won't feel the need to be creative anymore. Resources must be *available* in the company. Somewhere. Employees should be aware of where those resources are, and have access to them, although it shouldn't be too easy. Certainly, you should never *push* resources to the team. Let them fight for them. Let them be creative in obtaining resources they need, or reach their goals with what they already have. It will make them more creative.

BUREAUCRACY

You must fight bureaucracy like you fight the plague. However, you need to also be selective in the fights you choose. Not all bureaucracy is bad. The bureaucracy that kills creativity is made of strict processes, over-formalization, and internal politics. In order to fight those you must identify *where* processes should (and absolutely should not) exist, and *how* are they used.

You don't have to remove bureaucracy from the *entire* company altogether. Otherwise things could really get messy. As I said before, some areas in the company need bureaucracy to operate properly. Accounting and purchasing departments need bureaucracy, and so does manufacturing. However, you could give your support team more autonomy and reduce bureaucracy. You must definitely keep bureaucracy out of your product development and design team. This is the team whose creativity would be hurt the most by bureaucracy. Lax formalization helps. When employees feel they could talk to anyone in the organization, no matter how high or low they rank— they are more productive and creative.

Back at TI, I wanted to present the USB 3.0 plan to the Senior Vice President, two levels above me, who could allocate resources to it. I had to go through my boss. She, in turn, called his office to set up the meeting. "We have a meeting," she called and told me. "Great!" I said, "when?" "September 5th, 11am," she replied. I was stumped. "It's July now!" I reminded her, "we need to have the meeting much, much sooner!" My boss explained that she spoke with his administrative assistant, and that was his first available time for a meeting. He was very busy. "Do you mind if I try to get us an earlier meeting than that?" I asked, "This cannot wait six weeks." She agreed, but instead of calling his assistant, I walked to his office. As I stepped into his suite, I pointed to his open door and asked his assistant: "is he on the phone?" I didn't see anyone else in his office with him. She nodded no. I walked directly to his door. She stood up, but realized she was not quick enough to stop me. I poked my head through his open door. He saw me. I asked "can we meet to talk about USB 3.0?" "I believe my assistant scheduled a meeting for you on that," he said. "Yes, but it's in six weeks. This can't wait that long," I explained, and immediately asked "are you available anytime tomorrow?" He looked at his calendar and told me he had meetings from 8am to 8pm. "How about 7am?" I asked. "I'll be here if *you* will," he replied. So the meeting took place the next morning at 7. Formalization was about to get in the way and delay an important project by 6 weeks, if I had let it. Most corporate America employees would not do what I did. And it's up to you how much would you let formalization get in the way of progress. At that point, I lived up to my promise to another senior VP, C.S. Lee.

Where you absolutely must maintain a level of bureaucracy, mainly in the form of processes, make sure that those processes are derived by requirements and restrictions *outside* of the organization, and not internally-imposed. In my study, I found that the creative employees in startups were not process-free, but they believed those processes *helped* them do their job. On the other hand, employees in mature companies often complained that processes were used by other employees to gain organizational *power*. Those other employees were in position to stop progress until they were satisfied. They felt that processes became internal, counter-productive *challenges*.

Before I started *facilitating* ideation and strategy development workshops, I attended quite a few. Almost always, in the preparation packet, I would receive a page with description of the appropriate attire for the workshop. No shorts, sandals, or flip flops. Business casual. No Jeans. Sleeves should be at least… You saw lists like these before. What do they make you feel? Well, there is a perfectly good reason for those lists. They intend to make sure that no attendee would make other attendees uncomfortable, because that could be a recipe for disaster. The first time I facilitated a strategy development workshop, one of the attendees asked *me* what the appropriate attire would be. Realizing that I didn't address that in my original invitation to the workshop, I sent the following note which, since then, I sent before every workshop I facilitated: "Wear whatever makes you comfortable, as long as you don't make anyone else uncomfortable, and if you're not sure, ask them." What does such a statement make you feel? First of all, it makes you feel that the rule has a *purpose*. It is not arbitrary. There are no "buffers" built into it. It empowers you to do the right thing, and it tells you why. Make sure the processes in your organization are made to help, and even more important—that they are perceived as such.

There is absolutely no room for internal politics in a creative team. Frankly, there is no room for it anywhere in your company. Read how Facebook fights internal politics in chapter 10. You must nip it in the bud. When you hire employees, make sure you hire employees that would not increase internal politics levels. When you check references for candidates, ask whether they contributed to internal politics in their companies, or fought to eliminate it. Be very attentive to complaints about employees stirring internal politics, and make it very clear that this behavior is unacceptable. I regret not doing so in several cases. I know, you have an employee with strong technical skills, but one who is very political, and you don't want to go through hiring another one only because of that. So you compromise. This compromise will cost you. Dearly. You just don't know it yet.

INCENTIVES AND ENCOURAGEMENT

Teresa Amabile, among others, found that complex tasks, such as the ones requiring creativity, are supported by *intrinsic* rather than extrinsic motivation (see chapter 9). Incentives, for the most part, fall into the category of *extrinsic* motivation. The research that started with the Duncker's Candle Problem in 1945, through Glucksberg in 1962 and Dan Ariely in 2005 (chapter 7) found, similarly, that financial incentives could not increase creativity. Moreover—they could reduce it. That's good news, right? Not only will you be saving money by not giving bonuses, but you would also increase creativity levels at the same time! There are three types of incentives and encouragement that you should consider, with their impact on creativity: financial, promotions, and praise.

FINANCIAL INCENTIVES AND BONUSES

Financial incentives should be treated very carefully. Bonuses contingent upon successful completion of a complex project or a creative task are exactly the type that could hurt creativity. On the other hand, having visibility to the impact of the project success on the company and benefiting from it supports creativity. After all, Roethlisberger and Dickson (1939), summarizing the *Hawthorne Experiments*, stated that "none of the results… gave the slightest substantiation to the theory that the worker is primarily motivated by economic interests." On the other hand, they claimed that most dissatisfaction with wages in those experiments was based on *fairness*—differences between employees, and that wage incentives failed to work when they were not aligned with social values. Fairness and social value alignment were more important to employees than the rewards themselves. Stock options (or stock grants), given equitably (not with a 10:1 or 100:1 ratio between management and employees) to team members, based on company success rather than meeting milestones would work the best.

PROMOTIONS

You must also be careful with promotions. Those should be as disconnected from teamwork as possible. Otherwise, they could create internal competition within the team, withholding information, the "meeting after the meeting," back-stabbing, and other types of internal politics as team members are fighting over the available or expected promotion. This type of internal competition prevents open communications in the team, eliminates the possibility of true debate of ideas, and destroys creativity. How should you promote team members, then? Do it on an *equitable* basis. Give promotions based on performances and capabilities. Do it in consultation with the team. Better yet—let the team recommend it. And never, ever give promotions contingent upon reaching team milestones or certain performances. Finally, don't promote people to their level of incompetence. You will not be doing them any favor. Once you promoted someone to a level of their incompetence—there is no way back. Their egos won't let them go back. They would have to leave the team, and possibly even the company to avoid the embarrassment of being downgraded.

PRAISE AND ENCOURAGEMENT

The last type of incentives is the encouragement and praise you could give employees. Chapter 7 described the importance of those to team members. The most important praise comes from their peers. Those who fought with them in the trenches. The second most important comes from the team leader, or immediate supervisor. The last one comes from the higher levels of the organization, up to the CEO. While generally this is the hierarchy of importance, it is not always the case. Find out from team members what they care about the most, and in what order, and focus your efforts that way. A kind word could go a long way, if it comes from the right person at the right time and for the right reason. When times are tough, schedules are pressing, and budget is tight, it is hard to find the time and energy to give praise. Do it anyway. This is the time when it could have the biggest impact. Do it on an equitable basis. You don't want team members feeling left out and unappreciated, but give praise only when they deserve it. If you give praise regardless of performance—you would be perceived as disingenuous. If you have team members who don't contribute to the team, remove them from the team. Don't make them leave because they feel unappreciated. They may "poison the well" before they finally leave.

HIRE CREATIVE PEOPLE

I know I could get in trouble with your human resources department here. I know they would love to hire people without any prejudice. However, you shouldn't look at *creativity screening* as discrimination. Look at creativity the same way you look at any other technical job skills. For a programmer's job, is it fair to screen candidates based on their ability to program? For a driver's job, is it fair to screen candidates based on their driving record and years of experience? It is! Then why not screen candidates based on their creativity level, if you were hiring for a product development or design position? Of course, you may argue that *every* employee should be creative. And if so—you should screen *all* candidates for creativity. There are individual creativity tests (such as SparcIt, described in chapter 14), and you could give test assignments that would help you assess the candidate's creativity. I had candidates solve a problem before to see how creative their solutions were. Hire creative people.

RISK-TAKING

One driving factor for creativity is the willingness to assume risk, as described in chapter 14. This is one of the reasons why you find more creative people in startups than in mature and large companies. The willingness to assume risk drives you to experiment and accept failure, which is required for creativity. That same willingness also guides employees to work in the much riskier startup rather than the more stable large company (even though the recent recessions, starting in 2000, proved that the aforementioned "stability" is nothing but a myth). Although I haven't reviewed specific tools to measure risk-willingness, I recommend you find such a tool and evaluate risk-acceptance in the hiring process. Hire people who are willing to take risks. Even if they are not taking a risk (or at least not perceiving they do) by joining your company—make sure they are willing to experiment. They would be the people who ranks "do the right thing" higher than "do what I'm told." They would rank "do something about it" over "wait for it to happen in due time." They would have a bias toward action.

HIRING CREATIVE TEAMS

Hiring individuals that are already creative can shorten *time-to-creativity* of new hires. However, company-level ideas are generated at the cross-functional *team* level, for the most part. Developing the respect and trust required for creativity-supportive team dynamics can take a long time, possibly years (see chapter 10). You could shorten that time through one of two practices: hiring individuals through the perspective of a team, and acquiring an entire team.

HIRING INDIVIDUALS WITH THE TEAM IN MIND

The basis for this hiring practice is by starting with a perspective of a whole team. Some team members may already work in your company, and are already part of the team. Look for the 9 diversity factors required for the team, as described in chapter 10: demographic, multi-disciplinary (cross-functional), knowledge (education), experience, generalists vs. specialists, "extracurricular" activities, cognitive preferences (e.g., introverts vs. extroverts), risk-taking attitude, and visionaries vs. pragmatists. To have a truly creative team you need a well-diversified group of people. Make sure you know what is missing among the different factors and hire people who could complement each other and fill the gaps. Don't focus only on the required technical skills and experience. This would certainly makes hiring more complex. However, only a holistic view of the team during the hiring process would help build a team with good dynamics. Keep in mind that the team may not stay together long, and that members may move in and out of the team over time. Sometimes even in and out of the company. When the team loses a member, consider all 9 factors when recruiting a replacement, internally or externally. Lateral movements within the company by members of a diversified team may hurt the team, but would still support overall company creative diversity. One good source of hiring is *references* by current team members. Those members know the potential hires personally and can attest to their ability to complement the rest of the team. They also provide the "pre-qualification" that could shorten the time to build trust with the new members. More on the diversified selection of team members and the *Creative Diversity Optimizer* tool later in this chapter. Remember that new team members could be recruited from within the company, too. That's how Kelly Johnson recruited his successor, Ben Rich, to run Lockheed's Skunk Works.

ACQUIRING A WHOLE TEAM

Most acquisitions are done to acquire a new innovative product, service, process, or business model. Few are done to acquire a proven, innovative *team*, with a specific skill set, even if the company was not interested in the actual product that the team developed as a startup. The price of such acquisition would typically be linked to the number of *core* people in the acquired company (the ones who are responsible for innovation, rather than those in supporting roles) and the uniqueness of their skills, instead of an expected return on investment from the new products they bring with them. The acquiring company may discard those products altogether after the acquisition. The advantage of such an acquisition is that, for the most part, it brings in a team that is already *diversified*, has an already established *trust*, works well together, and has the right dynamics in place. You should validate those before the acquisition, using the tools recommended here, just like you would if you built an internal team. This team's trust and creativity were built over a long period of time and forged under the harsh circumstances of a startup. Make sure you assess the team not only based on their technical skills. Consider how they work together, and how they complement each other on the other 9 diversity factors.

You might be tempted to break the team apart and integrate individuals into different groups in the company. In one word: *don't!* While you may benefit from the *technical* characteristics of the different team members *individually*, you would lose the creativity of the team as a whole. Furthermore, one of the reasons that acquisitions fail is the clash between the acquired team and the existing team which leads to power struggles that nobody wins, while the company loses. The best is, if you acquired the team for its capabilities and creativity, to keep it intact and isolated from the company's bureaucracy. Make them feel at home, but make sure they feel it's *their* new home, and not as guests.

TEAM MEMBER AND TEAM LEADER SELECTION

Having the right team in place doesn't necessarily mean hiring *new* people. You may, for the most part, already have the right people in your organization. You have three options: hiring a new team (individually or as a whole), pulling people from all around the organization to form a new team, or changing the makeup of an existing team. The last one is the trickiest, since it could cause a disruption to an existing team. While team dynamics may not be the best, there is still "the devil you know" preference of team members to stay with others they know, even if they are not optimally productive together. The first two methods are the easiest, since they don't involve *removing* team members. Remember why you are doing this. You are doing this to improve team dynamics and increase team creativity. My study showed that both creativity and job satisfaction were results of positive team dynamics (see diagram in chapter 3). Therefore, when you create good team dynamics, not only will you have a productive team, but you would also increase job satisfaction. Two birds with one stone! And you would be using science to build the right team.

CREATIVE DIVERSITY OPTIMIZER

To increase team creativity through diversity of perspectives you must include all 9 diversity factors in your team. Add to those the technical skills required, and you have the dimensions along which you should maximize the orthogonality of team members. What does that mean? It means that your team must be diversified (different from one another) along as many dimensions as possible. You could do this mathematically (statistically). For every dimension you must assure as close as possible to normal distribution of the different possible values held by different team members. As a reminder, the 9 diversity dimensions are (see chapter 10 for details):

- Demographic
- Multi-disciplinary and cross-functional
- Knowledge & Education
- Experience
- Breadth vs. Depth
- Extra-curricular interests
- Cognitive Preferences
- Risk Taking
- Visionaries vs. Pragmatists

Each one of the 9 categories could have several items underneath. For example, the demographic category may include:

- **Demographic**
  - Age
  - Gender
  - Ethnic background
  - Education level
  - Etc...

The *cross-functional* dimension may represent the different disciplines existing in the company, as required for the completion of the project assigned to the team. Here, you may have a *tier 1* (core function) and *tier 2* (extended function). The following example would apply to a high-tech, electronic product company:

- **Multi-disciplinary and cross-functional**
  - Software engineering (tier 1)
  - Hardware engineering (tier 1)
  - Mechanical engineering (tier 1)
  - Product marketing (tier 1)
  - Finance (tier 2)
  - Human Resources (tier 2)
  - Etc...

Take the dimension of *cognitive preferences*, for example. As dimensions, you can use the 4 MBTI elements (it's easy to use this one since each dimension has exactly two possibilities):

- **Cognitive Preferences**
  - Extrovert (E) vs. Introvert (I)
  - Sensing (S) vs. Intuition (N)
  - Thinking (T) vs. Feeling (F)
  - Judging (J) vs. Perceiving (P)

When I had MBTI facilitated for my team (and myself) in 2004, we found that my team members all fit 4 types: ISTJ, ISFJ, ISTP, and ISFP (all in grey), while I was (and still am) an ENTJ (black). As a team, we left a lot of space between us. While assuring some diversity, it was just too polarized. I had the letters T and J common with some of my team members, only T with some of them, and nothing in common with two members.

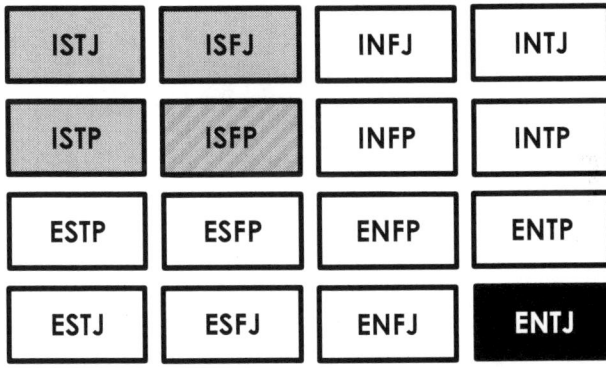

If you stare at the diagram above long enough, you would start seeing small circles in the intersections. It's an optical illusion. And it has nothing to do with this discussion…

To have good diversity, you should have the different types spread as much as possible across all team members. However, you should also make sure that there is enough *commonality* between different team members, or trust would never develop. In the following illustrated examples there are 5 team members (*M1* through *M5*), and

4 different diversity dimensions (*D1* through *D4*). For simplification, each dimension can have one of only two values, black or white.

	M1	M2	M3	M4	M5
D1		■			
D2					
D3					
D4	■	■		■	■

The first diagram above shows a team with too little *diversity*. Dimensions *D2* and *D3* do not show a good representation of the entire spectrum of characteristics. All members are white. Dimensions *D1* and *D4* do have representation, but it is not split evenly.

	M1	M2	M3	M4	M5
D1	■			■	
D2	■	■			
D3	■				
D4				■	■

The second diagram above represents good *diversity*, but not enough *commonality* among team members. Members *M2* and *M3* have a lot in common, and so do *M1* and *M4*, or *M3* and *M5*. Each of those pair would likely get along (each pair has 3 characteristics in common), but member pairs *M3* and *M4*, *M4* and *M5*, *M2* and *M4* would likely not get along, as they have very little, if at all, in common.

	M1	M2	M3	M4	M5
D1	■		■		■
D2		■		■	■
D3	■			■	
D4	■		■		■

The last diagram above represents good diversity that balances diversity of dimensions along with enough commonality among team members. Nothing would ever be perfect, but you should balance as much diversity *and* commonality as possible. As contradictory as it might sound.

How can you achieve that balance? Follow the following steps:

First, identify the diversity areas you should consider in your team. Those could be any or all of the 9 diversity areas I proposed in Chapter 10, plus additional dimensions you feel are needed in the team. For each one, identify the different values it could have (for the cross-disciplinary dimension, for example, you could have software engineers, hardware engineers, marketing, finance, etc.). Bear in mind that different businesses require different types of technical skills. You could give the different values numbers, or keep them as words. Make sure you included *tier 2* disciplines, and not only *tier 1*. For each discipline you should identify the importance of diversity in that discipline, and the importance of commonality there.

Second, for each team member write the values for each discipline.

Third, calculate the distribution across every dimension, weighted by the importance of diversity in that dimension. These numbers should be as high as possible, indicating strong *diversity* on the team.

Finally, take every pair of members and measure the *commonality* between the two members of the pair along the different dimensions. Four team members would produce 6 pairs. Eight members would make 28 pairs. The same rule as the number of possible new idea combinations described in chapter 12 applies here. Average those commonalities, weighted by the importance of commonality in those dimensions. These numbers should be as high as possible, as well. You should also average those for specific members and see if any member has very little in common with the others. Those could potentially be "problematic" team members, since having very little in common with others means that it would be hard for the others to trust them. Moreover, find specific pairs who have extremely little in common. Those could have high probability for interpersonal friction.

This tool can help in three ways: First, it can help you identify whether your team is *diverse* enough to be creative, but also if your team members have enough in *common* with one another to build respect, trust, and eliminate friction. Second, it can help you identify whether a new team member would fit into this team or not (whether the new team member adds to the diversity, while having enough in common with the others or not). Finally, it can help you identify the characteristics of a desired team member to help you in hiring or selection of new members for the team.

When you build a team, start with the core members, most likely based on their technical skills, and then identify what's missing, modeling the "ideal" new team member. You could then either find this member somewhere else in your company, or hire her externally. Either way—you would have identified much more than the desired technical skills for new hires. You would identify what would make a new member add to the creativity of the team.

TEAM LEADER SELECTION

The first part of team leader selection is a philosophical / ideological decision. Do you want your team leader to be "first among equals" or a higher-level manager? Both options are valid. The best structure I experienced was a *de-facto* team leader who emerges from the team through consensus ("first among equals"), supported by an executive sponsor outside the team, a higher-level executive in the company. The executive sponsor would provide "air cover" to the team and its leader, and add another layer of separation between the team and the company's bureaucracy. Lockheed's top management provided such "air cover" to Kelly Johnson, separating him from the government's bureaucracy and letting him lead his team.

For the role of the "first among equals" you should select a team leader just like you selected any other team member. The internal leader is an individual contributor, as well. Therefore, she should meet the same *diversity* and *commonality* requirements that any other team member is expected to meet. My preference is to let the team decide who the team leader should be. *Appointing* a team leader could violate the "no promotions" rule described in chapter 9 and earlier in this chapter. You could create resentment among team members, and cause more harm than good.

Beyond the diversity/commonality screening, you also need several additional characteristics for a strong team leader:

- The team leader must have great communication skills. He or she would need to help the team work together.
- The team leader should have one of the highest *commonality* ratings among all team members. In other words: he or she should have as much in common with as many of the others as possible. It helps communicating with them, understanding them, and being respected and trusted by them.
- The team leader must have already established trust with senior management. This is a critical factor. For senior management to trust the entire team with autonomy and resources, so desperately required for creativity and implementation, they must first trust the team leader. Only then would the team leader be able to become the buffer needed between management (and bureaucracy) and the team. If senior management doesn't trust the team leader, they would micro manage the team. If Lockheed's senior management didn't trust Kelly Johnson, we would likely never have seen the P80, U2, SR71, or F-117A.
- The team leader must possess facilitation skills and knowledge of ideation workshops. He/she would have to facilitate those for the team, solving tough problems and generating creative ideas. The good news is that facilitation skills can be learned and acquired.
- Finally, the team leader must possess business planning and presentation skills. She would likely be the one presenting the team's output to senior management (although, as I found, sometimes a

> *team* presentation, based on areas of expertise, works better). The team leader's ability to communicate solid, pragmatic, yet innovative ideas to management would build the trust she needs further.

TRAINING & COACHING

Like any muscle in your body, your creativity capabilities need exercise. There are 6 opportunities you have to conduct such training at the different levels of the organization: individual creativity training, team leader training, ideation workshops (practice and "real-time"), technical skill training, executive coaching, and team building.

INDIVIDUAL CREATIVITY

Chapter 12 covered the framework for idea generation. The process is simple and includes 4 steps: collect ideas, let them incubate, force trigger events, and then relax and let connections occur in your *medial prefrontal cortex*. Note that the second (incubate) and fourth (relax) stages are passive. There is nothing you could learn or practice to master those. However, the first (collect) and third (trigger) stages require some effort. An individual creativity training program should therefore include the following elements:

- Theoretical training. Explain how the process works. It is more effective to use the process once you understand it.
- Discuss sources of ideas. Propose sources. The collection of "old ideas" must become a habit, and thus once a week you should meet with team members (preferably as a group) to support this effort, and discuss what interesting ideas they encountered over the past week while "collecting." Three powerful questions that help spark ideas are: what have you learned that surprised you? What obstacles have you encountered, and what did they stop you from doing? And—what unexpected results did you get when you tried something and expected something else to happen?
- Encourage trigger events. Team-building activities serve as great trigger events, but they may be too few and far in between. Exercising,

- walking, or any other intense activity would do, but you must encourage your team members to do so.
- Provide formal creativity skill development courses. The State University of New York (SUNY) offers a massive open online course (MOOC) called *Ignite Your Everyday Creativity*[98], for the price of $49 (if a certificate is sought) or free of charge (without certificate). SUNY partnered with *SparcIt* for creativity quotient (CQ)[99] assessment. *SparcIt* is mentioned in chapter 14.
- Finally, on a regular basis, discuss the process and its effectiveness. What worked? What didn't work? What should change?

TEAM LEADER

The team leader needs the same training as any other team member. In fact, the team leader should be part of the team during training. However, the team leader must hone additional skills, some of which she may already have, and some of which she must develop. Team leader training would take place individually, separate from the rest of the team. Training for team leader should include:

- ***Facilitation skills***. The ability to facilitate workshops effectively and efficiently. These are "generic" facilitation skills, unrelated to specific ideation processes. They include the ability to make sure everyone got heard, nobody monopolized the discussion, conflict resolution, and other such skills. The ability to maintain objectivity when facilitating is important.
- ***Specific ideation processes***. Chapter 16 discusses six of those at a high level. The ability to facilitate an ideation workshop is important for a team leader. Otherwise, you would always have to rely on external facilitators. In chapter 11, I described how my own knowledge of the business helped prevent a scenario planning workshop from derailing. There are advantages when the team leader facilitates the ideation workshop.
- ***Business planning and presentation skills***. The team leader must be able to present to executive management the team's proposal

---

[98] https://www.coursera.org/learn/ignite-creativity
[99] http://www.24-7pressrelease.com/press-release/suny-buffalo-state-selects-sparcits-automated-creativity-assessment-tool-for-its-upcoming-mooc-on-creativity-401329.php

> in a clear, concise, and convincing way. Being able to predict questions that may be asked and build trust during the presentation are crucial for the team to maintain its autonomy.
>
> - **_Coaching_**. The team leader must be able to deal with team dynamics. Chapter 10 discussed those dynamics, and chapter 11 addressed the role of the team leader in assuring effective, productive, and creative teamwork. The ability to maintain those can be learned, and continuously coached.

IDEATION WORKSHOPS

Chapter 16 discusses ideation processes in greater detail. An ideation workshop is a great opportunity to provide any of the other types of training. The entire team is in one place, making it easy to conduct training.

TEAM BUILDING

Chapter 10 emphasized the importance of team-building for shortening the *respect-to-trust* time. You could "shave" years off that process through intense team-building activities. Yes, I am still aware that many companies, through this era of cost-cutting, refer to team-building as a boondoggle and an unnecessary expense. I can assure you that they are worth the investment. However, you should be careful with what you choose as team building activity. It must meet certain criteria:

> - Team building events must have high intensity. I'm sorry, all you avid golfers, but golf is *not* a high intensity activity. I'm a shooter, and can tell you that neither is shooting. There are two purposes why you need an intense team building activity. The first is that you want to get as close to a "life altering event" as possible (without putting anyone at risk), to shorten the *respect-to-trust* time. The second—the more intense the activity, the higher the likelihood that ideas resulting from the following ideation workshop would be groundbreaking. The team building activity would be the trigger for idea generation.

- The activities should be *team* activities rather than individual ones. Flying radio controlled airplanes, although an intense activity (trust me, flying a 10-pound jet at 130 mph is nothing if not intense), but would not bond the team. You need team activities, and preferably not competition among team members (such as a race). Furthermore, you should include activities in which team members have to trust each other. They have to develop an instant trust, and it could become sustainable later.
- Finally, the team building activity should be completely disconnected from the workplace. Although it's always cheaper to hold those events in one of the company's facilities, the temptation is always to stay in touch with your daily activities. Even if it costs more—do it in a remote location. Preferably in the countryside. Do not allow any connection to the world, unless it is a family emergency (do not allow "emergency calls" from the office. Imagine you are on a plane from Dallas to India. You would be on that plane for 17 hours and nobody could reach you. Your office should deal with whatever crisis they are facing without you). I am very strict about that rule.

I encourage you to include team-building activities with ideation workshops and training, for more reasons than one. The entire team is already in one location (if they are not normally collocated). However, if you organize those such that the intense team-building activity is immediately followed by an ideation workshop (of course, after taking a shower…), you are also guaranteed to increase the flow of ideas for two reasons: the team building activity would serve as a *trigger* event for better individual idea generation, and that team-building activity would have increased trust, making the team more cooperative during the ideation workshop. In my experience, ideation workshops that followed (or intertwined with) intense team-building activities produced better ideas than those who were independent of team building. You could feel the different dynamics.

TECHNICAL SKILLS

You learned the broad foundation for your education in school. Then you focused your career in college or in work through specialization. However, at some point you may have stopped learning. Your "state of affairs" knowledge became obsolete, and that could be dangerous. You think you know enough, and are unaware of new developments in the field, and new emerging trends. You, and the rest of the team, must continuously learn and improve your technical knowledge and skills. Keep sharpening your saw.

Companies used to have training budgets, and those were typically the first ones to go during cutbacks and reductions in force. After all, is your training budget more important than saving one job?

But it's a mistake. Training must continue. You must stay abreast of the latest developments in your field. Those are the ones that could make your ideas, products, services, business models, and processes competitive and relevant. Consider individual creativity training that includes the reading, viewing, or otherwise consuming information *outside* of your industry and technical discipline as *breadth*, while getting more in-tune with developments in your specific technical discipline and industry as *depth*. Chapter 10 explained why it was important to maintain *both* breadth and depth.

Few good sources for the latest developments in your industry are tradeshows, industry organization meetings, and standard-setting meetings. As I wrote in *Bowling with a Crystal Ball*, those meetings could give you an opportunity to learn what was not published anywhere yet. It's where you could see what other people (and companies) feel about new trends and developments, and therefore be able to separate true trends from hype.

EXECUTIVE COACHING

I said this earlier: change is hard. Culture is even harder to change, and the hardest to change is *your* own role in setting culture. Chapter 9 gave you the rationale and theory of the link between culture and creativity. Chapter 14 showed you how to *measure* how supportive is your company's culture of creativity. As a manager or executive in the company, you must follow the 80:20 rule: spend 100% effort on 20% of the items that could have 80% impact on creativity. However, the *consistency* of your actions is crucial. You are developing new habits. You are taking a leap of faith and trusting your employees before they earned it. There are many things I asked you to do that just don't feel comfortable. As I told you earlier, changing the culture to build a more creative organization is not achieved through the investment of money. You may wish it was. It's easy to sign checks. Changing culture requires hard emotional, psychological work on your side. Every little transgression of going back to your "old ways" could nullify everything you worked so hard for. There are two tools I can offer you that could help.

First, create a support group. There are other executives or business line managers in your company who are going through the same things are you are. Meet with them regularly. Let one of them (or more) be your sponsor, like in Alcoholics Anonymous. Here is an adaptation of the AA definition of a sponsor for an executive sponsor:

> "One of most powerful tools to help an *executive* be consistent throughout change is the sponsor. This individual is there to offer guidance and support to a sponsee. The sponsor is not only a person to guide the member through the *cultural change*, but to also be there to listen. Being able to rely on a sympathetic ear can be particularly important when the individual feels on the verge of relapse (*to the "old ways"*). Choosing the right sponsor is important, because otherwise the relationship could prove to be disastrous."[100]

Fits perfectly! You could have an internal sponsor who already went through the cultural changes you are about to, and would be there for you when you need them. Don't go through this alone. One mistake and you could fall off the wagon.

---

[100] Adapted from http://alcoholrehab.com/addiction-articles/how-to-choose-an-aa-sponsor/

16.

IDEATION: THE NEXT BIG THING

Everything I taught you to this point was aimed at creating the right organizational climate and team dynamics for creativity, and to acquire individual creativity skills. Here is where the rubber meets the road. It is time to generate novel, useful, and feasible ideas for your company. The tool of the trade for that is the *ideation workshop*. Done right, the ideation workshop takes one day. However, as you'll see, often there is preparatory work that leads into it, whether done by the facilitator or, as in many cases, by the participants. You need your best people there, and unfortunately they are busy. This means two things: one, that you can't hold ideation workshops too often, and two—that you should maximize what you get out of them. Besides, if done right, they would produce ideas that would take time and effort to implement by the participants themselves.

For that purpose, I recommend conducting two- or three-day ideation retreats, and include two more additional elements in them: training and team-building. In fact, the best ideation retreat would be structured as follows:

- Day 1: training and creativity exercises.
- At the last hour of Day 1: discuss the goal of the ideation workshop. What are you hoping to achieve at the end? Define the problem to be solved. Get the participants to start thinking.
- Day 2: team building.
- Day 3: ideation workshop.

Although not ideal, but if you only had two days for the retreat, you could combine the first and second days into one. Hold training in the morning, identify the problem right before lunch, and conduct a "qualified" team-building activity in the afternoon and evening. The second day would then be dedicated to the ideation workshop. Follow the recommendations for training and team building provided in the previous chapter.

There are different types of ideation processes. Some practitioners would swear by one, and not consider any other. The reality is that many are "good" ideation processes, but they each offer solutions to different problems and issues, and offer different perspectives on similar problems. Some vary by their *time horizon*, some are meant to solve difficult *problems*, some are made to generate *ideas* starting with a clean slate, etc. Choose the one that fits your specific situation.

An important note: the description provided in the following pages would give you a general sense of six different processes. It was not meant to be a comprehensive *how-to* guide. Books were written about each one of those processes, and scholars spent their entire careers (or are still doing so) developing and practicing them. One of them even spent 25 years in a Siberian Gulag for developing his method. There are consultants whose sole occupation is to facilitate those, have facilitated many, and are now very experienced. Don't take the following pages as enough for you to facilitate yourself to save money. Your biggest investment is not going to be the cost of a facilitator. It would be the precious time of your key employees who attend those workshops, and the opportunities your company might miss because you haven't facilitated it professionally enough. The first time I facilitated an ideation workshop I was at awe that the company was willing to pay my fee for that. Then I realized that my fee paled in comparison to the cost of having all participants spend three days with me, and the potential cost of poor results from the workshop.

Imagine that you read a one-page document describing the different functions, and all the buttons and handles in the cockpit of an F/A-18E Super Hornet fighter jet. After reading this one page—do you feel comfortable enough to climb into the cockpit, start the two powerful General Electric F414-400 engines, unleash 44,000 pounds of thrust, and take it for a joyride? This would be the equivalent of using what you learned from the following pages to facilitate an ideation workshop. Would you feel comfortable enough flying the jet after reading the entire user manual? You would know more, but still wouldn't have first-hand experience, and could easily get in trouble and crash. The following descriptions I provide in this book could give you a sense of what ideation process is best for your needs. Then, you should learn more about it. Read books, articles, and case studies. Then, use a professional facilitator, experienced with the specific process you believe is right for your company. Only then, once you feel comfortable enough—do it yourself. Starting yourself is not a way to save money.

A second important comment: don't be married to only one process. Don't swear by any single one. They are all good, but they are good for different purposes. Sometimes it might make sense to use several different processes to solve the same problem through different perspectives. I, for one, like to start with one ideation process (say TRIZ or IDEA), and once it yielded an idea for a new product, service, process, or business model—I would conduct war-game to simulate the market (and mainly competition) reaction to it.

	Design Thinking	Scenario Planning	War Games
Origin	IDEO	Shell Oil Peter Schwartz: *The Art of the Long View*.	Military Benjamin Gilad: *Business War Games*.
Objective	Problem-solving. Finding better ways for users to use products and services.	Identifying plausible long-term futures and strategies to win in them.	Simulating competitor behavior and planning strategic moves in response.
Time Horizon	Immediate. Solve existing problems. Less than 5 years.	At least 10 years. Sometimes up to 50 years.	Between 1 and 5 years.
Level of ideas	Very tactical. Specific products and/or services.	Very high level. It provides direction, but not specifics. Don't expect specific products to be defined.	Tactical. Identify specific products, services, but also strategic moves.
Pre-work	Observing how users use products and interviewing them. Moderate level of work.	Can be done without pre-work, if you select a diverse enough group of people. Otherwise—research driving forces.	Studying the competitors in great detail. Must be done by the participants.
# participants	One or more teams of 5-8 people each.	4 teams of 3-4 participants each.	2-5 Teams of 3-4 participants each. Plus judges.

TRIZ	Bowling with a Crystal Ball	IDEA
Russia, 1946, Genrikh Alshuler	*Bowling with a Crystal Ball* Yoram Solomon	Yoram Solomon
Problem-solving, based on solutions to similar problems solved in the past in other fields.	Finding opportunities for market disruption based on predicting the technology available in the future, especially aggressive trends.	Finding opportunities for the next product or service for the company, based on current assets.
Immediate.	Medium term (3-7 years)	Near-term (2-5 years)
Very tactical. Specific products and/or services.	Specific products or services.	Specific products or services.
Work is done at the workshop itself. No additional pre-work required.	Technology trend research must be done, typically by participants themselves, but could be done by other experts.	Some research should be done by participants, with possible help from other experts.
1-4 teams of 5-8 people each.	3-5 teams of 3-5 people each.	3 5 teams of 3-5 people each.

Although different sessions could vary in their specific flow of the "content" section, this is a generally recommended structure:

- Start with introductions (if needed) and ice-breaker (always needed).
- Ask for, capture, and summarize the expectations for the event: Your expectations, the company's expectations, and the participants' expectations. If any are not feasible—identify those right then.
- Establish ground rules (see chapter 10 for a recommended list). Make sure the participants "own" the ground rules. For example, give the participants yellow (or red, or any other color) cards, and ask them to raise the card if they feel that someone had violated a ground rule.
- Conduct the ideation session.
- Finalize the conclusions, and identify next steps.
- Go back to the list of expectations, and go one-by-one to assure that you met all of them, and talk about why some of them were not met.
- Throughout the event, keep a running list ("Parking Lot") of ideas and issues that are not directly related, but should be captured for future use.

Strong team dynamics would contribute to creativity much more than political correctness. "How to" guides for brainstorming advise you how to conduct a passion-free, worthless process. One guide provided a list of phrases you should *avoid*, such as "a good idea, *but…*" or "be practical!" However, think about it—if you heard those phrases from someone you trust, would it offend you or ruin your creativity as much as it would if you heard it from someone you don't trust? Another "guiding principle" you may often hear is: "defer judgement" during the initial idea brainstorming. The reason: if you judge, you might deter participants from proposing additional ideas. Bull! If you make sure that you have strong team dynamics that support trust and open, passionate debate—you don't have to avoid certain phrases or judgement. Those phrases would be acceptable and contribute to the overall goal. You must hold a passionate and involved workshop, or none at all. Don't hold a politically-correct workshop. That would be a waste of time. After all, "love means never having to say you're sorry…"[101]

Finally, a word about transcribing and taking notes. I typically take notes myself on flip charts. It's better than capturing them on a computer connected to a projector. The body language and interaction associated with writing on flip charts are better. If your handwriting is not legible, ask someone with better handwriting to do it. Either way, make sure you captured the comments said, *exactly* the way they were said. Don't alter them. If you weren't sure what was said—ask for clarification. If you change wording, ask the contributor whether this was what she meant. If not—revise. If her comment gave you an idea for a better one—capture the original comment first, and then yours. If you modify comments you hear, participants would stop suggesting them.

Before describing the specific processes that I use the most, I'll just say that facilitating those processes is very gratifying for me. Much more than generating ideas myself. It always amazes me to see a group of motivated people generate radical, competitive, brilliant ideas. I don't see my job as a facilitator to generate ideas, but rather to "extract" ideas hidden in particpants' collective heads

DESIGN THINKING

Design Thinking is also known as *Human-Centered Design*. It was created by David and Tom Kelley of IDEO[102]. The concepts were featured in TED videos, and in the book *Creative Confidence*, written by the Kelley brothers. The concepts of *Design Thinking* are used by Stanford University in its d.school[103], and are available online. I had

---

[101] Ali McGraw in *Love Story*, Paramount Pictures, 1970
[102] www.ideo.com
[103] http://scpd.stanford.edu/ppc/stanford-design-group-courses-workshops-and-programs?utm_source=google&utm_medium=ppc&utm_term=designthinking&utm_campaign=DT&_vsrefdom=Adwords-

my first exposure to it in a seminar delivered at the University of North Texas' Innovation lab. It is a problem-solving technique (meaning, you have to start with a problem) in 5 stages:

- *Empathize*: learn about the user, understand how they use your product (or any other product). You can reach a high level of empathy through observing users in action, and through interviews, preferably right after (or during) the user used the product.
- *Define*: understand what is wrong with how the products are used today. What can you do differently? Henry Ford is known to have said "If I had asked them what they wanted, they would have said 'faster horses'." Sometimes you can't ask the users how things *should* be done differently. For the most part, they can't imagine it. Besides, they are already used to how things work now. Users might have very short attention span. It either works well, or they're not going to use it. No user told Steve Jobs how to design the iPhone. It was through observing how users used other phones and imagining an alternative.
- *Ideate*: brainstorm as many ideas as possible. Crazy ideas are encouraged. How can things be done differently? Don't limit yourself to what you know. Don't eliminate a possible solution simply because you don't know how to implement it yet.
- *Prototype*: one of the most powerful tools in testing the viability of your solution is prototyping. In the class I took at UNT, we had to deliver a prototype within 3 hours of class start time. The prototype could be "quick and dirty" and not even operational, as long as it could give the user a sense of how the final product (or service) would work.
- *Test*: let the users use (or simulate using) your prototype to see what they feel about the new usage. Record their reaction. Refine your ideas, if needed.

In 1995, I had an idea for a startup. We would develop a device that connects the phones in your home to the Internet and allow you to place international calls for the price of local calls. This was 6 years before Vonage was created (2001), and 8 years before Skype was founded (2003). It was hard to explain the concept to people. Even to

---

Other&gclid=CjwKEAjwlZa9BRCw7cS66eTxlCkSJAC-
ddmwmsirJJFtVgkf6N2UFbqcLoYuD6ZyNHvoixkYKvK4LxoCSHfw_wcB

my wife. Internet Telephony was very sketchy at that time. I therefore built a crude-looking prototype that connected to the Internet on one side, and then dialed to my cell phone on the other side. It established a connection from Israel to someone in Florida who happened to be connected at the time (that's how you would connect with people then, just like ham radio…). I handed the phone to my wife, and she spoke with that Florida man. That's when she understood what the product was going to do.

In 2010, when I conceived the idea for penveu, I claimed that a camera on a pen could determine exactly where it was pointing on the screen using on-screen targets that were invisible to the human eye. This was never done before, and I expected skepticism. To convince the CEO and the board of directors, my team developed two demos. One demo showed that we could embed targets in a screen image that would be visible to a camera, but not to the human eye. The other demo showed that the camera could track a *visible* target on the screen and write exactly where it was pointing. I explained that all that was needed to be done was to combine the two demos into one product that would track invisible targets. I secured funding that day. Four years, ten million dollars, and many patents later, the product was launched.

Today we live in a world of mobile apps. I became involved with yet another startup, which may release a new mobile app in 2017. It was hard for me to explain how this app would look, feel, and work. Even to my partner. To my help came an app called POP App. It allowed me to draw screenshots on paper, take pictures of them, mark active areas that would switch to other images, and in minutes I could demonstrate the operation of the app and make it tangible. I spent a few days designing real-looking screenshots and uploaded them to that prototyping app. Later, when I demonstrated it, people found it hard to believe that it was only a mockup and not a real active app.

SCENARIO PLANNING

Scenario Planning is *not* a problem-solving technique. It is a method used to envision the long-term future and allow the company to plan for it and be competitive when it arrives. It is one of the ideation processes I enjoy the most. The resulting ideas are very high level, and mostly in the form of *direction*, rather than specific products or services. Shell Oil[104] uses this strategic tool often. Giving its industry, oil, it cannot change direction quickly, and therefore must "see" the future as far and as accurately as possible. Scenario Planning was described in Peter Schwartz's book *The Art of The Long View*. In Scenario Planning, you go through the following steps:

- **Develop a focusing question.** What do you want to know about the future? Is it the future of energy consumption? The future of Internet access? Where the automobile industry is heading? Before developing the question you cannot define driving forces, as those would emerge from the context of that question.

- **Brainstorm driving forces.** Knowing what you are looking for, ask the participants (in one large group) to brainstorm the forces that could impact the answer to the focusing question. In oil exploration, it could be the increased use of electric cars, increased environmental consciousness, government regulations, Middle-East geo-politics, etc. Each driving force should have two extremes. The use of electric cars could have "dominating" on one side, and "less than 1%" on the other. Err on the side of including many driving forces, rather than few. You could "go around the room" to collect ideas, until no new ideas emerge. At this point, it is very important to consolidate similar ideas and narrow the list down to 8-10 driving forces. Having several relatively similar forces might have an adverse effect on the ability to identify the top ones (since voting could split among relatively similar forces). Try to reach a list of forces that are as orthogonal to each other as possible.

- **Identify the most critical driving forces.** Of those, identify the ones that are the most *critical* to answering the focusing question. Some driving forces may not have a big impact. Some might have dramatic impact. Identify the latter. It could be all 8, or some of them.

---

[104] http://www.shell.com/energy-and-innovation/the-energy-future/scenarios.html

- **Rank top critical uncertainties**. Once the most critical driving forces were identified, identify those who are the most *uncertain*. Try to narrow it down to only 2. Those would be called *top critical uncertainties*. Identifying them based on uncertainty might prove to be tricky, as I learned from my own experience.
- **Define 4 scenarios**. Once the top two critical uncertainties were identified, they define 4 possible scenarios, one for every combination of the two extremes that each driving force has. If one critical uncertainty is whether government energy regulation would become more strict, and the other is whether the public becomes more environmentally-conscious, then one scenario might be that government regulation would be more strict while the public is more environmentally-conscious. A second scenario would be that government regulation would be stricter while the public becomes less environmentally-conscious, and so on[105].
- **Brainstorm how to win in each scenario**. This would be the time to split the participants into 4 different groups, and assign one plausible future scenario to each group. First, ask them to think about the scenario. Ask them to visualize what the world would feel like under that scenario. Instruct the different teams to write a few news headlines for a day in that future. Ask the teams to *name* their scenarios. The more they *feel* what the future might be under their scenario—the better they would develop a winning strategy for it. Ask them to write the narratives for their plans under that scenario. Not only suggest strategies. Ask the teams to read their narratives to the entire group.
- **Consolidate into a single winning strategy**. As a large group, consolidate the strategies resulting from the different scenarios into a single strategy that would allow your company to win under all 4 scenarios, or most of them.

The resulting strategy from scenario planning would provide a general, long-term direction. Specific products, services, processes, or business models could emerge from it later. You should repeat the scenario planning process every 5 years or so, as the future becomes the present. The result from a Scenario Planning workshop I facilitated in 2002 at Texas Instruments was a decision to enter the

---

[105] If those were actually two of the driving forces, I would expect those to be combined into one, as over the long run it is safe to assume that the government represents the will of the people. Although the government doesn't always do that...

almost non-existent market for mobile Wi-Fi. TI later became the leader in the market (with 60% market share) once it emerged.

WAR GAMES

A business war game is more tactical than scenario planning. Its goal is to help position the company better in its immediately competitive environment. Companies tend to *underestimate* their competitors and their motivation to win. The competitors are assumed to always be one step behind you. Other companies, albeit the minority, tend to *overestimate* their competitors and avoid trying to beat them. Most importantly—they don't really know their competitors, and as a result, develop strategies in a vacuum. A good source on this process is Benjamin Gilad's book *Business War Games*.

In March 2006 I facilitated a War Game. In preparation, I divided the participants into teams representing the major competitors in the field. I instructed them to study those competitors well, and start thinking about ways those competitors could beat our company. One of the engineers dismissed my request, explaining that he was afraid that if his war-game team devised a good way to beat our local team—we would have to revise our strategy and product roadmap and, being an engineer in the company—*he* would be the one who would have to implement it. He didn't want change. I realized that there was something missing: a strong enough motivation to win when you play one of the competitors, even if the motivation was extrinsic. I asked the business unit manager for a $2,000 bonus to be split among the 4 members of the winning team. The team that included that same engineer eventually won the game. The steps of a War Game are:

- ***Identify 3-5 competitors.*** Some of them could be *specific* companies, while others could be a combination of several competitors with relatively similar characteristics. Including 10 competitors in the game would make it a very long game, and not as productive.

- **Define the meaning of winning.** How does one team win? Highest market share? Biggest increase in market share? Winning a specific customer bid? Anything else? The definition of *winning* must be aligned with the real business unit's objectives.

- **Define the Judges.** Who should be judging what happened after every round of the game? Not only must you identify specific people, but you also must decide who they represent. Often, the judges represent the customers in that market.

- **Have the team become the competitors.** Once you assigned people to teams, they must learn who "their company" is. They must identify with that company. They must read biographies of the decision-makers in that company and become them. During the game, they must make decisions likely to be made by those people. Whenever I facilitate war games I ask the participants to identify themselves by the names of those executives. This increased their ability to project the behavior of the competitors in reality.

- **Play the game in rounds.** Each team opens with a short list of strategic actions they would take. Those could be product announcements, acquisitions, or anything else that makes sense. The judges determine whether those actions are realistic, but they are instructed to err on stretching imagination, to some extent. Once all teams announced their "moves" for the round, and after the judges "adjusted" their moves, if appropriate, the judges would announce how the market has changes as a result of those moves. Who gained market share? Who lost? What changed? The teams would now break to plan their moves for the next round in response to the results of the first round and with the goal (winning) in mind. A good time frame for a round is one year, but it depends on the industry's rhythm. If the game starts in 2016, play a round for 2016, 2017, 2018, etc. Play no more than 5 rounds, although once you start realizing that the moves are too unrealistic, or no new significant moves are created, let the teams know that the next round is the last round, so "give it everything you've got."

- **Determine who the winner is** It is important to make that decision, and give the bonus that motivated the teams to win.

- **Modify the strategy.** You are done with the game, and should now ask yourself: what should our team do to win in the real world, especially if it didn't win in the game. The strategy is easy to determine if your "local" team won the game, but in a well-executed game this might not happen. The entire team must now wear their original, "local team" hats and devise a strategy to win if the competitors acted as projected in the game. Don't fall back to underestimating them.

Our "local" team lost the 2006 war game. Unfortunately, the lessons learned from the game were not taken seriously, and the business unit continued "as usual." Quite a few of the events and strategic moves projected during the game took place in the following 2-3 years. One warning about war games: make sure you "unwind" the emotions that tend to build up during this highly adversarial workshop. Relationships have been known to be affected by such simulations. To read more about how a war-game can go terribly wrong, read about the Millennium Challenge military exercise, conducted in 2002. Don't just read what was officially published... Another tool that should be mentioned in this context is the use of game-theory. It is somewhat similar to conducting a war-game, but using computer simulation and game theory algorithms instead[106].

TRIZ

TRIZ is a unique problem-solving technique. It was created by Genrich Altshuler in Russia in 1946. The acronym (although in Russian[107]) stands for "Theory of Inventive Problem Solving." The basic premise of TRIZ is that history repeats itself, and therefore the problem in front of you was already solved in another time, another place, and another industry. All you must do is find how it was solved *there*, and apply that solution *here*. TRIZ development took decades (including 25 years that Alshuler spent in a Soviet Gulag after being arrested for suspicion of disclosing state secrets through his method, and was released only after Stalin's death) of reviewing millions of patents, extracting the *generic problems* that they solved and the *generic solutions* for them. The process is highly *prescriptive*. It is illustrated in the following diagram and includes 4 steps:

---

[106] www.openoptions.com
[107] теория решения изобретательских задач, pronounced: teoriya resheniya izobretatelskikh zadach.

- Identify your *specific problem*. You must identify the root problem. It often calls for asking "why?" many times, until you found that root problem.
- Find a *generic TRIZ problem* that is the most similar to your specific problem. The problem is typically defined as a *contradiction* between two conflicting characteristics or needs.
- Lookup the *generic TRIZ solution* (or several possible ones) for that generic TRIZ problem.
- Translate the possible TRIZ solution into the terms of your specific problem, and you have your *specific solution!*

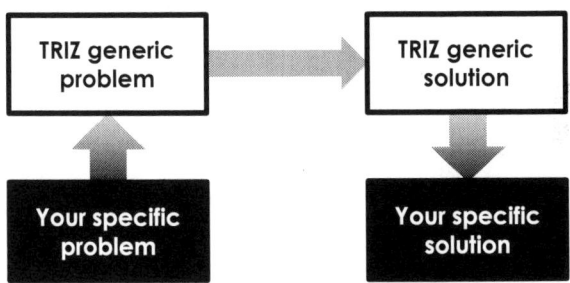

Sounds pretty simple, doesn't it? The most similar concept to TRIZ is the concept of the legal *precedent*, in which you find previous cases with relatively similar (and applicable) circumstances, and the court decisions that were rendered as a result. In fact, this method is so *prescriptive*, that an algorithm (*ARIZ, the Algorithm for Inventive Problem Solving*[108]) was developed to help automate the process.

One of TRIZ's key principles is that every problem could be described as a *contradiction*. Take, for example, an airplane's landing gear. In the early days (and in some planes today), the landing gear was fixed. Having a landing gear is a great feature for airplanes when they take off or land. Otherwise, the paint on the bottom of the plane can really get scratched… However, in the air, the landing gear adds drag, and as a result slows the plane down and increases fuel consumption. There is a contradiction between the need for the

---

[108] https://triz-journal.com/ariz-algorithm-inventive-problem-solving/

landing gear to be there for landing, and the need for it to not be there during flight.

Altshuler identified 39 different technical characteristics that could contradict with each other. He then, based on his review of millions of patents, identified 40 *Inventive Principles* that were used in those patents to solve those contradictions. He created a table that linked standard solutions to any possible contradiction. In the landing gear example, the appropriate standard solution would be *separation in time*. The landing gear would be down (and, preferably, locked…) at one time for takeoff and landing, and up (and aerodynamically covered) during another time—flight.

TRIZ has evolved over the years, as more patents were researched, and as practitioners continued to refine the technique.

There are two keys to the effective use of TRIZ. The first is the ability to use *analogies*. On one hand, you should be able to find an analogy to your problem in one of the TRIZ contradictions (or, if expanded, in any other problem that existed and was solved before). They may look very different, and your strength would be in realizing that they share a lot in common and suffer from the same basic root problem (or contradiction). On the other hand, you must be able to translate how the generic solution could apply to your specific circumstances. What would *separation in time* or *separation in space* mean to the problem at hand?

The second key is *breadth* of knowledge that was discussed in chapter 10. The TRIZ table might not always provide the answer, but the TRIZ principles may still be valid. As long as you have a broad enough knowledge of problems that were solved in other disciplines and industries, far remote from your area.

Here is a real example. As my team began developing penveu, I noticed in one of my visits to the lab that when the device was pointing at the screen, there were times in which the pointer was very jittery. I asked one of the developers why, and he explained that the camera on the pen was always looking for the best quality target (it could see more than one target at any time) and calculated position based on where that target was in the field of view. Sometimes the pen would "abandon" one target in favor of another one that was clearer to see, and the position calculation (due to rounding errors, among other things) would be slightly off, even if only by one pixel. That one pixel "jitter" was annoying to the human eye.

"Do you know how GPS positioning works?" I suddenly asked him. He didn't know. It was far from his area of expertise, computer vision. I explained that GPS systems faced a very similar problem, until GPS developers decided that the selection of the satellites used to calculate position would be done not only by the quality of signals received from them, but also by their relative position to one another, such that it would minimize triangulation errors.

"Why don't we use that here?" I asked. So he did, and the jittering problem disappeared. I used TRIZ principles to solve this problem. I found a problem in a different field with similar characteristics to our problem, and applied the generic solution used there to our case. We couldn't have done it had I not know how GPS works.

In 2000, after decades of cooperation with Russian scientists, Samsung decided to adopt TRIZ. In 2004 alone the company trained more than 1,000 engineers in using the technique, leading to 50 new patents, and saved the company over $100m in a single project[109]. Just sayin'...

---

[109] Forbes: *What Makes Samsung Such An Innovative Company?* http://www.forbes.com/sites/haydnshaughnessy/2013/03/07/why-is-samsung-such-an-innovative-company/2/#749a5dca7398

BOWLING WITH A CRYSTAL BALL

Once I was part of a panel at the University of Texas, faced with the question "where do great ideas come from?" Other panelists gave their answers, but when it was my turn, I said: "from the future, of course!" The fifth ideation method described here is based on forecasting the most aggressive technology trends, identifying future opportunities for market disruption, and acting on them now, as was described in my first book, now in a second edition, *Bowling with a Crystal Ball*.

In *The Innovator's Dilemma* Clayton Christensen focused on specific *markets*, and how technology could disrupt them. In 1998, in an executive briefing at Stanford University he told a story of when he consulted to Intel executives, right after *The Innovator's Dilemma* was published, and how Andrew grove, the founder and then Intel CEO said: "what you are describing is not *disruptive* technologies, but rather *trivial* technologies with disruptive *implementations*." Now, don't get me wrong, both Christensen and Grove are heroes of mine, but I have to disagree with both of them.

Technology disrupts markets. I agree with that. However, when I have to decide whether to focus on a *market* (like Christensen did) or the *technology*, I would focus on the technology every day of the week, and twice on Tuesday. Focusing on the market causes you to accept "the rules of the game." The more you know the market, current players, current product and technologies, the more you identify with the market with its dynamics, and the less you accept that it could be disrupted. When you are a market insider, it is hard for you to see what's outside that has the potential to disrupt it.

Case in point: in 1997, I was the CEO of a small Voice over IP (VoIP, except that back then it was called "Internet Telephony") startup. I visited Korea (South, even though I believe my birthday is celebrated in North Korea...) and met with the second largest telephone provider, trying to convince them that packet switching (VoIP) would eventually replace circuit switching (the old way of establishing a telephone connection) because it was more efficient and, therefore, less expensive. They refused to listen. Mostly because they were worried that due to its lower costs, this new technology might cannibalize their business. They were right. It did. But instead of doing it themselves—they allowed others to do it to them.

Now back to my disagreement with Christensen and Grove. I am a believer in disrupting markets with *cutting edge* technologies and not trivial ones. Trivial technologies are, well, trivial. More than anything they are *predictable* and somewhat obvious. Cutting edge technologies, with the fastest moving trends (such as processing power, storage capacity, silicon size, power consumption, and the like) are less obvious and appear, incorrectly, to be unpredictable, simply because of their fast pace of change. The fastest moving technologies enable today what could not have been imagined two years ago, and would enable in two years what could not be imagined today.

The foundation for this technique includes the forecasting of the fastest-paced technologies, taking an outsider's view of different markets they may disrupt, and identifying the new value they could bring to those markets through the introduction of new products, services, or business models that couldn't be implemented with today's technology performance. The process begins with technology forecasting and then shifts to markets. Not the other way around.

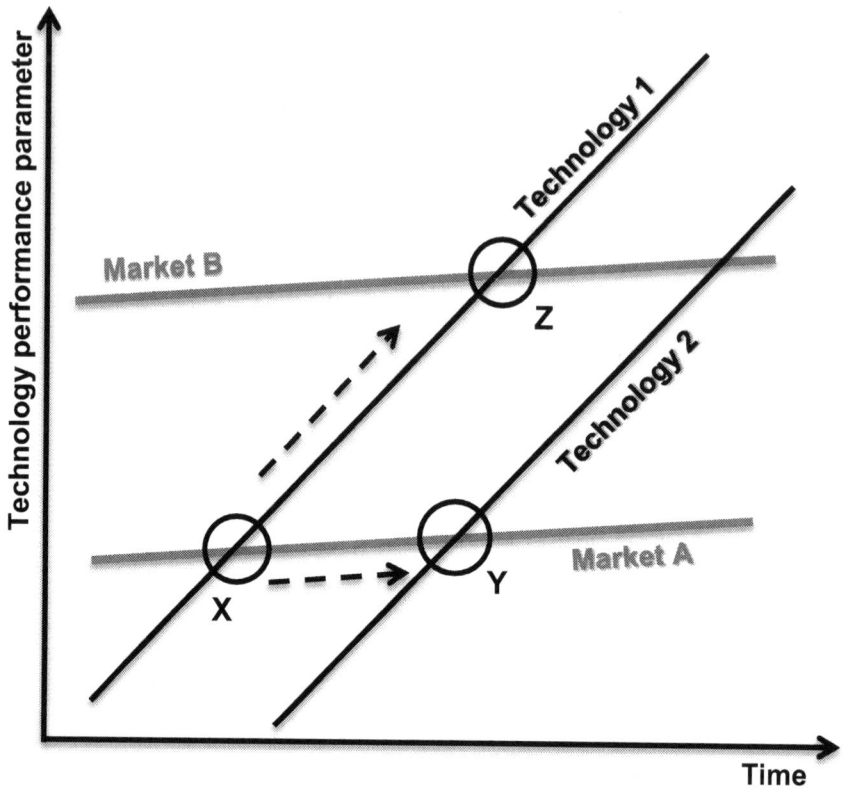

The diagram shows that Technology 1 would initially disrupt market A at point X. Christensen's approach warrants that you watch Market A and look for technologies that may disrupt it further (such as Technology 2 at point Y). However, it is hard to find which technology has such potential. Instead, I suggest following Technology 1 and identify additional markets it has the potential of disrupting. This is how you could identify point Z, in which it would disrupt Market B. Follow the *technology*, not the *Market*. The shrinking of hard disk drives, combined with continuously reducing power consumption, allowed Apple in 2001 to take a PC-based component (the hard disk drive) and disrupt the portable music player market with the first iPod, offering an unprecedented amount of music (1,000 songs) that could be stored on a single device, and a completely new way of selling, delivering, and consuming music. That same trend helped me, in 2004, find the opportunity to create USB 3.0.

Facilitating a *Bowling with a Crystal Ball* ideation workshop begins with research of technology trends. The book by that name explains how to do that. You must study technologies that have the potential to disrupt your market, even if you don't exactly know how. Forecasting battery or electric motor technology trends to predict disruptions to the automotive industry might be more obvious than researching processing power and storage capacity trends. The former would help envision an electric car, which already exists. The latter would help envision a self-driving car. Both should be done. Once those projections are made and trends plotted, move 7-10 years into the future along those trend lines. Focus on the opportunities then. The question to be asked (and answered) at the workshop is: "what could be done with the technologies that would be available in 7 years that couldn't be done today?"

IDEA

The purpose of the IDEA workshop is to find the next product or service for *your* company, but unlike some of the other processes described here—it is based on core capabilities and technology your company already owns, and things you already know. It is potentially more incremental than some of the other processes, but would still allow for some disruptive innovation to occur.

IDEA begins with research done by different people in the company, bringing their domain knowledge to the table, but also conducting research of *adjacent* technologies, applications, and capabilities.

On one hand (on the right of the diagram in the next page), this process brings knowledge of three "Tiers" of applications. Tier 1 includes the applications currently used in the industry, and that the company is involved with. Like with *Bowling with a Crystal Ball*, participants are asked to forecast trends in those. Tier 2 includes adjacent applications. For example, if the focus is on wireless communications, then adjacent applications may include non-wireless communications and their evolution trends. Tier 3 would include somewhat remote applications, for which it gets harder to see a relationship between those and the core applications that the company is currently involved with. In the example of communications, these could be non-communication electronics, processors, etc.

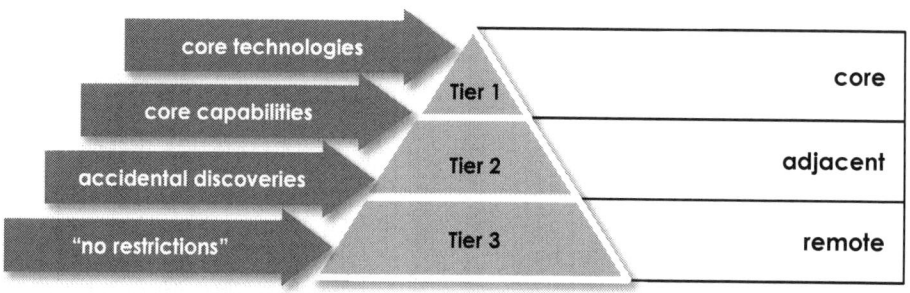

disrupting forces   **application tiers**

On the other hand (on the left), those trends are contrasted with 4 "disrupting forces" which, again, should be researched before the workshop. Those include:

- ***Core technologies*** that the company is involved with. Those have to be defined at their very basic technological level, disconnected from the applications they are used in. Defining the core technologies in terms of the applications they serve could bias and limit the thought process.

- ***Core capabilities*** that company employees (typically, but not limited to, the engineers) have. Those, too, must be disconnected from applications and technologies in which those capabilities are used.

- ***Accidental discoveries***. Often engineers make accidental discoveries "in the line of duty," and typically put them aside or forget them because they did not solve a problem they had at the time. Employees should be interviewed to find what accidental discoveries they made.

Those are legitimate discoveries, and may apply to future products or services the company is seeking to invent.

- **"No restriction" ideas.** Often people tend to assume restrictions that do not exist. Sometimes those restrictions do exist, though. "What could I do if restriction X didn't exist?" is a question not asked often enough. However, for the purpose of the IDEA workshop, it should.

During this ideation workshop, the 7 elements (3 on the right and 4 on the left) would be contrasted to generate new ideas.

DON'T GO BACK TO SQUARE ONE

In 2009, I facilitated an ideation workshop in a public technology company. By the end of the first half day I realized that the solutions proposed by the different teams were "safe." They were not imaginative enough. They were not far-fetching enough. In fact, they were pretty incremental. I then joined one of the teams to see how they brainstormed, and that's when I had an epiphany. The team was doing all the right things. They started by defining the problem they wanted to solve. One team member proposed an idea. Another had built on it, they all got excited, and the idea kept developing with growing excitement, until someone (the team's designated "devil's advocate") pointed out that the idea would generate a secondary problem. This would sound something like this: "guys, if we did X, then Y would happen..." Everybody seemed deflated. As if they celebrated too soon. He was right—if they had tried their solution, they may have solved the initial problem, but would have created a secondary problem with their initial solution.

"Back to the drawing board!" was the team consensus.

And there lies the problem. We are conditioned to only solve one problem at a time. The effort to solve the initial problem came to a complete halt when the initial solution created a secondary problem, and the team went *back to square one.*

There is a very simple thing you must do to avoid this conundrum. Think of creative problem solving as playing a board game. You start at square one. You throw the dice, and overcome a hurdle that takes you all the way to square five. However, there is another problem in square five. In the game you wouldn't go back to square one, but rather keep fighting the new problem in square 5.

Why not do the same in creative problem solving? When you encounter a secondary problem—try solving the secondary problem. Don't immediately abandon the first solution and go back to square one. Maybe the solution to the secondary problem is not very difficult? Maybe once you solved the secondary problem you would be home free with a new, very creative solution to the original problem you were set out to solve? Give yourself (and your team) some rope in how far (and how long) you should go before you finally decide to go back to square one. Don't give up after encountering the first secondary problem. Start down a path, and keep solving problems until you reached a dead end. Or until the solution becomes unattractive anymore, or you have spent too much time without seeing the end in sight. Only then go back to square one. Not sooner.

THE STRENGTH OF THE IDEATION WORKSHOP FACILITATOR

The skills required by the workshop facilitator were discussed earlier in this chapter, as well as in chapter 11. One of the strengths of a great ideation workshop facilitator has is the mastery of many tools, and ability to combine and customize them to the specific problem or goals of the specific workshop, and to the specific technologies and markets the company is in. A facilitator who only knows how to use one tool and swears by it would not be as effective as the master of many tools who can combine them.

17.

IMPLEMENTATION: RUBBER MEETS THE ROAD

So you have a great idea. Or your team has a great idea. How do you know if it's really great? What do you do with it now?

THE FAILURE OF THE INNOVATION FUNNEL

In chapter 9 I told you the story of the Texas Instruments engineer in Israel who felt that his management failed to see the value of the many product ideas he brought to them. He was frustrated, but at the same time he failed to pursue his ideas beyond presenting them to his management, "uncooked," and expecting them to take it from there which, in this case, they didn't.

You see, most companies deploy the classic "innovation funnel." Employees bring ideas to the "judges" at management, who decide whether they have value or not, and what to do with them. There are three problems with that practice. The first is that management has some of the most *unqualified* people to judge those ideas. I'm not being cynical, nor am I trying to berate management. I really mean it. This applied to me, as well. Think about it: the management "evaluator" doesn't know the technology half as much (probably not even tenth as much) as the engineer who brought the idea, and had never done a thorough market research. How is he expected to know if this is a good idea or not?

Stevens and Burley's article (*3,000 raw ideas = 1 commercial success!*) suggested that for every single business success—3,000 ideas were brought forward. This brings the second problem: how much time do you think management has to spend on screening those ideas, knowing that it would take 3,000 of them to get one right? Given that they probably cannot spend more than 5 minutes on each (the amount of time it took evaluators I observed to decide whether an idea presented to them was worth filing as a patent or not), how long do you think it would take them to judge 3,000 ideas? (Don't bother, I'll tell you: more than 31 full working days.) And finally, the third problem is that since the "judges" have no more than 5 minutes to spend evaluating every idea, what do you think are the probabilities of false negatives (rejecting good ideas) or false positives (accepting bad ones)?

Here is what you must do as a manager to avoid those three problems altogether. First—eliminate two sentences from your lexicon: "I'll be the judge of that" and "I'll know it when I see it." Second, when an employee comes to you with what she believes is a great idea, don't discourage her. Don't tell her it's a great idea, either. You don't know that. Simply ask "what do you need to get it done?" In most cases employees would not know what it takes to get it done. At least not right then. Send them to find out. They would have to collaborate with others to find the answer. They may not like what they learn. Once they find the answer (if they didn't already know it), say the following. Repeat after me:

"This is what it would take for me to say *yes* and give you the resources you need."

At this point, hand them a piece of paper that includes your conditions to fund the project and allocate the required resources. Those conditions may include market size, competitiveness, alignment with company core competencies, development of new skills, and everything you consider when *you* make those decisions.

You would be amazed at the impact of this empowering statement. One of your conditions could certainly be that this cannot be at the expense of their existing commitments and projects. That's fair game. Another could be that they must get "buy in" from others who are needed to get the product to market. That helps in the "self-selection" and "self-evaluation" of projects. Think about it—if you knew that the employees who would have to manufacture that product, those who would have to sell it to customers, and even those who have to find a budget for it within the company's overall budget have "bought into" this idea—why would you say no to it? If you could still find a reason to say no—make sure that it is part of the conditions listed upfront on that piece of paper.

When I worked on launching USB 3.0 at Texas Instruments, I didn't get management approval. In that 7am meeting, the senior VP said *no*. But I ignored the rejection. I approached the best engineers in our group and told each one of them: "I need your help on this project. Management did not approve it. You can't tell anyone, and if you do—you could get in trouble, and I can't help you then." Little did I know that this was a value proposition to them... People like to be involved in mysterious, secretive, and exciting programs. That was the whole attraction at Lockheed to join the Skunk Works group.

Reduce to writing the conditions under which you would be willing to fund the project, and when someone comes to you with an idea—give them that sheet and tell them "here is what it would take for me to say *yes* and give you the resources you need." That document is the boundary agreement, and in the following pages I will discuss what it should contain.

Let me just be clear about one thing. I know exactly what I'm asking you to do. I'm asking you to empower your employees to make funding decision themselves. I know, it's a scary thought, but let me summarize the advantages and disadvantages of replacing the current, classic *innovation funnel* and review committee with a *boundary agreement*. Here are the advantages:

- More qualified evaluators. Managers and executives are the least qualified to judge those ideas. They do that merely because they control budget and resources. When you move the decision point to the employees, you moved it to the people who know the technology, the market, and the customers the most.

- If those who are the most qualified to evaluate projects would make funding decisions, the probability of false positives (funding a bad project) or false negatives (rejecting a good project) would be minimized.

- Giving employees the "big picture" view (how projects fit within the entire company) and the understanding of their impact on the company's success would give them autonomy that, in turn, would positively affect their creativity.

- Giving employees the power to make funding decisions empowers them. They would feel like partners, and would consider things just like you do. You are not the only person who can make informed decisions. Your employees would stop asking you for things that you think are unreasonable. Finally, they would understand what it feels to be you.

- Giving employees the decision power would also teach them new things, such as budgeting, project management, communications, and managerial responsibilities. Things they would otherwise never learn. With that—you would be developing the next generation of leaders, managers, and executives in the company. Maybe even the next CEO.

- Allowing employees to make funding and resource allocation decisions would increase the throughput of the company's ability to make such decisions. You would no longer be the bottleneck. Decision-making would become scalable.

- Finally, it would reduce your own workload and stress. No longer would you need to make funding decisions for projects you know very little about. Your time could free up to set the vision and direction for the company and develop employees.

However, I cannot discuss the advantages without the disadvantages of moving decision-making to the employees. There is only one:

- You must trust the employees, and create an environment in which they will earn this trust. See chapter 9.

I would offer a word of caution, though. Just like not all employees embrace autonomy—some would not want to take decision-making responsibility, either. In many cases, it could be tied to their fear of you, or fear that was instilled in them by a previous boss who made failure very painful for them. Don't give employees decision-making powers if they are not ready or willing to accept it.

THE BOUNDARY AGREEMENT

In 2000, PCTEL was on track to reach $100 million in sales. The company was founded only five years earlier, which made that milestone all the more impressive. That year, the company was named the second fastest growing company in Silicon Valley, following Yahoo! I had just sold Voyager Technologies to PCTEL, and became one of the company's director-level leaders. One afternoon I was asked by the CEO's executive assistant to go to one of the larger conference rooms. Eighteen of my peers, across all functions, from engineering to marketing, human resources, finance, and more were gathered there. Nobody seemed to know why we were summoned, until the CEO walked into the room. He told us that we were selected to develop a plan for the company to reach $120 million of revenue in 2001. There were no further rules, except that this work could not come at the expense of our other responsibilities. There was not a single executive in that room. We were all director-level and below. We were extremely busy people, but nobody complained about this extra work. This was one of the most empowering moments of my professional career.

That piece of paper that you give employees when you say "here is what it would take for me to say *yes* and give you the resources you need" is called the *boundary agreement*. It defines all the terms and conditions that, if met, would guarantee (I realized this is a strong word) funding and resource allocation.

Developing the boundary agreement sounds a lot simpler than it really is. When I proposed to an executive who attended one of my workshops to reduce his resource-allocation decision process to writing, it was clear to both of us that it was not going to be a simple task. The funding and resource allocation decisions are some of the most important processes in the life of a company. They are also evolving processes, which changes over time, as circumstances change. For those reasons, they almost never exist in written form. How are you expected to reduce these to writing? Plus, part of it is *intuitive*, isn't it? You use your gut to guide you in making those decisions, don't you? How do I expect you to reduce that to writing if you can't even explain why your gut told you that one project should be funded while another shouldn't?

However, some parts of this process could be reduced to writing and provided to your creative employees. Here are a few examples:

- The fundamentals of a good business plan. As an investor, I can relatively quickly tell you what makes a good business plan. You have to show 4 things: that you are proposing something *different* (preferably *very* different) than anything existing today; You must show that there is *value* in those differences to a specific segment of the target market; You must show that you have a way to gain and maintain *competitive advantage* over competitors, current and potential; Finally, you have to demonstrate a strong return on investment. First and foremost—to your customers. Then to your company, and then to investors or shareholders, as applicable. While initially this was going to be a significant part of this book, I decided not to include it here, and instead turned it into an online course titled *Business Plan through investors' eyes*[110]. These are the fundamentals. These can be reduced to writing. Simply demand that a business plan is created that meets those 4 criteria.

---

[110] https://www.udemy.com/business-plan-through-investors-eyes/

- Certain realities in the company could be stated quite clearly as well. For one, you know what the budget constraints are, what the cash-flow limitations are, and also debt and investment restrictions. Identify those, and require that any proposed new business complies with them. If your company has $200 million in liquid assets, a $2 billion budget is unlikely to be feasible. Probably even a $100 million budget is not feasible. What is?

- It is fair game to state that the new business cannot come at the expense of existing businesses or work-in-progress, unless the existing projects are specifically abandoned. In other words—this cannot come at the expense of your "day job." The new project is always shinier than the current one, but if there is no reason to abandon the existing project, which still meets the criteria as it did the day it was funded—don't abandon it! I'll prepare you: you will always have employees propose a project, and once you get excited, will ask to work on that project full time. Don't allow that. You would find that if they are truly excited about the prospects of the new project, they would find a way to do both. They would borrow and steal resources, but do both. If they are not willing to step back from the ultimatum—they don't believe in the new project enough. Self-selection in action! At the same time, never say "I'll take it from here." Never take the new project off their hands. I've been there. It's not fun. I would be perfectly happy in maintaining my "day job" along with the new project.

- As one of the conditions, you may require that an "all-star" team within the company would be involved in the project. This would significantly increase the probability of success (and reduce false positives and false negatives in the selection). Don't name specific people. Let the proposers find a team, but insist this would be an "all-star" team. Define "all-star" for them.

- Don't build *bargaining room* in the boundary agreement. Don't include a rule stating that a project cannot take more than 6 months and cost no more than $250,000, and then approve exceptions when they tell you it is impossible. It makes the entire boundary agreement seem arbitrary and non-binding. Don't be too specific and don't over-complicate it. Instead, try to stay at the conceptual, principle level. Leave it somewhat to interpretation. Leave room for tradeoffs. You should convey the *philosophy* behind resource allocation decisions rather than strict, arbitrarily guidelines. The more high-level, conceptual, and principle-based the boundary agreement is, the less you would have to change it over time. Modifications to it should be rare, and be the exception, not the rule.

- Despite that last point, especially in the early days (or years) of the boundary agreement—accept that it might have to change as "rubber meets the road." The agreement might look great on paper, but as Field marshal Helmuth Karl Bernhard Graf von Moltke (1800-1891) said: "no campaign plan survives first contact with the enemy."[111] Involve the employees in making changes to the boundary agreement. Whenever you encounter a situation that is not covered by the boundary agreement, instead of unilaterally changing it, involve the employees and discuss the changes to the agreement. In fact, get them involved from the initial creation of the boundary agreement. That level of ownership in the creation of that agreement would make them treat it differently.

So, instead of asking your employees to propose new business ideas to you, forcing you to make the needed resource-allocation decisions, involve them in the creation of a high-level, principle-based boundary agreement, and ask them to only present businesses that meet the criteria of that agreement. Remember the "success curve" by which 3,000 ideas became one market success? As the following figure shows, the current "handoff" happens when 3,000 ideas are presented to managers, who start making decisions. Using a boundary agreement would move the "handoff" point at least to where only 125 small-scale projects are presented to get more significant funding. That change alone represents a 24-fold reduction in management effort, and reduces the probability of false positives and false negatives, since decisions leading to that point would be made by those who have the best information and expertise to make them.

---

[111] https://steveblank.com/2010/04/08/no-plan-survives-first-contact-with-customers-%E2%80%93-business-plans-versus-business-models/

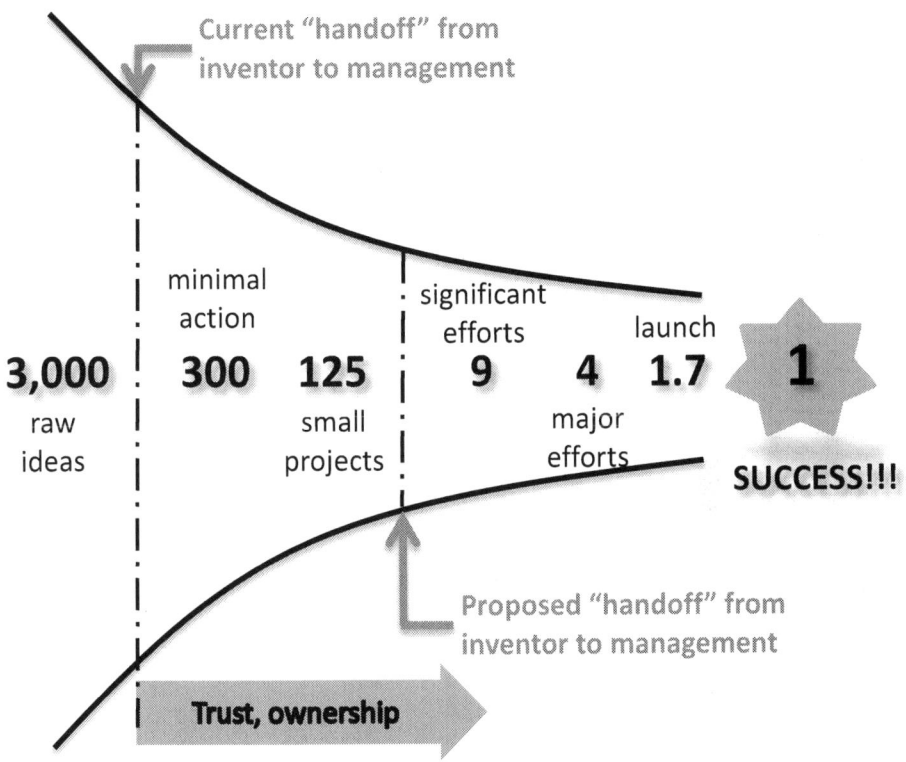

All it takes is giving employees the authority to allocate resources to the magnitude of 1-3 man-years and limited funding, within the confines of the boundary agreement. You haven't yet authorized, nor does the boundary agreement require you to give a blank check to fund millions of dollars or more. Note that there is a huge difference between *forcing* employees to spend one day a week being creative, and *allowing* them to authorize 1-3 man years for a small proof-of-concept project. As Ben Rich, who took over Lockheed's Skunk Works group after Kelly Johnson and delivered the stealth F-117A fighter jet, wrote[112]:

---

[112] *Skunk Works: A Personal Memoir of My Years of Lockheed* by Ben R. Rich, Leo Janos

"Lockheed's management agreed that Kelly could keep his tiny research and development operation running—the first in the aviation industry—as long as it was kept on a shoestring budget and didn't distract the chief engineer from his principal duties."

Once this process proved itself, trust would start building between the management who "owns" the resources and the employees who are now authorized to allocated them (at least in part), as chapter 9 showed, and as that trust builds—that point of demarcation could move further to the right, leaving bigger decisions in the hands of those are have the most information and expertise. And as this continues—the boundary agreement would continue to evolve.

18.

DO IT AGAIN

Chapter 13 described the 4 phases of increasing employee creativity and organizational innovation in your company. Those were introspection, intervention, ideation, and implementation. The 4 phases were described in detail in chapters 14-17. However, this should forever be an ongoing task, and you must continue executing all 4 phases. First of all, continue to assess employee creativity, the company's level of innovation, the organizational climate, and team dynamics. You should create an annual plan to do those. It would likely take at least a year before you could start observing real change.

After a while, the efforts in the intervention, ideation, and implementation phases would start showing results. Measure them. This is not something you would do only once. If you lose momentum, you would have lost every improvement you gained. You must continue to press on. The hardest task is to maintain the level of effort and work.

Chapter 13 recommended that you don't try to roll out a program to the entire company. At least don't do it in year one. However, as positive results start to show, it would be a great opportunity to start introducing this work to other areas in the company. Don't *force* other departments to follow suit. Entice them. Show them how *they* can change, based on what you had achieved in your group.

Your assessments in the second year should link to specific intervention and training efforts done in the first year. This would be an opportunity for you to see which intervention and training efforts helped, and which didn't. Drop what didn't work, and do more of what did, until it doesn't improve anymore. Remember to implement new hiring processes.

YEAR 1 PLAN

At this time, you should put together a "plan of attack" with a simple goal: *increase employee creativity and company innovation*. The plan must have the following characteristics:

- The objectives for the short term (one year) and long term (5-10 years) must be clearly stated. Short-term objectives may focus less on *outcomes*, since it would take more than one year to see significant impact on outcomes. The short-term objectives should focus on specific *activities* that must take place. For example, objectives may include: complete an innovation index and corporate culture assessment and establish a baseline for both; hold 4 ideation sessions for the business unit, etc. An objective such as "increase innovation index by 20%" should be avoided in the first year, especially since you haven't established a baseline yet.

- The plan should be *achievable*. You must find the "middle of the road" between unattainable goals and goals that are too easy to achieve. Read the definition of BHAG (Big Hairy Audacious Goals) in *Built to Last*. The goals should be *stretch* goals.

- The plan should be limited in *scope*. Don't try to roll out the plan to the entire company. Start small. Choose one business unit or team that needs to produce new ideas and work with that business unit. In most likelihood—this would be *your* business unit.

- Remember the 80:20 rule. The plan must allow you to spend 100% of the effort on 20% of the areas that would deliver 80% of the results.

- Once the plan is done, communicate it continuously, and implement is consistently and persistently. Don't slack off. Every minor transgression could have devastating consequences to innovation.

- The plan should include elements of all 4 stages to be complete.

The following is an example of a year 1 plan. It is only an example. Your year 1 plan could be different from it. It's a good starting point to make sure you didn't forget anything:

- **Introspection**
  - Establish a baseline *Growth Innovation Index* in Q1 and create instructions and rubrics to repeat it annually and consistently. In Q4, decide what would be the GII target for next year.
  - Perform KEYS assessment with 90%+ participation of employees in business unit A.
  - Use the *Creative Diversity Optimizer* to assess the product/design team in business unit A.
- **Intervention**
  - Using the *Creative Diversity Optimizer*, make team member changes to the product/design team in business unit A.
  - Revisit team leader selection, and make a change if needed.
  - Conduct executive leadership training workshops on organizational climate for creativity in Q1 and in Q3 to reinforce the importance.
  - Develop and conduct a creative team leadership training program for the team leader in Q1.
  - Modify hiring procedures to include creativity and risk-acceptance assessments, using the *Creative Diversity Optimizer* guidelines.
  - Assure that each team member creates and executes a technical training plan in their respective disciplines. The plan should be completed in Q1. Execution could start in Q1 or Q2.
- **Ideation**
  - Facilitate a *Scenario Planning* workshop in Q1.
  - Facilitate a short-term ideation workshop (*TRIZ, IDEA, Bowling with a Crystal Ball*, etc.) in Q2.
  - Facilitate a second short-term ideation workshop in Q3.
  - Select the best ideas from the ideation workshops and conduct a *War Game* workshop to simulate market acceptance in Q4.
  - Each ideation workshop above should include employee creativity training and team-building.
- **Implementation**
  - Develop a basic boundary agreement by Q2.
  - Have at least one team prepare a business plan that meets the boundary agreement terms and present it to management by Q3.
- **Overall**
  - Document what worked and what didn't. Present a report at the end of the year to the executive management.

YEAR 2 PLAN

Year 2 plan would differ from year 1 plan in several areas. First of all, it would require less introspection-assessment efforts. Some of the assessment efforts should be repeated every other year, or less often than that. Some of the intervention efforts may change, or be replaced with other efforts, depending on the assessment findings from year 1. Year 2 would be a great year to have a growth innovation index goal for the year, once its baseline was established in year 1. A different mix of ideation workshops could be used. Scenario Planning should not be facilitated more than once in five years. Year 2 would also present a great opportunity to "show off" successes to other business units and other areas in the company and help them start implementing the 4-step process as well.

Finally, in year 2 you should start including goals for *major* product development, and possibly product launches, depending on your industry and type of product, service, process, or business model your company develops.

epilogue.

MYTH BUSTING

This book opened with a few myths, considered common wisdom in Corporate America. Throughout the book I hope I busted those myths. It is only fair that in this epilogue, as a summary, I would revisit them and contrast them with reality, as it was described in the book. For each myth I included a reference to the chapter in which it was described (and debunked) in greater detail.

INNOVATION = CREATIVITY

Reality: while related, those are two different things. Innovation is the *organizational* function of introducing new, useful, and feasible products, services, processes, or business models. Creativity is the *individual* (or team of individuals') function that incorporates the cognitive ability to transcend traditional ideas, rules, patterns, and create meaningful and original new ideas. The relationship between the two can be described as: innovation is the implementation of creative ideas (Chapter 1).

INNOVATION = ENTREPRENEURSHIP AND STARTUPS

Reality: while most innovation originates in startup companies, some of the most innovative companies are mature and large (Apple was founded in 1976 and generates $228b. Google: 1998, $78b, Microsoft: 1975, $87b). The myth acts as a self-fulfilling prophecy and deters large companies from attempting to innovate like startups. 57% of the participants in my study experienced higher creativity levels in startups. However, 9% felt more creativity in mature companies. The rest experienced equal levels. Innovation is not restricted to startups. Large, mature companies can innovate (Chapter 3).

YOU WERE EITHER BORN CREATIVE, OR NOT. CREATIVITY CANNOT BE LEARNED OR EXERCISED.

Reality: this, as well, became a self-fulfilling prophecy, this time at the *personal* level, causing some to believe they are not creative, and shouldn't even try to be. In fact, creativity *is* learned, and can be exercised, like any other muscle in your body and cognitive process in your brain. It can be affected by your practices, by how you expose yourself to different ideas, let them incubate, trigger the executive part of your brain, and then relaxing to let it combine those old ideas into new ones. Great ideas may feel accidental, but they are not. You can put yourself where the likelihood of such "accidents" is greater (Chapter 12).

THERE IS NOTHING YOU CAN DO TO INCREASE INNOVATION ORGANICALLY IN YOUR COMPANY

Reality: just like individuals can increase their creativity levels through practicing certain things, so can companies. Since innovation is the implementation of individual (and team) creative ideas—an organization has three general degrees of freedom to increase creativity. The first is to hire more creative people. Hire people who already invested efforts to become more creative and are therefore more creative *now*. The second is to create a climate that motivates those individuals (and teams) to be more creative. The third is to institute an effective mechanism of self-selection of creative ideas to implement them, instead of the archaic "innovation funnel" (Chapters 13-18).

YOU MUST DRIVE INNOVATION

Reality: *driving* innovation is ineffective. Innovation is less like golf, and more like curling. You must *allow* it to happen. You cannot mandate it. You cannot force employees to be creative, but you could let them know that experimenting and failing are acceptable, as long as they learned from them. You could promote the behaviors that increase creativity, and discourage and eliminate the behaviors that reduce it. You must eradicate bureaucracy, internal politics, and internal competition (Chapter 9).

YOU MUST ESTABLISH INNOVATION SPACE AND ALLOCATE TIME FOR INNOVATION

Reality: Google was known to have allocated a day a week for employees to be creative and generate new ideas that are unrelated to their current assignment. Many companies have established innovation labs to provide physical space for employees to be creative. In reality, those didn't work since you couldn't control when and where ideas occur. The best you could do is to create a *climate* in which employees and teams become more creative, and the organization would implement the best ideas. This climate must exist 24 hours a day, 7 days a week (Chapter 9).

FINANCIAL INCENTIVES INCREASE CREATIVITY

Reality: financial incentives do not increase creativity. Experiments showed that monetary incentives *reduce* creativity. Financial incentives have been proven to increase productivity of simple and repetitive tasks. They fall under the category of *extrinsic* motivation. However, complex tasks, especially the creation of new ideas, are motivated *intrinsically*, from within the task itself. Supervisor and organizational encouragement, autonomy, and the right amount of resources would encourage creativity, while monetary bonuses would destroy it (Chapter 9).

INNOVATION REQUIRES SIGNIFICANT RESOURCES AND FUNDING

Reality: for decades companies measured innovation by the percentage of their sales that is reinvested in research & development (R&D). There is no evidence that the amount of money invested in R&D yielded better creativity. On the contrary—some companies proved that increasing the R&D investment correlated with lower increases in profitability. There is no doubt that employees need a minimum amount of resources to try new ideas. However, beyond a certain amount of resources the law of diminishing returns comes into play, and furthermore—you *could* have too many resources that would make you think less. As one of my research participants said: "…you have to be more creative when you have less resources, because you have to do more with less and it kind of spurs the creativity process."

INNOVATION INITIATIVES MUST BE IMPLEMENTED THROUGHOUT THE ENTIRE ORGANIZATION

Reality: The last thing you want to hear is that you have a "creative accounting" department… Recent regulations imposed more scrutiny on companies, and forced implementation of more stringent internal processes. The company must comply with those external regulations, but your "creative core," the product design team (or teams), responsible for developing new products, must be free from bureaucracy and regulations that do not apply to them. Your manufacturing and accounting teams would be subject to stringent regulations, but even they should treat those as *external* regulations, and not internal formalization that has built-in slack or buffers beyond what is mandated externally.

post-epilogue.
THREE TAKEAWAYS

FROM FEAR TO IMPLEMENTATION

Throughout this book I dissected employee creativity and company-level innovation piece by piece. I shared what research said about every piece, and offered ideas on how you should address each one. It is time to put it together again and show, at a very high level, how those pieces fit together. The next figure illustrates the big picture.

Creativity and innovation occur, and are affected at three levels: corporate, team, and individual. The flow diagram illustrates that you start with creativity (on the left side), affecting all three levels, starting with corporate climate, driven initially by fear, down to increasing the individual creativity level. Once there, you turn creativity into innovation (on the right side), by which individual creative ideas are implemented. The following diagram should be quite self-explanatory and clear at this point, but I will add references to chapters in this book. First, the company needs fear as a motivator (chapter 9). Because of that fear and having no other choice, it creates the right climate for employees to be creative (chapters 3 and 9). Team dynamics play an important role as well (chapters 10, 11, and 15). Finally, individuals are responsible for their own level of creativity through their actions (chapter 12). Sparking creative ideas is done through ideation workshops (chapter 16), the results of which are then turned into prototypes and business plans. A self-selection boundary agreement-based implementation mechanism replaces the traditional innovation funnel process (chapter 17).

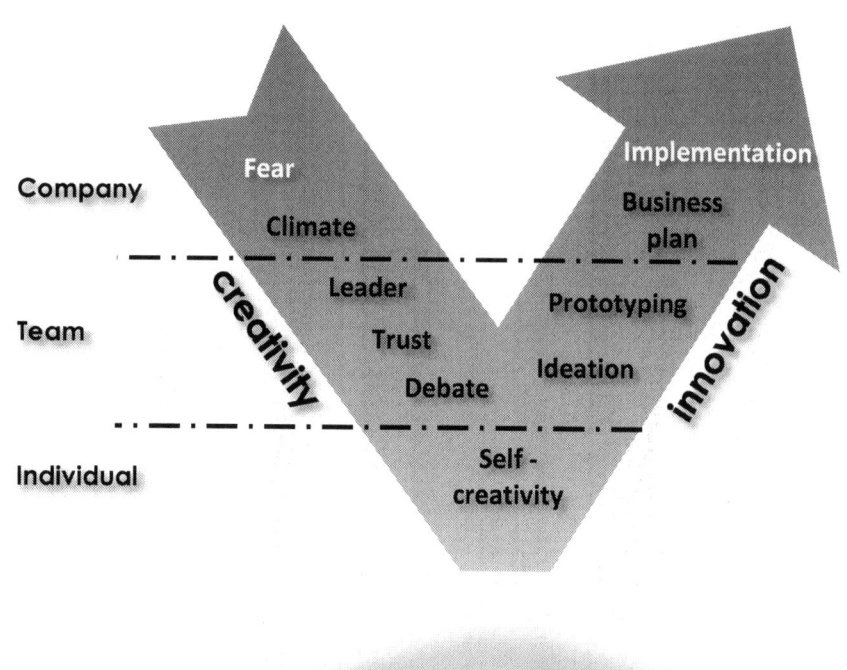

I hate saying goodbye, but it's time. In early 2016, I delivered my *un-kill creativity* executive workshop to an executive team of a Fortune 500 technology company in Florida. At the end, I was asked for the three key takeaways. Somehow, remembering three things is easier than remembering a long list. Here are the top three things that would increase innovation in your company the most. They are *small* things. They require no significant investment or budget. They don't require you to roll out a new infrastructure. They don't require company-wide training. All they require is a change of *attitude*. Yours. If you get a strong feeling of déjà vu, it's only because I repeated those many, many times throughout this book.

1. Accept that your job is not to *drive* innovation. Your job is to *allow* it. Your employees already know how important innovation is.

They know it's good. You don't have to sell it to them. All they need is the *freedom* to do it. Innovation is more like curling and less like golf. It's not the driving of the stone that gets it there—it's the swiping and altering the state of the ice in front of it that allows the stone to reach its destination. You can only make small adjustments.

2. Ask yourself: how would I react when one of my employees tells me that he tried something I didn't authorize and failed? If you react severely, demanding that next time he asks you first, and threatening consequences for trying unauthorized things—he would never do it again. However, you know who never fails? Those who never try. Accept that there would be trial and error on the way to success. Let your employees try, and help them get on their feet after they fail. This would give them the creative freedom to try again. When my year-old Maya started walking, she started running. Very quickly she fell. What was the first thing she did after she fell? No, she didn't cry. Instead, she looked at me to see how *I* reacted. My reaction clued her whether she should cry, or get up and keep going. When I yelled "oh, no!"—she would start crying. But when I called "get up! keep going!" she would get up and go.

3. When an employee comes to you with an idea, avoid saying "I'll be the judge of that." Replace it with "here is what would make me say *yes* to this." One of the most powerful factors affecting creativity (and thus innovation) is the sharing of the "big picture." If you share the big picture with your employees and let them know what would make you approve a product idea (and the budget and other resources they need)—you would force them to consider all aspects of their idea, and not just throw it over the fence for approval. You also reduce your workload (what a concept…), empower your employees, increase the probability that ideas are well vetted (your employees are in the front line of technology and customers, and are better positioned to assess the viability of their ideas. I'm sorry to say, but you are highly *unqualified* to vet an idea in your position…)

Do those three things and you are guaranteed to increase the level of innovation in your company by orders of magnitude. As a participant in one of my workshop said: it would be *transformative* to the company.

Try it.

ACKNOWLEDGEMENTS

In the middle of one night in 1995, I had an *aha!* moment. I had an idea for a product that connected your phones to the Internet and allowed you to place international calls for the price of a local call to your Internet service provider. In 1996, I thought it would be great if I could control my air-conditioner remotely, using my mobile phone, and started yet another company. This one happened 14 years before Tony Fadel left Apple to launch Nest. Both those companies eventually failed. They were too far ahead of their time. When I moved to the US in 1998, I joined Voyager Technologies, a tiny wireless engineering-for-hire company in Silicon Valley. It had 7 employees. I suggested we focused the company on two new emerging, yet barely heard of, wireless standards: 802.11b (which would later be branded *Wi-Fi*) and *Bluetooth*. That bet led to selling Voyager to PCTEL for almost $22 million in 2000, only a few months before the "dot-com" bubble burst, which hit Silicon Valley the hardest.

Bill Gross is the founder of *IdeaLab* in South California, responsible to the launch of companies such as tickets.com, Picasa, NetZero, and many more. He found that *timing* was the most deciding factor in the success of a company[113]. Timing accounted for 42% of the difference between success and failure[114]. Being at the right place at the right time.

---

[113]https://www.ted.com/talks/bill_gross_the_single_biggest_reason_why_startups _succeed?language=en#t-163802
[114]Followed by Team/Execution (32%), the quality of the idea (28%), the business model (24%), and funding (only 14%).

I found that there was another factor, not one bit less important: meeting the right *people*. As I look back at my professional career, and at what led to the writing of this book, I was fortunate to be at the right place, at the tight time, so I could meet the right *people*. I could write an entire book only to thank all the people who helped me get to where I am today, but here I would focus only on those who helped make this book come to life.

The book and the name for it were inspired by Professor Teresa Amabile from the Harvard Business School. Specifically, by an article she published in the Harvard Business School Review in 1998, the year I moved from Israel to Silicon Valley, called *How to Kill Creativity*. We never met, and only communicated once when I worked on my PhD dissertation, but she would forever be an inspiration to me. I read almost everything she ever wrote. The same applies to another Harvard Business School Professor, Clayton Christensen. I followed his work all the way back to his own Doctoral Research in 1992, and his tremendous contribution to the understanding of the dynamics of disruptive technologies.

Speaking of doctoral research, I wish to thank all those who helped me in mine. My initial plan was to study how certain content made people open emails with commercial value and forward them to friends. It was Dr. Cortlandt (Corty) Cammann, my mentor and dissertation committee chair, who helped me find my true passion for creativity in the workplace, which resulted in my two-year study (*From Startup to Maturity*), my new practice, and this book. Whenever I was stuck—he was my sounding board. He was my guide, and my friend. However, unexpectedly, three days before I submitted my complete dissertation to him, he passed away. I miss my conversations with him, and I miss his friendship.

He wasn't alone. My dissertation committee included Dr. Shelley Robbins from Capella University, Dr. Joe Picken from the University of Texas at Dallas, and Dr. John Whitlock, the head of Capella's research department, who took over as a committee chair after Corty's passing. They provided me with valuable feedback, and assured I kept my own voice. I also want to use this opportunity to thank 21 anonymous participants who were willing to meet with me and share their stories. One of them, too, had passed away since then in an accident. I could not have completed my research and reached my conclusions without their openness. They met me in their offices, their homes, and anywhere imaginable. They lived in Texas, Florida, California, Oregon, Washington, China, Israel, and other places. They kept me honest when they thought I was making up my mind before hearing them. Many of them said during the interviews: "maybe I am not your *typical* participant". To them I would like to say: You are all *unique*, and each of you in your own way and experiences helped me understand this complex topic and make sense of this study. I hope that in return this study could help you with your career, be it in a startup or a Fortune 500 company.

I wanted to thank those who took a chance on me and helped me share my knowledge and experience with their students and their readers. Sharing what I knew helped me learn more. Dr. Joe Picken who, after serving on my dissertation committee, asked me to teach a class at the Institute of Innovation and Entrepreneurship at the University of Texas at Dallas and kept inviting me every year to talk to his new classes, Mari Anixter, Braden Kelley, Rowan Gibson, and the team at *Innovation Excellence* who published my innovation articles and named me one of the top 40 Innovation Bloggers in 2015; Lindsay Blakely, the Los Angeles Bureau Chief at *Inc. Magazine* who gave me my own column there; and the event team at the Association for Strategic Planning who invited me to share my insights on creativity at their national conference, twice.

I'm an extrovert. As such, I need people to be my sounding boards. There have been so many people in my life that I was fortunate to meet at the right time, who helped me make the right decisions, and helped me focus my direction. They are HJ Li, Lee Colan, Jill Johnson, Bill Adams, Mark Sinclair, Ray Shook, and many more. They shared their precious time and experience with me selflessly, and for that I'm grateful.

The cover photo for this book was created with the help of my friend David Downs who, other than being one of the best photographers I ever met, also serves as a Plano City Councilman.

Finally, I wanted to thank my wife and lifelong friend Anat, and my daughters Maya and Shira, who always stood by me, even when I didn't know what I was doing. This book was dedicated to Anat's parents, my in-laws, Moshe and Margalit, who always believed in me, and gave me their unwavering support whenever I needed it the most. Nobody could ask for better in-laws.

I couldn't have done it without you.

what? where?

INDEX

acquisition, 10, 43, 49, 50, 52, 53, 54, 55, 56, 57, 58, 59, 102, 151, 152, 278

Altshuler, 306, 308

Amazon, 4, 61, 62

Andrew Grove, 142, 311

AOL, 50, 51

Apple, 4, 5, 6, 17, 61, 62, 97, 133, 135, 142, 180, 193, 236, 331

Autonomy, 33, 38, 40, 46, 99, 104, 106, 133, 266, 268

big picture, 38, 41, 45, 85, 100, 101, 102, 122, 127, 129, 160, 180, 268, 320, 335, 337

Bill Gates, 52, 194

Bill Joy, 52, 194

Bluetooth, 205, 339

BMW, 61, 62, 233

Boston Consulting Group, 6, 24, 61

Bowling with a Crystal Ball, 263, 290, 297, 310, 313, 314, 346

Bureaucracy, 33, 83, 106, 270, 333

Burgelman, 99, 142

Clayton Christensen, 17, 22, 33, 45, 126, 217, 310

Creative Team Optimizer, 10

CrossPoint, 185, 186

Daimler, 61, 62

Dallas, 59, 60, 71, 73, 116, 172, 181, 182, 197, 289, 341

Debate, 33, 145, 150

Design Thinking, 179, 296, 299

dissertation, 1, 5, 20, 21, 24, 33, 34, 36, 79, 116, 185, 250, 253

diversity, 41, 82, 87, 131, 137, 138, 140, 143, 144, 145, 146, 158, 163, 195, 200, 252, 277, 278, 279, 281, 282, 283, 284, 285

Ekvall, 99, 145, 146, 150

Emerson, 124, 164

encouragement, 32, 38, 82, 124, 273, 275, 333

exit strategy, 49, 52, 53, 251

extroverts, 76, 143, 150, 192, 193, 252, 277

Facebook, 165, 218, 272

Flip camera, 53, 58

Gilead, 61, 62

Google, 8, 36, 49, 61, 62, 118, 331, 333

GPS, 230, 309

ground rules, 168, 169, 298

Growth Innovation Index, 9, 240, 241, 246

Harvard, 3, 17, 21, 30, 45, 53, 165, 171, 191

ICQ, 50, 51

IDEO, 179, 212, 296, 299

incentives, 8, 76, 77, 78, 79, 80, 121, 122, 124, 266, 273, 275, 333

Interphase, 1, 3, 4, 5, 44, 80, 98, 175, 196, 256

Introverts, 76, 252

iPad, 7, 218, 312

Israel, 3, 18, 50, 71, 95, 104, 126, 129, 150, 151, 159, 214, 301, 317, 341

Kelly Johnson, 81, 177, 186, 187, 268, 277, 285, 325

Marshmallow Challenge, 179

MBTI, 173, 193, 253, 281

McKinsey, 25, 137, 235

Michael Dell, 52

Microsoft, 61, 62, 331

Mirabilis, 50, 51

MOOC, 249, 287

NASDAQ, 4, 50

PCTEL, 3, 23, 42, 59, 214, 321, 339

penveu, 4, 5, 153, 175, 185, 196, 197, 301, 309

Plano, 4, 5, 182, 233, 256, 342

praise, 124, 125, 187, 275

profit, 2, 26, 27, 28, 29, 30, 50, 57, 62, 67, 180, 228, 236, 262

resources, 8, 22, 39, 40, 52, 57, 69, 70, 81, 86, 89, 96, 101, 114, 115, 116, 117, 119, 120, 128, 129, 130, 138, 139, 165, 178, 187, 224, 236, 255, 257, 259, 266, 270, 275, 285, 318, 333, 334, 337

risk, 25, 26, 41, 46, 73, 86, 87, 92, 95, 96, 97, 129, 143, 148, 156, 174, 175, 210, 251, 252, 276, 277, 288

Runco, 247, 248

Samsung, 61, 62, 309

Santa Rosa, 4, 212, 213

Sarbanes Oxley, 46

SEC, 51

Silicon Valley, 3, 4, 18, 42, 59, 159, 181, 214, 321, 339

Skunk Works, 7, 81, 120, 135, 136, 176, 177, 186, 268, 277, 319, 325

Solram, 3, 50

SparcIt, 248, 249, 276, 287

Steve Jobs, 7, 52, 97, 173, 177, 194, 300

SUNY, 249, 287

SWWC, 2, 3, 11

team building, 153, 161, 227, 286, 288, 289, 293, 294

Team dynamics, 33, 89

Teresa Amabile, 3, 21, 45, 80, 91, 99, 121, 124, 126, 145, 273

Tesla, 61, 62

Texas Instruments, 1, 3, 4, 5, 15, 42, 44, 59, 68, 102, 120, 126, 129, 173, 180, 181, 212, 236, 250, 268, 303, 319

Toyota, 6, 61, 62

trust, 38, 39, 54, 55, 56, 81, 86, 87, 89, 91, 96, 97, 98, 113, 124, 126, 127, 128, 141, 145, 148, 149, 150, 151, 152, 156, 157, 158, 159, 160, 161, 162, 163, 164, 167, 171, 172, 257, 258, 264, 266, 267, 268, 269, 276, 277, 278, 281, 284, 285, 288, 289, 291, 298, 321, 326

TTCT, 219, 247, 248, 249

USB 3.0, 44, 70, 102, 129, 263, 271, 313, 319, 346

VoIP, 310

Voyager, 43, 214, 321, 339

Wi-Fi, 42, 131, 169, 182, 183, 304, 339

Yahoo, 43, 321

homework.

OTHER BOOKS BY YORAM SOLOMON

From Startup to Maturity is a reformatted version of Yoram Solomon's 2008-2010 doctoral research. This exploratory, interview-based case study used a sample of 21 participants who worked in both startup and mature companies, and explored the differences in the participants' experiences of creativity and the factors contributing to, or inhibiting it. This study found that people experienced higher degree of creativity in startups than in mature companies, and more important—*why*. This book is one of the main foundations for *un-kill creativity*.

When asked in a panel "where do great ideas come from?" author Yoram Solomon replied: "from the future!" A significant, timely, and ambitious endeavor, *Bowling with a Crystal Ball* is relevant to developers, strategists, marketers, venture capitalists and academia alike. The book examines the impact of state-of-the-art technologies on consumer-driven markets. Delivered in a personal manner, the book teaches the art of accurately forecasting fast-moving technology trends, creating value-add market disruptions, and navigating them through the industry maze to success. Originally published in 2007, it served as a textbook for a technology and industry forecasting university class. This 2015 edition adds the story behind the creation of USB 3.0, as well as a 2014 validation of the original 2007 trends presented in the first edition.

The reason you couldn't lose weight until now was that the present value of your long-term health is lower than the effort required for losing weight. In simple words: it's just too hard. There is no silver bullet that could reduce the effort. You know what you must do to lose weight. The problem is that you lack motivation. The author of this book is not an expert on nutrition or physical training, but is a researcher of motivation. He shows how to add external motivation enough to expend the effort required for losing weight, and how to turn that effort into habit such that you could sustain it for the rest of your life. The book is built upon numerous models and research in health, psychology, and economics, and told through the author's personal journey, through the stories of Alex, Valerie, Matthew, Don, Beth, and Joe, and through a survey of 222 participants. Although in the context of weight-loss, this book teaches you how to find the motivation to do what's important, yet long-term.

ONLINE RESOURCES:

Website: www.largescalecreativity.com

Inc. Magazine articles: www.inc.com/author/yoram-solomon

Innovation Excellence articles:
innovationexcellence.com/blog/author/yoram-solomon/

Facebook page: www.facebook.com/largescalecreativity

Newsletter: http://www.largescalecreativity.com/sign-up

Made in the USA
Lexington, KY
16 September 2017